# Figures of Alterity

# FIGURES
# OF ALTERITY
*French Realism*
*and Its Others*

LAWRENCE R. SCHEHR

*Stanford University Press*
*Stanford, California   2003*

Stanford University Press
Stanford, California

© 2003 by the Board of Trustees of the
Leland Stanford Junior University.
All rights reserved.

Printed in the United States of America
on acid-free, archival-quality paper.

Library of Congress Cataloging-in-Publication Data
Schehr, Lawrence R.
Figures of alterity: French realism and its others/
Lawrence R. Schehr
p. cm.
Includes bibliographical references and index.
ISBN 0-8047-4333-9 (alk. paper)
1. French fiction—19th century—History and criticism.
2. French fiction—20th century—History and criticism.
3. Realism in literature.   4. Outsiders in literature.   5. Identity
(Psychology) in literature.   I. Title.
PQ663.S35 2003
943'70912—dc21
2002009777

Original Printing 2003
Last figure below indicates year of this printing:
11   10   09   08   07   06   05   04   03

Typeset by Alan Noyes in 10 / 12.5 Janson text

*For my mother
and in memory
of my father.*

# Contents

# Preface

During the nineteenth century, as French fiction set about describing the world, a multitude of realist depictions of society, its figures, its structures, and its laws came into being. Single novels tried to describe a whole, but Balzac needed close to one hundred novels and short stories to develop his world of the human comedy. And in so doing, he scratched only the surface. Early on, and in part because it was founded on the historical novel, realist narrative looked beyond the immediate, examined the past, or reached toward an unknown that would be tamed and assimilated. Realism was seldom content with being a mirror of the local; in its search to provide general laws, realism repeatedly went beyond the immediate to describe as much as it could.

Doing so meant finding a language and a set of rules that could tame the other by bringing it into the fold, thereby normalizing it. It was not adequate simply to mark the other as exotic and leave it at that. For the other was not only something different or foreign, it was also what was most immediately and clearly present, part of everyday life. It is not an exaggeration to say that the feminine is the first and most enduring "other" faced by realism. For realism is predicated on a model of metaphysical presence, a phallocentrism based on the assumption that the writer is male, that the world is male-structured, that its rules are written by men, for men, and for the good of men. And in consequence, everyone else and everything else is second or secondary.

To say that the world depicted and the means depicting that world are male-oriented is not enough. For the rules are not only male-centered but also white, Christian, Western, and straight, to mention only a few possibilities. Each time that realism seeks to describe something, it is faced with that multiple textuality. That is to say, its methods are dominated by a particular ideology and metaphysical position but the object it seeks to include is other to that metaphysics and ideology. And moreover, this other object—and by "object" I mean the constructed referent that is an object of realist discourse—has perforce its own, different discursive structure, a different function in other ideologies, and even a different metaphysical position that does not see white, straight, Christian male assertion of dominance and transparence as necessary.

Realism thus assimilates the other by dint of its role as the nineteenth century's only superpower, but in so doing it never fully negates the structures and processes of alterity of the other. Though carefully constructed within the discourses of Western metaphysics and narrative, Salammbô's *zaimph*, for example, is never fully assimilated. The difference and the otherness remain, as does a tension between what it is supposed to be and the narrative that seeks to tame it. This is not to say that the object exists outside the narrative but rather that the narrative, in positing the other, posits that difference from itself as never completely overcome. The tension is within the writing, a tension that marks the act of assimilation of the other as a rhetorical move, perhaps one of the primary ones of realism.

This book is a study of a number of acts of assimilation by realist writing. My aim is to show how, through the construction and deployment of textual and rhetorical figures, the assimilation happens, works, and/or fails. By and large, I have chosen quite canonic works, with even the least known or the least central to the canon, *Le Jardin des supplices*, being a familiar work to most specialists in nineteenth-century French literature. In focusing on canonic works, I have hoped to show how the mechanisms of realism function at the heart of the enterprise.

Several parts of this work have appeared in print and have since been revised and expanded for this book. I should like to acknowledge permission to reprint here. Part of the material on Flaubert's *Salammbô* appeared as "*Salammbô* as the Novel of Alterity," *Nineteenth-Century French Studies* 17:3–4 (1989): 326–41. I should like to thank Marshall Olds and *Nineteenth-Century French Studies* for permission to reuse this article. Some of the material on Mirbeau appeared as "Mirbeau's Ultraviolence," *SubStance* 86 (1998): 106–27. This is reprinted by permission of the University of Wisconsin Press. Some of the material on Proust appeared in an earlier form in "Rachel, quand du Seigneur," *L'Esprit Créateur* 37:4 (1997): 83–93. I should like to thank John Erickson and *L'Esprit Créateur* for permission to reuse this material. And some of the work on Gide appeared in French in "André Gide et les figures de l'homosexualité," *Le Désir à l'œuvre: André Gide à Cambridge 1918, 1998*, ed. Naomi Segal (Amsterdam: Rodopi, 2001), 326–45. I should like to thank Rodopi BV for permission to use this material.

My gratitude for support, friendship, feedback, comments, and suggestions extends to colleagues and friends on various campuses. At the University of South Alabama, special thanks for many years of support and interest go to Calvin N. Jones, Caryl Lloyd, and Bernie Quinn. During my time at North Carolina State University, I got great help and feedback from Michael Garval, Debora Godfrey, Dudley Marchi, and Yvonne B. Rollins. My new colleagues at the University of Illinois have been extremely generous with their time and interest. Special thanks here to Jean-Philippe Mathy, head of the Department of French, and to Matti Bunzl, Tim Dean, Andrea Goulet, Doug Kibbee, Laurence Mall, Armine Mortimer, David O'Brien, Adam Sutcliffe, Emile Talbot, and the whole "Friday group" who have provided a new academic home for me. Thanks as well to the Department of French and the College of Liberal Arts and Sciences for their very tangible support for this project.

Helen Tartar continues to be a supportive and understanding editor, whose interest in my work has been unflagging over the years. And, as production editor, Tim Roberts has been most helpful and easy to work with.

David Bell and Charles Stivale read earlier forms of this manuscript, and their suggestions and comments proved extremely useful in the process of revision. Thanks, too, to others who listened, read, commented, asked, told, marked, and remarked: Éric Bordas, Jean-François Fourny, Anne Garreta, Alessandro Grilli, Robert Harvey, Alex Hughes, Lynne Huffer, Kevin Kopelson, Elisabeth Ladenson, Richard Macksey, Gerald Prince, Mireille Rosello, Beryl Schlossman, the late Naomi Schor, Franc Schuerewegen, Naomi Segal, Marc Smeets, Chantal Thomas, Margaret Waller, and Allen Weiss.

# Introduction:
# The Place of the Other

There are as many definitions of realism as there are literary critics and theorists interested in the subject. These definitions can be characterized according to a schematic model. Certainly the earliest definitions came out of a polemical position that developed during the period of realism itself. However, this last statement is tautological. In the narrow, historical sense, realism may quickly be defined as a literary practice associated with the narratives of Gustave Flaubert and other (perhaps "lesser") authors and epitomized by his watershed work *Madame Bovary*. But one would do well to consider many aspects of Stendhal's and Balzac's work realist, and, in an extension toward the present, one would include not only the Naturalists such as Zola and Maupassant but also the last great narratives of direct representation, such as those by Proust and Gide, for whom realism is personalized but still true to the grand narrative.

Let us now try to offer a simple, and somewhat naïve, formal definition relating more to what the realist narrative purports to do rather than to when it was written: realism is the accurate representation of the world in which it arises, the modes for that representation being given according to the models afforded by the nineteenth century. Realism, then—or more likely realist praxis, for no one narrative is complete—reflects not only the surface of the world it describes but also what forms, controls, and limits these narratives. Such paradigms and materials include the underlying laws at work: laws of history, economy, psychology, and exchange that are believed to be universals at the time of writing. Such laws govern the processes of change reflected in narrative, defined simply and elegantly by Gerald Prince as "the representation of real or fictive events and situations in a time sequence" (1). It is these laws, then, that provide the norm or the nature that narrative is supposed to reflect. Whether it is Grandet's business deals or Emma Bovary's increasing debt, the development of narrative follows the laws of the world it describes. A logical difference between the narrative and the laws underlying it may lead the narrative to being perceived as a change of genres. A trope, a figure (about which more below), or a deconstructible difference will necessarily be a reconsideration of the realist model itself.

Following a time line from Stendhal to Gide and Proust, we can see that a corpus exists, though it is neither homogeneous nor inclusive. Thus romanticism lasts long after its heyday, and there are arguments to be made about traces of romantic practice in the work of Flaubert, even as he tries to extirpate it in *L'Éducation sentimentale*. And realist practices, albeit in a rather banal form, continue to this day in what one might disdainfully call middlebrow literature that pretends to direct representation of human reality and that ignores any artistic developments associated with modernism and postmodernism.

The working definition of realism served merely as a means of gathering some narratives together in a noncontinuous praxis over the course of a century. But what are the characteristics of realism so defined? In "Un discours contraint," Philippe Hamon sketches out Roman Jakobson's uses of the word *realism*, which include the "realism of the project of the author," "the realism perceived by the reader," "realism as an artistic school," "realism as a process of 'inessential characterization,'" and realism as "consequent motivation" (414). Such a division need not concern us here, because the various categories clearly overlap insofar as the field in question is concerned. The canon of French realism, though perhaps fitting the narrowest of the definitions, has limits that can be generally agreed on by most contemporary readers. Even with Stendhal and Proust, most readers would buy into the notions of their writing as realist textuality. So realism would include a commonly agreed-on praxis that stretches over a century from the logical motivation of Stendhal to the retrospective synthesis of Proust and Gide. If elements of different praxes appear at both ends, this is not consequential, for any narrative is going to be crossed by heterogeneous textualities and informed by heterogeneous material praxes.

Hamon asserts that the question of realism should be different from the ones asked heretofore about copying the real. He wonders if one can "reproduce through semiological mediation (with signs) a nonsemiological immediacy" (416). The answer is no, except where language can imitate language in reality or where speech or writing can approximate certain elements of the real, such as sounds, noises, movements, and lines. So, for Hamon the question of realism becomes one in which realism is still somehow mimetically related to the real. Still, he suggests that realism is not simply a question of how literature copies reality but how literature makes us believe that it copies reality (421). By that modification, realism becomes a performative—a coercive speech act—that, through various mechanisms, informs the reader that what he or she is reading is believable as the mimetic representation of part of a world from which he or she generalizes a real reality behind the words.

This copying is realism's motto. As Furst (77) says, "The motive underlying realism's self-image that *all is true*, like its assertions about faithfulness and mirroring qualities . . . is to affirm the proximity of realist fiction to a contemporary actuality close to hand." From the very beginning, the realist space is a virtual one that looks like commonly defined reality, at least that agreed on by superreaders (Riffaterre 203) removed in time from a postmodern world, growing along with the change in time that corresponds with the century of bourgeois development from 1830 to 1930, from the invention of the photograph to the invention of talking films, from the fulfillment of the bourgeois monarchy to the fulfillment of the bourgeois republic. Strangely, the twinned birth of the invention of the photograph and realist narrative both values and denigrates approaches used theretofore. At that moment, one could say that visual fields separate into two competing fields, each of which is supposed to represent truthfully, one through direct depiction, one through analysis and completion. The realist work is that locus in which everything that exists is supposed to be representable. Yet, just as the fields propose two different readings of the real, each is related to the other by what it represents. So rather than having a separation of fields, one winds up with an interrelated field of representation: photographs will use techniques of the novel to tell a story, and novels will certainly be marked not only by the photographic but also by the cinematic, even before the latter fully exists. So, competing fields end up being complementary ones, interrelated by figures and techniques. As Jonathan Crary points out, "The circulation and reception of *all* visual imagery is so closely interrelated by the middle of the century that any single medium or form of visual representation no longer has a significant autonomous identity" (23).

Looking at a sharply delimited (though again neither homogeneous nor completely impermeable) corpus, such writers have, with great success, determined the characteristics of that corpus and deduced a series of rules or characteristics for it. A novel would be realist if it obeys all the rules deduced about that corpus. This schematic is an effective device for understanding the ways in which realism works. But what if one rule is not obeyed or one characteristic is not adhered to? Is the work any less realist? Somewhat realist? Are there *sine qua nons*? Are there hard and fast rules that must be obeyed, whereas others are optional? Are any of these rules themselves subject to interpretation? Do rules purporting to be an objective description of a work themselves conform because a critical decision has to be made that depends on a sense of similitude, belonging, or normative reading?

Finally, is an author realist, or are his or her writings realist? Think of Flaubert. Does he write realism with *Madame Bovary*, reject it with *Salammbô*, return to it for *L'Éducation sentimentale* (in spite of the fact that this novel is as much a writing *against* romanticism as it is within realism), and do something entirely else with it in *Bouvard et Pécuchet*? The last two novels mentioned are cases in point. In the former, the argument that the author is writing as much against a kind of textuality and ideology as he is writing within another is neither a radical nor a particularly divisive comment. But to what extent does realist praxis as it is defined by a set of rules allow for such writing against? With the latter work, the question might be asked differently: to what extent does realist praxis allow its own allegorization within the confines of realist praxis?[1] Does this or does this not change any definitions of the realist work?

The idea of writing against, just invoked in the case of *L'Éducation sentimentale*, brings us to a quite different way of imagining the realist enterprise, in a set of readings directly or indirectly influenced by one of the two great master thinkers of the period in question: Marx and Freud. For the former, one would invoke the creation of a textual world that was not merely the direct representation of the world, and preferably that of the poor (Eugène Sue, for example, or naïve interpretations of Stendhal's mirror), but in a more sophisticated way the representation of the contradictions of a political, social, economic, and materialist reality. These contradictions comprise the clue to an understanding of the realist representation of the real in this sort of argument: whereas the prose seems to be constructed of dominant discourses and ideologies, the "counterdiscourses" at work, to use Richard Terdiman's felicitous expression, are visible, or made visible, so as to show the contradictions inherent in any hegemony. Let us consider Georg Lukács's reading of the historical novel: despite the incredible romanticism associated with an author such as Walter Scott, the great historical novelist, it is undeniable that the epic sense of history in his work corresponds to what many would consider a protorealist position. What is risky here is the implicit Marxist sense of history, which is that of a progress narrative grounded in the Hegelian and Marxist sense of the historical moving from a more primitive to a more advanced position. In the Marxist evolutionary model, the capital "H" of history toward which humanity strives is the final overcoming of contradiction (Hegelian history become the abolition of the class structure, the dictatorship of the proletariat). The Marxist model is at odds with realist practice, for the latter is anything but a progress narrative. Indeed, it is likely that it not be one for realism to function. Friedrich Engels's oft-quoted famous letter to Margaret Harkness epitomizes that problematic: comparing Zola and Balzac, Engels (pointing out along the way that Balzac was Marx's favorite writer) underlines the irony in Balzac, an irony that undercuts the sense of progress with a good amount of puncturing of ideological balloons.[2] Thus, for a Marxist reading to be correct, the reading cannot resolve the contradictions with the sense of progress but can do so only through a metatextual troping.

The other master thinker, Freud, might be similarly invoked, although with Freud, the importance of contradiction is never denied, and, except in a progress narrative fostered and promulgated by an American brand of psychoanalysis, complete resolution is never sought. With a Freudian sense of realism, realism depends less on the material or social world than it does on the inner psychology of characters: a realist work is one in which characters think along lines considered by psychology and psychoanalysis to be real or realistic, with or without any need for a secondary abstraction toward a general set of rules of the workings of the psyche. This "with or without" can be easily explained through the invocation both of the temporal and the ahistorical. In purest Freudian terms, the psyche is constructed ahistorically, and the psyche of a human being a thousand years ago is the same as that of someone today. Along those lines, Hamlet would be as much of a realist(ic) character as Emma Bovary. But as Deleuze and Guattari showed in *L'Anti-Œdipe*, objections can be made on historic grounds to the ahistoricity of the Freudian psyche. More generally, from Heidegger through Sartre to Foucault, a critique of this ahistoricism would insist, much as Marxism does, on the specific historic circumstances of a situation. Thus, a social constructivist would sharply criticize such an equivalence, because everyone is a product of the discourses and ideologies into which he or she was born. But, even if one is not a social constructivist, such an equivalence clouds the difference between something or someone real (or even verisimilar) and something or someone realist. As easy as that objection is to make, it is not without its linguistic shoals. Even if Hamlet is not a real, sentient being, his psychoanalytic structure is verisimilar. Yet what ostensibly defines the realist work is its own verisimilitude, even if the truth is not certain. The gap is linguistic: no word distinguishes between these two kinds of verisimilitude, one that is a similitude, what is perceived as the truth—and even here, a Nietzschean would argue, there is a severe problem—and one that is a similitude to a specific kind of reality. It is in that specific kind of reality that realism is invoked.

So, again, what could realism be? Definitions have evolved again according to the development of literary criticism, and in the heyday of literary theory many other changes would influence current perceptions of realism. Paradoxically (coming from the work of Barthes), one of the most sophisticated definitions of realism is that it is the literary practice that most clearly shows the artifice of literature, for that is the most real position inscribable within the literary work or, to use the word most favored by literary theory, the text. Since the text is that which is woven and unwoven—from Ariadne's thread and Penelope's weavings and unweavings, through James's "The Figure in the Carpet," or in a metaphor of the same, from Valmont using his latest paramour as a writing desk through Borges's unwritings and unreadings—realism would be that which most clearly shows the incompatibility of the real (or even the Real, in the Lacanian sense) with the literary. Narrative can inscribe the absence of the real, so that anything that rewrites this act of inscription is rewriting the primary gestures of literature. A deconstructive reading of any such "strong" text brings to light the ideological structures, or more generally the phallogocentrism—a metaphysics of presence conflating phallus, logos, presence, and being—inscribed as the master trope of any such work or "text."[3] From Barthes's concept of the "effect of the real" to Derrida's grammatology, such efforts universalize the gesture of writing that makes it one with the world it seeks to represent but simultaneously make an impossible gesture to re-present or inscribe presence.[4]

Yet, before getting to the specificity of the realist project, I must state the obvious: realism happens in language. This seems, perhaps, to be a *vérité de La Palisse*. But it is, at least implicitly, a criticism of some recent trends in areas of criticism that, after the heyday of "theory," for all its strengths and weaknesses, somehow envision a return to a transparent signifier. No longer viewed as a semiautonomous (secondary) modeling system with its own rules, literature has, for some, become the handmaiden to history. Literature is thus perceived often as being a weaker version of the truth, one that needs to be buffeted by historical data, facts, or transcendental truth. Although there is not a complete independence of the aesthetic from the real, literature, as Barthes and Derrida among others have told us, has its own rules and follows a time line not necessarily synchronous with history and often in opposition to it. The time of the aesthetic and the timeliness and untimeliness of the aesthetic are far more complicated matters than a theorization of literature as direct reflection or as handmaiden would allow.

The specific problem here is that realism predicts or argues for its own *rature*. Read me, the realist novel seems to say, and I will disappear to create reality before your very eyes. The relation of literature to the truth is not anything new to realism, and one of the long-standing arguments about literary value is that somehow (depending on age, culture, praxis) literature is a witness to the truth. As recently as the late eighteenth century, with all France in turmoil, as Allan Pasco has pointed out in two works, novel after novel presents itself as a mirror of the world or a window on the truth. With realism (and especially after Romanticism whose truth was elsewhere), the truth becomes very specific: not only a general truth, not only an eternal truth but also, and especially, a detailed truth represented by a mirror that offers verisimilar reflection. Thus the argument about the realist project becomes even more compelling. The temptation to dismiss the order to "read me" to find the truth ever more insistently seems to say "cross out the text." Realism predicts its own disappearance in favor of the truth and in favor of a representation that is given as re-presentation, as one said in the seventies.

That disappearance or re-presentation is not the truth of the realist project, nor could it be. Let us leave to one side the more theoretical argument, where the very impulse and the appeal to cross out the signifier in favor of the signified are themselves highly coded rhetorical moves. The signifier cannot simply vanish in favor of the real, and the codes of the signifier cannot be abolished. The signifier will continue to have its own rules of representation, rules that, although not contradicting the laws of form relative to which literature becomes literature, retain an independence against the imposition of the real. Or with Marx and Engels mentioned above, matters might be troped thus: reality is not ironic, literature is. So, to read the real under realism, realism must continue to be read *sous rature*, for it cannot be crossed out, and its signifiers and codes cannot be made magically to dissolve into a sea of historicity, materiality, or reality.

Let us spend a few more moments on the rules of the signifier before turning to the specificity of the realist project, for even within the realm of language, a game is afoot. The best demonstration comes from the realist art of description—specifically, ekphrasis. Indeed, realism gets to the "thickness" of the real through description and through the care taken in detailing the uniqueness of an object.

Ekphrasis has traditionally been defined as a long, detailed description of an object within the course of a narrative (be it prose or lyric). The ongoing flow of the narrative stops, so to speak, and the narrator gives free rein to his or her powers of description to "paint" the object in words. The most well-known classical example is the description of the shield in *The Iliad*, in which Homer pauses in his description of the action to paint a very detailed portrait of what is depicted on the shield. More recent examples are Flaubert's description of Charles's cap and, in a lengthier vein, many of Balzac's descriptions, including that of the Maison Vauquer in *Le Père Goriot* and that of the antique store in *La Peau de chagrin*. One strategic outcome is that the use of ekphrasis brings order, be it logical or aesthetic, to a visual scene. Balzac describes the antique dealer's warehouse as a *capharnaüm*. His description, logically ordered for us to read the scene as if it were a series of vignettes, orders the reading; even in the description of one object, such as Charles's cap, a logical order has been brought to an object—the eyes seeing it, as opposed to those now reading it, would perceive it more holistically (Ricardou 32). Thus the object is ordered for us by language. At the same time, the introduction of the ekphrastic moment is an attempt to create a picture out of words, as if that logic imposed by language were not there. So, if the logic of narrative order must remain, other trappings of narrative are pushed to one side. Most striking is that there can be no representation of a character as a living or conscious subject during an ekphrastic moment. As Jean-Paul Sartre shows in his classic ekphrastic description of a human being, it is the very antithesis to a humanized description. Roquentin's sight of himself in a mirror is the quintessence of the human perceived as an object.

Within the framework of realism in particular, one more component seems to come to the fore because of the very structures by which realism attempts to present the subject as independent monad of action and enunciation and the deconstruction of that monadicity. In realism, ekphrasis is a way of continuing the narrative by other means and of firming up the narrative structuring of the universe. Whether it is Charles's cap, the Pension Vauquer, the description of the barbarians in *Salammbô*, or the descriptions of various kinds of torture in Mirbeau's *Le Jardin des supplices*, ekphrasis orders us. Instead of opening the narrative to an invasive figurality (*vide infra*), it tends to reinforce the closed, thematic, or limited connotative nature of the narrative. Ekphrasis is a strategy that substitutes a feigned image for that which cannot be said. The question of ekphrasis is a repeated one in Balzac's *La Comédie humaine*, and often Balzac will stop at a description to convey a generalized mood even if that very mood is meant as an evocation rather than as a means of predicting a turn of events or developing a psychological portrait.

How then is the specificity of the realist project attained to ascertain what is unique to realism while including this gesture of the moving finger, the sense of truth and the universal, and that of the material, the political, the social, and the economic? How is the historical grounding of realism itself troped, a realism that is compossible with Marx and Freud? It is not for nought that Marx, Freud, and realism itself are all master narratives, pretending to the universal; outside of science, they are the last three figures to do so. It is finally that: like Marx, like Freud, realism pretends to have the capacity to be universal. In a material world already moving to globalization, already moving to the universalizing of the Western subject, that move makes sense. In a world where everything is fungible, where everything can be exchanged, and where there is a set of universal signifiers that are interchangeable and to which everyone has access, realism makes sense. Anyone can be a realist subject: he (sexist for now) *just* has to write, *just* has to have access to capital (cultural, social, symbolic, economic, political), *just* has to believe in the capability for capacity, for capaciousness, and for inclusion.

The general logic that governs the establishment of realist narrative is a set of laws of form (Spencer-Brown); there is also a general and particular material ground of material, technique, and cultures that provides the verisimilar realia for that narrative. This is what David Bell ("Pessimism" 28), in a felicitous phrase, calls "the thick complexity and specificity of the real," that is also fundamental to realist narrative. This double base exists or is presumed to exist. Its transmissibility and communicability do not exist outside the codes that represent it. Giving someone a lump of coal is not the same as having a system of coal-based heat that keeps a community or a household warm in winter.[5] So, the material base, as real as it may potentially be, needs to be seen through its representations. It can be envisioned as a direct and an indirect set of signifieds and referents that the narrative conjures through its prose. Transformed ever more frequently into a world of commodities, the world of objects—and each object in particular—is the material base of the world described in these narratives. The object taken as commodity has both a value of exchange (with all the attendant figures of value and surplus value) and a historical value: the history of production of each object is equivalent to the production of history. In realist narrative, history is sometimes, if not often, perceived to have a teleological value that guides the development of plot in a progress narrative that leads, naturally, and fatefully, to the production of the contemporary moment.

Implicit therefore in the object as commodity is the object as *telos*: history has led to the present moment, even if the present moment is perceived as a moment of decadence. Within realism, the idea of "progress" is not necessarily related to an augmentation of the good, and many a realist author sees his or her contemporary world as a falling off from a better time. Progress, in such a world, is often equated with what Heidegger will come to see as the means by which technology distances us from the unveiled truth, the *aletheia*. In what Lukács calls "the novel of disillusionment" (*Theory* 112–31), the narrative, paired with an interruption of the speculative, while still conforming to the laws governing the universe, distances itself from the individual and the singular. Zola, for example, translates the individual into a complex machine of which he or she is more and more an anonymous part: Gervaise gets swallowed by the *assommoir*, Nana by the industry of desiring machines, the miners by the mining industry and its quintessence, the aptly named mine, Le Voreux. It is with the end of realism, with its retrospective glances on history itself, and the advent of the modern that the material tends to disappear in favor of a new complex figure that will be the founding figure of modernity: not only the relation of the individual to the material and the laws governing the universe but also the relation of the individual only to those laws, in the eclipse of the material. That such an eclipse is itself an ideological structure is clear; high modernism and surrealism, more or less contemporaneous in their chronological arrival on the scene, are testimony to this.

The bases of realist discourses are not only the objects themselves but also the material discourses, themselves codes, praxes, and semiotic systems, each of which has its own logics and illogics and each of which is only more or less translatable into the discourses of fictional narrative. These material discourses may be local or general in nature. Locally, they approach the Lyotardian concept of a local history, a set of rules and regulations, a collection of images, or a range of *astuces* that mark a system. More generally, but as yet not reaching the level of a universal, a set of modern material discourses develops that will revolutionize the very representational systems on which classical knowledge is founded: the invention of photography that provides an alternative to narrative prose, the development of high-speed means of transport such as trains, and the development of industrial processes of production. This even includes the development of a code of fashion (Waller) that can be widely distributed through drawings, daguerreotypes, and eventually photographs, so that Emma Bovary knows what chic Parisian women are wearing as soon as they are wearing it, or even before.[6] Together these categories form a version of the episteme described by Foucault in *Les Mots et les choses*, defined as the total set of contemporaneous discourses including their attendant contradictions. Yet where this concept is a modification of the Foucauldian episteme is in its insistence on the presence of the material taken as images, figures, codes, and memes.[7] It is a generalized episteme not limited to the discursive but always modulated through it. In the end, the narrative refers to other discourses and to the episteme in general; it is self-referential and exhibits a measure of self-justification (as if it were complete) and freeplay, which shows that it is never wholly determinable.[8]

Freeplay is not anarchy; along with the laws of form, along with a glance at representability, along with a consideration of sense and nonsense, transcendental signifiers and taboos confer validity and meaning on the system.[9] By orienting various interpretative strategies, by limiting various kinds of misinterpretation, by distinguishing the heterodox from the orthodox, transcendental signifiers and signifieds, along with all the other parameters indicated, reduce the possible entropy and anarchy of freeplay. That these transcendental signifiers are ideological constructions (in the material and historical sense) and marks of a more pervasive generalized metaphysics (what Derrida called *phallogocentrism*) will come as a surprise to no one. Instead of limiting freeplay, transcendental values may lead critics, if not all members of the interpretative community, to the deconstruction of the system. Thus a transcendental system, be it Balzac's "altar and throne," Flaubert's "book on nothing" (for why could "nothing" not be a transcendental value?), Zola's laws of naturalism, Proust's time, or Gide's purity, should be the mechanism by which the terminal flight of the signifier is restricted. Fixed meaning flees, is inverted, changed, figured, troped, and refigured. The transcendental figures and the taboos are just signifiers pretending to be the origins, definitions, and limits of meaning.

The preceding pages have shown how complex the construction of the site of realism is and to what extent it involves the depiction of a material reality. In a work like *Salammbô*, one might argue (and certainly Flaubert would) that the representation of the religion of the Carthaginians is itself part of that material reality to be depicted. Reality exists for realism, but it is always already interpreted: subject to laws of form and laws of discourse, limited in its own anarchy by those laws and by various mechanisms that transcend that materiality, marked in its coherence and at least posited as potentially continuous. Insofar as realism is concerned, reality is subject to a kind of material and discursive history or archeology. One can imagine literary systems in which the immanence of the object (or individual) is all that is necessary and where no discursive archeology is necessary.[10] But, just as objects have their continuity and laws of form, and just as the real has its discursive praxes, so too does literature have its own semiautonomous coherences that relate both to its status as a secondary modeling system and to its capacities for ambiguity, irony, freeplay, polyphony, and rhetoric in general.

Realism, as the literary process most suited *sine qua non* to the expansion of capitalism, is endlessly trying to have its reach exceed its grasp.[11] Perhaps the most significant development in realism is its expansion. Realism is a narrative method that corresponds to an ever-widening vision of the universe, an increasing realm considered appropriate as subject matter for narrative. Narrative starts to include alterity in a striking way that marks realism as a praxis distinct from other literary endeavors. Alterity, quite simply, is the other: the previously unknown, the previously unrepresented but also that which had had a cachet of the exotic or of the different. Yet it is not merely a matter of reducing the other to the same by smoothing its asperities and by removing its perceived dangers. Instead of reducing the

other to a version of the same, by which it is considered an inferior
version of that which shows identity, realist narrative attempts a double movement: an extension of narrative toward the other and an inclusion of the other within a universal. Realist narrative seeks to
maintain the particular nature of that which it discovers, describes,
or represents while making itself the universal discourse that contains all others. Realism thus begins to extend its narratives to others, and spaces change in which the others are accommodated. In
some cases, what had been perceived to be exotic even becomes a viable subject for enunciation, action, or judgment. In others, the very
space of representation is reformulated because the variable subjects
bring their own laws of representation and form: as it moves toward
a universal, or at least a sum, realism is its own undoing.

No one narrative can entertain the realist enterprise; works multiply; perspectives double, treble, and finally become a hall of mirrors. Even at the beginning, the universal is implied in an epic vision,
itself a translation in part of the *mathesis universalis* of the eighteenth
century, the encyclopedia, or a hypertext. Each moment, praxis, or
discourse would itself imply the entire history thereof. That translation and history of mathesis into a universe of psyche and commodity are themselves already daunting and scarcely containable. Stendhal may posit a mirror, but when it truly comes down to
considering what that mirror implicitly and explicitly reflects, he
steps back. Showing what is in the mirror takes the multiple layers of
Balzac's *La Comédie humaine*. Incapable of including all human comedy in one novel, regardless of length, Balzac extends his writing
over about a hundred works. Zola, more modest, goes for twenty but
implies a myriad of technical discourses in each one. Between the
two, perhaps most tellingly, is the *mise-en-abyme* of realism in
Flaubert's *Bouvard et Pécuchet*: how many discourses figure in every
paragraph of that novel (Donato)?

Narratives extend back in time, usurping or engulfing the past
with the techniques of the present: though often retrospective in
some of the earlier *études philosophiques*, Balzac never shies away from
retrospective glances in later works, even so far as the very structure
of the work is considered. Take, as an example, *Eugénie Grandet*,
more about which later, or *Le Père Goriot*, each of which includes a
long retrospective history to get the reader to understand the present

moment (the narrated moment, not the moment of narration). The retrospection does not have to be cumulative, and Flaubert writes such a novel, an archaeological work, right after *Madame Bovary* in the Carthaginian work, *Salammbô*. Such a work is different from the historical novels of Walter Scott and those of Balzac (Lukács, *Historical*). In novels of that world, the narrative fiction is measured against the received facts of history, which is perceived as having transcendental validity. For Flaubert, writing retrospectively, or for someone such as Villiers de l'Isle-Adam (in *L'Ève future*, for example) or Jules Verne, writing prospectively, the grounding of the work is not in the historical reality itself (as if that could be defined apart from narrative) or even in a projective science but in the universalizing narrative of the present. Realism extends its realm into various alterities by including those others (whatever their form) as entities or structures predictable by an ever-expanding set of parameters and praxes.

Realism normalizes textual relations, makes the exotic the known, and gives histories and stories to various incarnations of the other. Thus realism is seeking to extend the idea of the universal to other realms from the implicit center of the white, male, bourgeois subject. It could be argued that realism's making of that gesture continues to reinforce a hierarchy of values and that the inclusion of other subjects is always done relative to the hierarchic subject that sits on top, the metonymy of the transcendental signifier, and the guarantor of the system, the white European male and his consort, she who bears him white children. Arguably then, the frontiersman attitude in much American literature of the time, even through the Gilded Age, would be a troping of this process in which the domination of the continent (or the ocean or the Mississippi River) is metaphorically the domination of the other in all its forms (Sundquist). In France, such an effect is readable in Chateaubriand, for example, even though no one would accuse Chateaubriand of being a realist. Yet, an author such as Flaubert can recuperate Chateaubriand's gesture. But, whereas the earlier author mystifies the exotic or subjugates it to the Christian universal, Flaubert tames most of it not by gallicizing it, for the "horrors" remain, but by indicating that it is representable, if not fully explicable.[12] No matter how rude on the frontier, civilization is always an approach to the white European ideal, a process of inclusion and domination that sees its apotheosis in Henry James, in whose work Americans (naïve, faced with Europeans and their so-phistication—which means their whiteness and their comprehension of the laws of the representation of the subject) are tamed by Euro-peans just as the Americans have tamed the river, the Indians, and the Wild West.

At the level of the character as subject, a simultaneous process still undercuts the act of domination. The subject brings some laws that are his or hers, laws of representation that do not abide and do not fit into the paradigm. Montaigne recognizes this process as early as his essay "Des cannibales," and Montesquieu gives an ironic spin to the interrelations between the phenomenology of otherness and the perception of knowledge and exoticism in *Les Lettres persanes*. Closer to the era in question is Melville's Queequeg in *Moby-Dick* or, within the realm of French narrative, Flaubert's Salammbô, who functions in a world in which heterogeneity is never resolvable into a simple binary code, a world in which ritual, sacred objects do not ever fit into the representational paradigms of realism. Realism is its own re-versal, its own undoing, and its own deconstruction. By pretending to move toward the universal, realism includes laws that are anti-thetical to the establishment of a homogeneous system.

Numerous examples exist of an understanding of critique of real-ism from that angle. Whether it is Bakhtin's carnivalesque het-eroglossia or Richard Terdiman's concept of counterdiscourse, whether it is Ross Chambers's concept of writing as opposition or even the bald-faced existence of a poem in prose, whether it is the Konstanz school of textual gaps (Iser, Jauss) or my own concept of the limitations of realism (*Rendering*), this implosion, cleaving, sepa-ration, and contradiction have long been studied. For some, the con-tradiction arises because the reality given as universal is always told, represented, and recounted from one (dominant) point of view: real-ist narratives have counterdiscourses because the other is always pre-sent, if not always heard—that is, the other of the exploited, those who are made to be silent. For others, no position can ever aspire to the universal. Thus, the irony of Flaubert's "Un Cœur simple" can never be fully measured, because readers are always off, behind, or askew.

With working definitions in place, with some sense of what is at stake, with some recognition of the ambiguities associated with realist representation, and with some vision of the gesture of realism to include the other, let us return to the initial words of this chapter relating to the space of realism. In the space given to realism, something changes as realism develops: realism itself changes, develops, and ultimately winds up a narrative of a world far different from the one that gave birth to it. It is still not certain what that realist enterprise is, other than the recognition of its limits (in its unlimited thirst for expansion), and the endless redefinition of its subject as the field of the subject expands, changes, reconfigures.

The space allotted to realism, the world, locus, or virtual reality deemed correct for now, a space originally of low culture, of utilitarian communication, is also a space of prose and of the prosaic (Bordas, "Question"). This is a space reflecting the useful, the mercantile, and the less than lofty, a space marked by the children of Candide, less innocent and white (*candida*) than he, marking their difference, marking the difference of their difference (or their *différance*), making their way in the world. All come to be defined as subjects whose very existence as such is made possible by a utilitarian world that equates subject with independent consumer, by a world in which the possession of discourse can be imagined as the creation of a unique *parole* that relates to a sense of self, a radical independence from the system, and a singular psychology. This radical independence does not mean that subjects do not interrelate but simply that the sense of identity, as a projection of Aristotelian logic, can or may be a radical one: a character can make his way without the socius into which he is born or the habitus in which he functions (the masculine pronoun is *de rigueur* here). He may be alone.

The narrator is always alone in the realist narrative, since he defines himself as a subject without the subjective. His *parole* approaches discourse and initially subjects and subjugates other individual, subjective discourses, even as these develop and proliferate. The narrator's *parole*, with its pretense to the universal, establishes a hierarchy of discourses. His discourse—his narrative—is seen as a totalizing discourse with access to the truth; rules of time that apply to mere mortals do not apply to him. Through the conventions of narrative, even tense itself, so interrelated for the characters to time, is freed of its temporal constraints to mark the literary as opposed to the human (Weinrich, Hamburger). While giving a multiplicity of points of view, the realist narrator still implicitly proposes his own universalizing discourse as a monophony instead of as a voice within the polyphonic (and rightfully so, for that is one of the aesthetic high points of realist narrative).

Another example is Flaubert's extensive use of *discours indirect libre* as a means of representing a character's thoughts or observations in a singular vocabulary that stays, nevertheless, in the third person. *Discours indirect libre* moves the narrative from a supposedly objective stance external to the characters to an internal one reflective of the character's mind or view of the world. By definition, that tactic is always initially subject to control of a "purer," dominant discourse.

As the century develops, the position of the narrator is less objective than it once seemed, and the multiplication of discourses essentially impedes the total subjugation of the same. The reemergence of the first-person narrative at the beginning of the twentieth century, which had largely been eclipsed in realist praxis by a third-person omniscient narrator, could be seen as the impossibility of the third-person narrative to continue. Where "Balzacian" third-person narratives are found, such novels are often perceived, especially in the contemporary era (post–World War II), as an impossible writing in or of a world in which history maintains its transcendental value and in which the objective voice doubles (ventriloquizes, mimics) that dominant voice, which is also the voice of dominance and domination.

Included are characters, implied authors, implied readers, and narrators alike, as well as more intangible figures of discourse and image discussed below. These are all included for the moment in a concatenation of assumed figures for the integral nature of the character is not certain. Michel Foucault questioned what an author is: in his radical critique of subjectivity, the author is replaced as an agent by a concatenation of discourses. The same could be said, *a fortiori*, for the character, which could be considered to be a collection of discourse(s) that may or may not correspond to a distinct psychology or delimit an individual subject.

The difference between a distinct psychology or an individual subject and a locus for discourse is developed in a telling passage in *La Volonté de savoir*, the first volume of Foucault's *Histoire de la sexualité*, a passage that wound up being a clarion call for gay rights

(58–60). In that passage, Foucault develops the idea of the gay individual with his (or her) own psychology, as a distinctly historical invention of the nineteenth century. For Foucault, then, the gay individual becomes a subject at that point (situated, conveniently for us, at the dawn of realism). Yet, for me, this beginning is somewhat different from that posited by a post-Foucauldian movement of social constructivists. First, it is not only the gay individual but also a whole host of others who are able to mark individual subjectivity. Second, it is not so much that the subject did not exist before but that the discursive means of expressing what, *from the outside*, from the point of view of the external observer or the omniscient narrator, could not coherently articulate what would appear to be the essence of the individual. Thus, while same-sex desire certainly existed, it is perhaps not until the early nineteenth century that a subject can articulate that desire in a way that is controlled or validated by the outside observer. Third, and a confirmation of the second point, whereas the discourse—again of same-sex desire, for that is the lightning rod of social constructivism—is possible in the early nineteenth century, it is still possible only relative to a rhetoric of medical and juridical normativity and abnormality. Only much later does the noncriminal, nonalienated subject emerge with rights to a realist discourse, one with the same rights to represent reality as those of other less exotic, more normal individuals.

Even if the purported focus and coherence of realist narrative depend on the existence of that unified subject, the narrative itself may undermine that unity in several ways. The unity of the character is partly subjected to the artificial dominance of the supposedly objective discourse that serves as the guarantee or *garde-fou* for the limits or the extensions of the subject. As that very objectivity comes into question, both epistemologically and ontologically, the unity, finite nature, or independence of the narrative subject is also doubtful. Changes in the presentation of the subjects, including the extension of subjectivity to other discourses, bring the independence and unity again to the forefront and into question. The chapter on Zola and Mirbeau will show how the discursive subject is scattered. Questioning the subject means recognizing the existence of various discursive practices (again, in the Foucauldian sense) that may or may not correspond to the finite unity required for a subject of action. There is no necessary unity between the subject of discourse and the subject of action as agent or protagonist or secondary character in realist narrative. Insofar as some might consider the individual subject of action and enunciation historically determined or conditioned, the independence and unity are again countered by the means of production (of discourse, of objects) and the historical conditions of the subject.

In sum, four possible reasons exist for not assuming the unity of the subject. First, the relative independence of discourses and epistemes makes the subject always beholden both to the set of possible discourses shared by the character, narrator, or implied figure and to the fiction of the existence of an objective discourse *not* subject to those constraints. Second, the historical determination of a character, figured by some real means of production and representation— again, in the sense that Foucault or Bourdieu (in a work like *La Distinction*, for example) find people conditioned by the praxes that surround them and that "pigeon-hole" them—removes a greater or lesser degree of freedom from the individual. To be perceived as being psychologically true, the character must have some degree of predictability, and, insofar as that predictability is present, the character is less independent. Third is the narrative itself, which, in a deconstructive turn, for example, follows its own laws and has, as Jacques Derrida pointed out in his early essays, its own freeplay that subverts determination and structure ("Structure"). The fourth motif, which will be discussed below, is the figure that erupts in a narrative between language, where representation is not possible, where there are yet no words for desire or subjectivity.

This space is first of all the space given to realism, a space authorized by discursive praxes, epistemological givens for the ways and means of perception, and the presumptions and assumptions of what is just or given to be just: the space in which the laws of verisimilitude are deemed to apply. The lyric mode is exempt from the laws of verisimilitude, given a space in which rhetoric can flower without any infraction to the law. Yet prose has to obey that law, in a space thought appropriate, a locus that keeps some things behind closed doors or, more accurately, a space that determines the space of the private as a marked locus in which one can enter with an invitation— *scènes de la vie privée* corresponding to the more originally authorized *scènes de la vie publique*. So it is a space in which prose is allowed to flower, to grow, and to represent, a space allotted to representation. There is nothing more realist than an invitation proffered and accepted, a welcome into a space within a space, nothing more realist than the means by which that invitation is one relative to the law, to a change in the local economy. It is the recognition within a narrative of a subject as such; at the same time, it is the *mise-en-abyme* of the reader's acceptance of realism's *captatio benevolentiae*, the willful suspension of disbelief. Some classic examples: Julien Sorel becoming a subject in the household of Mlle de la Mole, Emma accepting and acting on an invitation to the Château de la Vaubyessard, Marcel at any number of occasions, the Duc de Guermantes's insistence that an invitation once accepted cannot be subsequently unaccepted, and the famous consignment to perdition of Rastignac by the Comte de Restaud. A final, irresistible example is from "Combray," recalling all the previous hospitality in the novel ("Combray" is about invitations to eat with others) and predicting all those to come in the *Recherche*: Swann's ringing of the back-gate bell leads the informed reader to think of the gift of sparkling Asti wine, the suspension of the laws of politeness as one sends over to Swann's house for something or some information at the drop of a hat, Odette's invitations to Marcel, the invitation to tea made and forgotten by Charlus, the offer of bread by the Princesse de Luxembourg, the orangeade, the *matinée de la Princesse de Guermantes*, and so forth.

The subject of discourse, the subject of action, and the subject of the law, be it local or general, are at stake as the widening of the space of realism occurs through the transformation of that space by the admission of others. If the subject finds a single voice anew in Gide and Proust, perhaps because the previous discursive praxes had finally exploded from all that alterity, it is at the price of the purported guarantee of reliability, of objectivity, of any possible univocal resolution of truth and falsity, and of meaning and discovery: how else could the narrator of *A l'ombre des jeunes filles en fleur* "forget" to tell the readers that Charlus is gay?

Still, there is another space, a second locus: the space of representation, the space given by, created from, and engendered by representation. This is a space produced by the lay of language, by the representation that produces its own internal laws of form and process that move away from the space given to realism for representation. Simple examples will serve well, for it is not yet clear how the figures working in this space will be coded: the development of plot, the happy ending or not, the resolution, the death of Emma Bovary, the death of Nana, and the non-endings of the *Recherche* or *Les Faux-Monnayeurs*. Fiction produces its own laws even as they repeat the laws given to it. If Emma dies pathetically or if the narrator goes on to write a book such as the *Recherche*, it is because there must be closure, resolution, punishment, or reward. Vautrin must be carted off to prison, but only a cynic or a more mature writer would let him out to become the head of the secret police. One could question whether the Vautrin who goes to prison, duly punished by the young Balzac, is the same one who, a few years later, is modeled after Vidocq. This is the space given, but what realism does with it is completely other: if retribution and reward are exacted for the sake of justice in the novels, by the time realism fully engages that reward and retribution, it is obeying its own internal need for coherence, not the laws of propriety and property or exactly those of verisimilitude. In the real world, Emmas sometimes survive, Rastignacs sometimes fail, and insomniac would-be writers sometimes never write a line. So the space of realism, the space created by realism is not necessarily that given to realism, nor coterminous with it. The space produced by realism creates lacunae, differences, marks of alterity, black holes, and limits to its own supposed capaciousness (Iser 3–30; Schehr, *Rendering*): incapacities issue from its own capacity to talk about anything within reason.

Let us return to the first entrance of a figure from a side door, a figure not necessarily predicted by the realist paradigm. This figure is not really first but a nodal moment, a less than accidental introduction that makes an encounter, that makes the plot, that helps determine the role of money, wealth, and poverty. It is, in the real world, one of two emblematic moments. First, as befits a study of narrative, the example shall come from the realm of the narrative, from the first novel discussed here, *Eugénie Grandet*. Grandet's impoverished nephew Charles lands quite unceremoniously in his uncle's house. Through a financial crisis, as opposed to a spiritual or political fiasco, Charles's father has brought scandal to the family name and has just committed suicide. Dispatched before the father's act,

Charles winds up in his avaricious uncle's house in Saumur. In an instant, Eugénie falls in love with this stranger from a world other than her own. Even though his cousin Eugénie is in love with him, Charles must go, for his uncle will not have an extra mouth to feed. There is a simple solution: send Charles away, let him make his fortune, and, in so doing, he will buy back his nuclear family's honor. To keep him would be a sign that such dishonor could be spread to Grandet himself and secondarily to his daughter for whom he would hope eventually to arrange a good marriage. It would certainly not do to keep Charles in the house or to let Eugénie follow her feelings and become tainted by the dishonored Charles.

For all intents and purposes, Charles is banished by his uncle, and he ships out in one of nineteenth-century realism's earliest tones of alterity to wind up in the mysterious East. Charles soon learns that this world, unpolished by the gentility of Parisian foppery, is one in which everyone has to work to survive. He quickly learns what his uncle has always known: work is not merely labor; it can be trade. Hence, he sets out to buy and sell the most available commodity: Charles "realizes that the best way of making one's fortune, in these intertropical regions as in Europe, was buying and selling men" (1181). People are chattel, dehumanized objects to be traded like any other product. In this relatively early reference to expansionist, mercantile imperialism, the other is first seen as a dehumanized subject. No longer the conquered lesser beings of the Americas and Africa who need Christianity to bring them to salvation and humanity, no longer the noble savage, the trace of the exotic, and not yet the erotic oriental other, these beings are just fallen humans with no other purpose than serving in Charles's trade. Or are they human? Were they ever human? Balzac seems to be saying the unsayable as he implies that even white people can be bought and sold. Balzac thus immediately, if only momentarily, puts whiteness into question. Charles learns what his uncle already knows, all shown through the reflective glass of Balzacian irony.

Realism changes the contexts and paradigms. In a realist novel, being human means having a locus in which to speak, a language to speak, and the possibility of interacting with others. Decidedly Charles's goods do not fit into that category. Silent, they are sold as slaves in a world where such behavior is tolerated but in a novel where it is not; again, this distinction between worlds underlines the difference between the real and realist representation. The requirement of the realist paradigm, which is that the representation of a human be able to speak, is countered by the reality of a world in which this is not a necessity. Charles buys the slaves' silence and buys them as well. Such sales may have a connotative value of exoticism but these slaves are far from being humans capable of discourse: Charles "sold Chinese, negroes, swallows' nests, children, artists" (1181). This is a congeries of heterogeneous categories, as exotic, if not more so, than the antique dealer's shop in *La Peau de chagrin*. But where that novel, as an *étude philosophique*, flirts with fantasy and with unreality, *Eugénie Grandet* is a realist work. Let us put aside the swallows' nests now, as caprice or simply as something that connotes the exotic (suitably displaced from the human to the nonhuman). In normalized discourse, each of the others is somehow deprived of a proper language: Negroes and Chinese as foreigners or barbarians speaking some non-Western and therefore lesser tongue, children babbling or being *in-fans*, artists communicating in metaphor or media other than mundane prose discourse.

Important here is that these figures, shadows at best, are at the edge of the novel, barely introduced into the human world, presented *en passant* or introduced only to be immediately banished. Their very presence, shadowy or apparitional though it may be, at least gives the possibility that they eventually may have discourse. Negroes, Chinese, and children will eventually talk in novels, as will other characters marginalized for various reasons. How they will talk, how they will come to language, and how they will be guaranteed the possibility of subjectivity are all products of the development and the extension of the realist discourse, an extension that could be called, anachronistically, "inclusive." Seeking to reach its goals of attaining a universal, discursive realism winds up, almost without conscious knowledge on the part of authors or readers, including those silent ones within the realm of the discursively possible.

The possibility of the existence of the other and the possibility of the other having discourse, if not necessarily coterminous, are simultaneous. It is precisely because they are simultaneous that they are not coterminous. The presence of the discourse of the other, moving from silence toward sign, moving from circumlocution toward connotation toward denotation, is a repetitive practice, a performance over time of a discursive set (Butler 134–41). Yet for there to be a coterminous coherence, the other has to be posited first as having the possibility of language and of being a subject. In simpler terms, the coming to presence of the other within language, while occurring at the same time as the production of that language itself, does not necessarily (if ever) completely cover the territory of the other.

Let us take as an example something from the far end of the spectrum of books examined in this study: the discourse of the homosexual as depicted in the works of Gide. Despite the variety of approaches he uses in various prose forms (essays, autobiography, autofictions, confessions, *soties*, and novel), Gide does not give the gay man (for it is invariably a question of the man) as a whole, preconceived, finished being in possession of a language that is his in which he can express desire and subjectivity, thought, belief, definition, and opposition. The Gidean gay character is both more and less than the discourse he uses: more because the language is not yet adequate to describing all that may be eventually expressed, less because the language, in its own semiotic ramifications, and in the relative independence of the semiotic system from the referent, has its own consequences. If the gay man is opposed to the straight man, and the discourse of alterity that defines the former is opposed to the discourse of dominance and hegemony that defines the latter, it is neither certain nor predictable that these two situations are coterminous. Narrative can provide us with characters who are not complete living, breathing human beings or verisimilar representations thereof. Narrative provides us with a discourse that goes beyond the individual character and that is both less and more than that character. Narrative provides us with what life does not: a narrative supposedly given (but how is narrative given? by whom? to whom?) as the posit of neutrality.

The subject of this book is the extension of realist writing toward the other, toward alterity, toward otherness. Close readings of six authors from Balzac to Proust will demonstrate how realist narrative engaged the question of bringing the other into the realm of the discursively representable. The acts of representation involved in that development are not necessarily coterminous with either the representation of the exotic and its attendant stereotypes or even with the representation of an individual. The representation of the other is in reality the extension of discourse to the unrepresentable or to that which was previously unrepresentable. That the unrepresentable is perceived as oppositional is the result of the structurings of discourse by hierarchies and by metaphysics, whereby any bivalent pair is made into an oppositional pair.

By relying on an oppositional model, one would be inclined to make a preliminary conclusion that the first other is the woman, a woman, women. And yet it is not so simple. Let us consider a work from the same moment as Balzac's *Eugénie Grandet* but from another representational realm: Delacroix's famous painting, *Les Femmes d'Alger*. Admittedly, this is not a narrative, but my point can be made by examining the figuration and figurality of the women in that painting in a more immediate fashion. Delacroix's 1834 painting depicts four women in a feminized space, ostensibly a harem room decorated with and divided by various fabrics, in which their individual attire and an Oriental rug are the most striking, with their varied rich luxurious patterns and textures. In the left foreground, sitting on a rug, and noticeably separated from the other three figures, is a woman who *seems* more European than the others. She is looking out of the canvas, toward the spectator, ostensibly to bring his eye and his desire into the harem space. She bridges the gap between the world of identity outside the canvas and the world of alterity within. She is thus, by that engaged gaze, making herself more desirable and coding the exotic space as one that can be invaded and ultimately mastered by the masculine gaze that perceives it. In the center of the canvas, on a pair of rugs, sit the two slightly more exotic women; they are talking to each other and there is a hookah, an object that is both mark of the exotic and the sensual, in front of them. Not engaged with the spectator of the canvas, interested in each other, indeed rapt with each other, the oriental dyad is marked both by the presence of the hookah (drugs, dream states, and the dissolution of the individual subject) and by its own impenetrability. Finally—there is a temporal notion here, because post-Renaissance Western art often demands to be read from left to right, as if it were writing—on the far right, is the fourth woman. The depiction is of a black woman standing up and thus occupying a different plane from the other three characters as well as a larger space on the canvas than any of the others. She is turned away, with her back to the spectator, and her head is turned somewhat over her shoulder and gazing toward the back of the canvas, specifically toward a door—the door of the harem room that figures the background. Although she could not catch the observer's gaze (and *vice versa*), she is not blind, just impervious to the Western glance that identifies the other as a subject; she was, is, or will be chattel like those whom Charles Grandet trades. Delacroix gives us a gesture, that of the servant—from Cervantes's Sancho Panza to Mozart and da Ponte's Leporello to Proust's Françoise—all of whom can see what the master can, though without the ideological clouding that goes with his position. In this case, she perceives at least one of the two Algerian women (the less well-lit of the two), who occupies the geographic center of the canvas and who is thus the object of gazes of possession.

The painting is a complicated one, and the various gazes that are present, along with those implied, correspond to lines of force and power marking the other in various fashions.[13] The implied spectators, rhetorical observers, or intended gazers do not actually fully occupy the position of the dominant male as they do in mirroring the King in Foucault's analysis of Velasquez's *Las Meninas* (*Mots* 19–31). Yet the male gaze does dominate the whole spectrum of women. The male gaze possesses them as it keeps them desubjectified and alienated. A preliminary reading of the painting would indicate that the feminine figure, always subjected to and therefore always intertwined with the masculine gaze, has no independence from that gaze and, more generally, from the masculine position of dominance that reduces the feminine to a secondary other. Certainly—to return to the literary—deconstructing this belief has been one of the mainstays of contemporary criticism. Perhaps taking their figural clue from Virginia Woolf's idea of "a room of one's own," a space in which one can be oneself, or more exactly, in which "she" can be "herself," and, in a physical metalepsis of that self, write, Gilbert and Gubar develop an impassioned argument in their ground-breaking volume, *The Madwoman in the Attic*. They effectively elucidate the idea of confinement of women, confinement in all senses of the word: the woman is ultimately dangerous and always borderline hysterical; she must be confined. It is no accident that in the moment of birth in which she, in the realm of masculine fantasy, is most female, that is, in the moment of giving birth, that she is the most soiled and the most potentially dangerous. It is certainly not coincidental that the English language at least talks of confinement for a woman giving birth, for someone with psychological disorders to be locked away, and for the criminal, who, in the most dire situations winds up in solitary confinement.

Thus, Gilbert and Gubar's argument can be generalized: just as Delacroix has neatly circumscribed feminine space, no matter how luxurious it is, as a space protected by and dominated by the masculine gaze that owns that space and that invisibly (because not in the space of representation) determines its limits, the feminine space is always one carved out by the male, determining what the other will be. The space for representation is given to the other (the woman). The space for representation is not necessarily the space created by the praxis of representation. The space developed or that developed over the course of a century from *Corinne* to *The Awakening* challenges the masculine construction of the universe.

A profound difference gives one pause: the feminine is always already there. Women have always been represented. That the space given to them is not the space that they will choose, develop, or remark is not the same thing as saying that they are not there. There is a difference between the representation of women and the lack of representation of the Jew as anything but a stereotypical figure before realist narrative. Yet, to say that is already to go too quickly, because Jews are represented. Perhaps the difference here is one of degree, at least with this opposition: there are Jews in novels, even as protagonists, but they remain distinct individuals unassimilable to the universal subject. And there are homosexuals in novels (consider Balzac's Vautrin, put on stage as early as *Le Père Goriot*), but they are fleeting appearances, scattered representations that never form a discrete discourse of subjectivity, what Terry Castle calls the flickering image of the "apparitional lesbian," a concept extendible to all these others. However, the representation of women is a continuous and evolving matter parallel to the development of the bourgeois novel itself, as Ian Watt has shown.

The spaces of representation of and for women, though configured as secondary, are always and already figured for realism within its praxis of realism and before it as well. There is a space in which feminine desire can be fit, even if that space is one of masculine fantasy. Emma Bovary, the first literary example of shop till you drop, occurs in a literary space, neither reducible to a stereotypical figure nor imprisoned in a fixed locus. The mutability of that space, part of the original and originary dyad and opposition is given with the formation and deformation of that space. In other cases, the space is not given with the birth of realism, the inscription of realist praxis, or even the concomitant ideology that frames the spaces of representation. Certain figures occur where there has been potential for representation but no language for it. Realism moves the stereotypical toward the subjective, just as it will move the nonrepresented (that which was previously considered unrepresentable) toward the represented.

With that movement comes simultaneous loss: a loss of the truly other. By bringing the unrepresentable toward the realm of realist narrative and thus into the realm of unrepresentability, the very possibility of unrepresentability is lost. Where this remains, in fragments, traces, and haunting figures, will also be the subject of this study. There is a *horla* at every turn, whatever one sees or does not see.

The space of representation of realism seeks to go beyond dyadic opposition as a means to its own fulfillment. At first this search means that the very idea of binary opposition, and even dialectical opposition, is superseded by a set of tensions or differences that cannot be accounted for within the framework of a binary system. It means therefore that these additional others occur in a way that may be—and I am suggesting is—different from that standard opposition. This coming to prose has several components. First of all, the space in which the new discourse occurs is not wholly a discursive one but a figural one. Second, the space may occur as a traumatic one, at a locus of trauma, of suturing, or both. Third, the discourse, because of the not-yet-subjectified nature of that discourse is not necessarily wholly attached to the production of a discretely identified single individual. Fourth, in the most extreme cases, even as late as André Gide, who for many typifies high modernism, not realism, the discourse may occur at loci among discrete works, just as it does occur between or among characters.

Describing this space as figural as Lyotard defines that word in his ground-breaking study *Discours, figure* is to proceed quickly.[14] For Lyotard, the space of the text—be it a nonfictional discourse, a narrative, a play, or a poem—is marked and interrupted by figures that make the text something revolutionary, forcing it to reside not wholly within the realm of denotative, or even connotative, language. For Lyotard, the figure surges up and disrupts the text. A figure is the mark of the other that has not settled into a fixed textual structure. The figure makes the text question the bases of its own structures, the limits of the discourse, and the finite nature necessary for a thematic understanding.

Lyotard's basic opposition in *Discours, figure* between the discursive, the written, and the legible on the one hand and the figural, which involves depth and desire, on the other is, as Geoff Bennington points out, not merely a simplistic opposition but also a relation of difference (20). The figural ultimately interrupts and disrupts the lexical and the referential (22). While Lyotard limits the figural to the unconscious, it is arguably not justifiable to restrict it to that: the figural could represent not only the individual unconscious of a producer of text but also a kind of discursive unconscious, the mark of contradictions within a sign system or an episteme. Beyond that, the figure is also the mark of the unrepresented within discourse. The figural interrupts and differs from the flow of the discursive by introducing what is not comfortably represented in discourse. The figural corresponds to the freeplay of the signifier but is not a product of *signifiance* as much as it is a product of the gaps in representability.

Figures and figurality mark difference, and that difference can be approached in a variety of ways. Thus, although homosexuality is obviously one of the most important leitmotifs of the novel and one of the most profound structuring mechanisms, it is not a theme as such, unless it is understood reductively.[15] Proust's writing opens up the inscription of homosexuality in a myriad of tropings and movements that prevent closure. A subject becomes a theme when that closure is present to turn it into what Julia Kristeva called an ideologem (*Texte* 12). The word "subject" is problematic because it is used interchangeably for a character or for a motif. Perhaps the word "figure" is far more apt, because it shows the extent to which the position of the subject in the realist novel is not identical to the depiction of a leaky monad as character. This figure of subjectivity is found in the tissue of the novel, in the discourses that may *or* may not (or may *and* may not, again, in what Kristeva calls nondisjunction) correspond to a point-by-point description of a character.[16]

In realist narrative, there is an endless regression away from the instance, insistence, and instant of writing, a multiple path of connotations, tropes, and intertextual references that spiral away from completion; all these phenomena mark the written work as a locus that is both a self-reflexive *mise-en-abyme* and an infinite, heterological expansion. The realist work is particularly marked by this figurality because of its implicit (and sometimes explicit, as in the case of Balzac) claim to being a universal, complete discourse that matches the referential world. This figural disruption is not the only means of textual disruption, but it is a cardinal one to examine in light of the realist enterprise. The figural disruption or emergence is a way for realist praxis, even despite itself, to represent negation and contradiction and to leave a negative field within the textual space. It is a complement to Bakhtinian dialogism that views the written space of the narrative as a locus in which various discourses vie to create a heterology and to insist on the way in which the subjective experience of the world is viewed in an oppositional fashion. On another level, the tropes and rhetorical figures mark the textual space as one in which a reversal occurs through language, and an undoing—deconstruction in the most banal sense of the word—takes place within the space of the narrative. Despite the denotative model central to the realist project, there is always a space of reversibility, Barthes's symbolic code (*S/Z* 26). Because of the primacy given to the act of reference as act, writing itself as a signifying process, the realist work becomes a space in which misreading coexists with a correct univocal reading—or, more accurately, is a space in which there is no graspable correct reading. No reading of realism can maintain its univocal signification.

The figure reinforces the notion of the negation of the discourse, the insistence of the otherness of the narrative to itself, and the destruction of anything even resembling the closure that verisimilitude requires for the act of representation. The figure opens up realist narrative to a verisimilitude including the unknown and that for which there is no name. The figure is the coming to presence of the representation of otherness, of the remarking of that for which there is still no language. Whether the figure occurs at a locus of trauma or is that trauma itself depends on the plausibility of there being a correct reading. The surging of the figural occurs at a spot at which the realist work finds its breach as that which had not been included (which is not the same as that which had been excluded, even if they cover the same territory). The point of that breach, which is always a remarking through suturing, ideological or otherwise, of the insistence of the same, is the point at which that otherness creates its challenge.

Precisely because the figure arrives at a moment, locus, or site at which there had been no name given theretofore, it is not surprising that it does not arrive as something discretely incarnate. The other does not necessarily, if ever, sit comfortably within a subject, within a character. In that any individual character is always marked by a Bakhtinian dialogism renders problematic the identity of that character to himself or herself. Beyond that, the figure is a destruction of any purported identity, even when that Bakhtinian dialogism is bracketed. Thus the figure happens between characters and between a character and the narration against which that character is set and from which he or she is ostensibly but not really placed in the foreground.

After this overview of a certain number of critical matters in an assessment of realism's figures of the other, this study focuses on Balzac's *Eugénie Grandet*. In this most normative of novels, Balzac subtly and convincingly shows the reader how he constructs valid subjects of action and discourse. In particular, he demonstrates how various subjects are included and how they relate to repositories of values. It is thus that Eugénie herself is constructed as a viable figure. With the construction of Eugénie comes much reflection on the interrelation of gender roles and social roles: from her father's point of view, Eugénie must remain a dutiful daughter, but within the context of the society of wealth, he has brought her up to be an independent son. The remainder of the chapter is devoted to the strange introduction to *Pierrette* and to the meeting between Yautrin, now the Abbé Herrera, and the despondent Lucien de Rubempré, who has been thinking about committing suicide.

The next chapter looks at Flaubert. After several pages devoted to the figuration of desire in *Madame Bovary*, the study focuses on the novel of complete alterity, *Salammbô*. In this radical departure, Flaubert attempts to develop a verisimilar reconstruction of the historical moment of Carthage during the Punic Wars, a moment in which no underlying logical or rational base can be invoked to stabilize the system. This study shows how Flaubert, writing the absolute other of Carthage, constantly undercuts the means by which the reader might lessen the ambiguities of the narrative. The final part of the chapter is devoted to the "deconstruction" of the Kantian transcendental category of time in *Bouvard et Pécuchet* and the implications for narrative: time of narration, tense, and logical order of cause and effect.

The fourth chapter focuses on the dehumanized other as an *ersatz* subject. The first part of the chapter is devoted to the developing sense of the object in late nineteenth-century narrative. Specifically, Zola uses the object as the equivalent of a subject. In Zola's world of depsychologized narration, the various characters lose a sense of essential subjectivity as they are complemented by the objects that constitute their world. Zola invests objects with memory, traces of subjective presence, and even morality: the object can be invested with evil. The chapter ends with a study of the pervasiveness of evil as motive force in Mirbeau's *Le Jardin des supplices*. In that novel, the only real subject of action and discourse is evil itself.

The final chapter is devoted to two high modern narratives as the last heirs of the realist tradition: each invests in developing and destabilizing discourses in which there no longer can be any absolute knowledge about the viability of a subject. Specific focus is on the construction of the Jewish woman in Proust's *Recherche* and Gide's writing about homosexuality in *Les Faux-Monnayeurs* and elsewhere. In both these cases, the authors show how narrative has expanded to include a wide variety of positions and how no single position can ever be absolutely grounded.

# Just Balzac

## I. Prologue

Balzac's massive undertaking, *La Comédie humaine*, is a representation of the laws of the universe that Balzac is constructing. At first glance, these laws, obeying the constraints of verisimilitude in most of the *Comédie*, are those governing the world that he seeks to represent. Thus, in his world, parallel lines do not intersect, Newton's laws are observed, and Napoleon was emperor. Balzac's Paris looks like a reasonable semblance of the Paris of the Restoration, and his characters, for all their poetic souls, base motivations, involvement in lucre, and ideological stances, resemble the human beings of the world he is depicting.[1] In specific, their concepts of self, or more accurately, the concept of self ascribed to these characters, is consonant with the way in which the subject is viewed in a contemporaneous setting. This, in particular, means that the subject considers himself or herself a reasonably independent individual in whom the constraints of background, family, group, and social standing relate to an exercise of free will.

Certainly, the way in which various characters are cast into situations makes the exercise of free will a difficult choice at times; the personal desires of a character to succeed *quibiscum viis* (3:1182) are contrasted with the character's personality as limned by the author and with a sense of moral obligation, honor, a political agenda, and ideals of justice.[2] For example, despite his desire to succeed, to make his way in French/Parisian society, to regain his family fortunes, and to repay the sacrifices his family has made for him, Eugène de Rastignac in *Le Père Goriot* draws the line at condoning or consenting to a murder. Vautrin proposes arranging an accidental death for M. de Taillefer (junior) after Rastignac will have wooed the estranged Mlle de Taillefer whom her father believes illegitimate. If his courtship of this disenfranchised and impoverished young lady is successful, Vautrin suggests, when she suddenly becomes an heiress, she will not think Rastignac a gold digger but will marry him anyway. Rastignac will have no part of this pact with the devil and cannot accept that murder be committed for his sake, no matter how much he wants to succeed. Thus, his desire to succeed is tempered in part by his ideas of justice and universal laws pertaining thereto.

In that example, the laws of justice as a universal for all subjects are consonant with the laws of verisimilitude that control the unrolling of the novel, its descriptions, and its means of representation. In general, this is the case. Where there is a seeming conflict between action and justice, in works as diverse as "El Verdugo," "L'Auberge rouge," *La Peau de chagrin*, and "La Fille aux yeux d'or," two initial explanations seem sufficient. The first is a generic explanation of melodramatic excess (Brooks). If Balzac's writing veers at times toward a melodramatic conclusion, it is not so much that he is undermining the realist project at hand. One might posit the reverse: Balzac's success as a realist happens sometimes despite himself. He has none of the aesthetic impulse that Flaubert will have, and realism happens in his work despite any melodramatic impulsions on the part of the author. Balzac's realist impulse and his irony succeed where melodrama ebbs.[3]

What of the mechanism, structure, or hinges involved in the gargantuan project of *La Comédie humaine*? The parts certainly do not always fit together neatly. If this makes for a more complex opus, it also makes for a contradictory one, and, specifically, some of the *études philosophiques* do not neatly fit the patterns of the Parisian writings. The sense of power and loss, and reading as a negative exercise that ultimately depletes the world, contrast starkly with the power to read and the power to force a misreading in *Le Père Goriot*, in the second part of *Illusions perdues*, and ultimately in the cynicism and irony of *La Cousine Bette*. One could certainly find a common measure among the various parts, but Balzac's contribution to the realist project arguably begins with *Le Père Goriot* and the work that immediately follows, "La Fille aux yeux d'or." Earlier works and even occasional contemporaneous ones that seek a philosophical solution could retrospectively be perceived as one path—the search for the absolute—whose success is always mitigated by the ironic reversal and relativism of success in Balzac's more mature works. *Le Père Goriot* inscribes the project as a whole, attempts to give a microcosm, establishes the narrative techniques of background and description, and provides the mechanism for the recurring character. It also furnishes what will become the archetypal plot for a Balzac novel, the material/social success (or its opposite, failure) of a protagonist. This plot involves a change of state, social success, and financial gain. This novel also makes the first attempt at an inscription of the other, in the form of Vautrin, cast clearly, although not at all exotically, as homosexual. The following work, "La Fille aux yeux d'or," though ending with a melodramatic *coup de théâtre* and marked throughout by a willful exoticism, still reinscribes the other, again, in the form of the homosexual, within the tissue of the narrative. With these works, Balzac successfully introduces the other as equivalent of the same to the extent that it can be represented.

From *Le Père Goriot* onward, one of Balzac's chief concerns is what we would now term the coming to presence of the subject as such in all its guises. In specific, that means the arrival on stage of the subject as subject of enunciation and of action but also as a viable economical, political, philosophical, and juridical subject. These versions of the subject are not necessarily coterminous, and in some cases they are in conflict, as has already been seen in the brief example from *Le Père Goriot*. Again, in that novel, the viability of the homosexual Vautrin as a subject of action and enunciation is not matched point for point by his validity in certain economic, juridical, or social schemas (Schehr, *Rendering* 91–104). Vautrin, the marginalized figure, guarantees the system; he seeks to escape its oppositional nature by fantasizing becoming a landowner and slave owner in the antebellum American South, thereby installing himself as absolute subject in a carnivalesque reinscription of himself as Sun King.[4]

That marginality guarantees the binary opposition only briefly. In *Le Père Goriot*, the post-purge boarding house will function as this opposition guaranteeing binary couples and values only because all the others have been purged, sent to a purgatory, and deprived of their burgeoning subjectivity. *Le Père Goriot* is haunted by those thousands of posited slaves necessary for Vautrin and by the silent multitudes in the final scene of the novel. As the reader will remember, Rastignac's challenge to society is witnessed, so to speak, by all the dead in the cemetery at Père Lachaise, spirits of the past haunting the present, serving as a silent Greek chorus, marking the oppositional world, once again, as one that finds its opposition by marginalizing the impossible or uncomfortable third.

Not coincidentally, "La Fille aux yeux d'or" follows quickly on the heels of *Le Père Goriot*, as it represents the return of that melodramatic reversal mentioned above: in a game of changing gender roles, the only solution in the tale is the dramatic one of murder as the Marquise de San Réal kills her one-time lover, Paquita, pursued by the feminized Henri de Marsay. Rather than re-engaging and pursuing the marginality of a figure like Vautrin, in whom marginality can be understood as a coming in or a going out (Schehr, *Alcibiades* 5–22), Balzac chooses to make a literal haunting by invoking the act of murder: the insecurity of the truly other will not be accepted; the continuing marginality of the third entering and reconfiguring the representational work cannot be abided.

Perhaps then there is a danger in the feminine, and perhaps all these mysterious absolute others, all those that haunt, and all those that will enter are avatars of the feminine seeking to destroy, corrupt, or change masculine domination. The solution is as tempting as it is deficient: the feminine is always already there, always already within the representational schema, secondary to the masculine though it be. No: the introduction of the radically other is a *mise-en-question* of that position of dominance and submission along with the questioning of the concordance of laws.

In *Eugénie Grandet*, Balzac takes up the question again. It would not be too radical a statement to posit the following: dissatisfied with the melodramatic solution and as yet incapable of instilling as much irony as he will need to balance the question of the marginalized figure, Balzac sets out in *Eugénie Grandet* to undo the opposition between masculine and feminine, between male and female as they stand in supposed opposition to each other and as they stand as subjects before the law(s). Only then will Balzac know how to introduce complete alterity; only then will Balzac be able to trope his narrative with irony. He cannot pull a rabbit out of the proverbial hat or produce a *deus ex machina*. It is not they that haunt this work but all the others, those voices as yet unheard, those potential voices of the human comedy, of realism itself, as Balzac begins to shape it in his writing.

This time there will be no magic solution of disappearance: the potential escape of Vautrin to the southern United States or the real capture of Vautrin to take him safely off to jail. Nor will there be the melodramatic resolution of murder, evoked and effected but to no end, as the death of Taillefer does not result in Rastignac's happy marriage. Nor will there be the murder to end the difference of difference, the otherness of the other as occurs in "La Fille aux yeux d'or." There is no absolute to be sought, nor is there a total dissipation (*Louis Lambert, La Peau de chagrin*). Otherness must be understood, invoked, evoked, and included here and now. The solution will be a material one. The thesis can be thus rephrased as a set of questions. Subject to the economic law (material law, capitalist law, and the law of the family [*oikos-nomos*]), is Eugénie masculine or feminine? Is she her own subject, or is she subject to the will of another? Can Eugénie somehow prove to be the incarnation of the law of the feminine, both to mark territory as hers and to allow the absolute other or the mysterious third, to stop its haunting and take its place?

Let us see what is at stake in *Eugénie Grandet*. This is Balzac's normative novel, a novel of family values, the predictable novel that goes according to game plan, a novel where the charm or the genius is in the details. On the surface, this novel would appear to be among the most normative of Balzac's works. According to Lilian Furst (152–53), who chooses it as one of the model works for her discussion of realism, it illustrates Balzacian technique at work and shows the "density" of the realist novel by giving layer on layer of narrative against which the characters are presumably set. Perhaps the novel is too normal; yet it ironizes those norms by blowing them up from within. So much normality might not even be healthy to the reader. Reading *Eugénie Grandet*, Jean-Paul Sartre's hapless Roquentin tells us, is not much, but it is better than doing nothing. He writes: "I am going to read *Eugénie Grandet*. It's not that I take great pleasure in it: but one has to do something. I open the book at random" (75). To counteract the predictability of Balzacian plotting, Roquentin resorts to bibliomancy or *le sort virgilien*, and he opens to a discussion of Eugénie's growing love for her unfortunate cousin Charles, a discussion in which, as a sign of that love, she wants Charles to have strong coffee with cream for his breakfast. But horrors: to have that, the faithful servant Nanon will have to spend money, and that is just too far out of the range of the acceptable. The counts and accounts must be balanced, no money can be found wanting, no unnecessary expense can be made because the money must grow.

Sartre does not resort to bibliomancy; he chooses a moment in the book that is the epitome of the plot, of capitalist hoarding, of miserly attitudes, and of indentured servitude. Sartre wants to render a judgment and justice: human life is worth more than this and is what you make of it. Money, or filthy lucre, while useful in what he will eventually call the practico-inert, is an illusion of value. The individual must choose. However, Sartre never seems to wonder here who is an individual or who can choose. For Sartre, universalizing his own position as a Western, male subject with his inalienable rights, everyone is an individual who should be able to choose and therefore, who *can* choose. Even if the Western subjects all believe this, it is not necessarily the case that every author and every character agree.[5] Charles Grandet, for example, will not be above treating people as chattel.[6] Thus Sartre fails to realize that there is a history to the perception of subjectivity within the dominant discourse. It is precisely this that Balzac understands and illustrates in *Eugénie Grandet*, for that nascent subjectivity is the focus of the novel. Who is a subject? Who can decide? Who has a right to hospitality?

How can an individual have freedom, and how can justice be rendered to an individual? The question of justice seems to be present for two reasons. First, justice relates both to money (the novel's leitmotif) and Grandet's concomitant vice of avarice; he personifies not only wealth but also its miserly misuse.[7] This novel, whose theme is money, naturally lends itself to a kind of ethical retrospection epitomized in the question of justice. But also, and perhaps more importantly, this novel is ultimately far less normal than Sartre suggests, for it involves nothing less than the construction of its titular heroine in a way previously reserved by Balzac for his male characters.

Among the many great productions of *La Comédie humaine*, this novel stands out as being the first women's novel. It is the first important Balzacian novel in which the protagonist/title character is a woman. These heroines are few when compared to the heroes with whom Balzac peoples his works. Balzac's conception of action tends to relate to the male of the species; the man acts and the woman reacts. Thus, in *Le Père Goriot*, for example, Balzac gives the actions to Rastignac and to Vautrin, the latter more in theory than in reality, for he is ultimately limited in his ability to act, given his arrest. In the past of the novel, Goriot was the one, through his speculation and war profiteering, who acted at a propitious moment. In contrast, Delphine and Anastasie tend to react to the actions of men, as does Mme de Beauséant both in this novel, as she reacts to the actions of Ajuda-Pinto, and later, in "La Femme abandonnée."

For Balzac, the lack of action is not the same as a reaction, and one needs to go no farther than *La Peau de chagrin* to see this. In this work, which is not truly subject to the realist paradigm, Raphaël de Valentin chooses not to act as a means of prolonging, if not saving, his life. But that, too, in its perverse translation of an act of volition into an insistence that there be neither will nor action, is itself a kind of action, albeit negative in nature. Raphaël's abnegation of will is equivalent to an expression of male will, even as all his needs are met before he has to make a request. It is also a reaffirmation of the system: a man does not have to say anything for his needs to be met; the rest of the system, characters and objects alike, is subjected to him, dominated by him, even without will, representation, or enunciation. The system reaffirms androcentric discourse and power, but the system is doomed to disappear: at the metaphysical level, the reading/misreading has its consequences. Reading means there is representation and absence; the immediate is no longer manageable or presentable. The disappearance of Raphaël through an act of will (or the absent expression thereof) means that such beings will disappear. No independent subject or any subject that requires immediacy will last for very long in this new narrative and this new world.

Raphaël's successors, Rastignac, Vautrin, and Eugénie, will attain their successes or accede to their positions as subjects by an inclusion of the other, by an acceptance that they are part of a figural schema that includes alterity, and by a refusal of immediacy. Similarly, Lucien fails in *Illusions perdues* because he insists on the immediacy of his talent (his writing, and thus his acts of representation) as a key to the expression of the subject and his intrinsic worth. If Vautrin (as Herrera) teaches him a more ambiguous system, he will eventually return to a belief in his own worth, and thus he will fail.

With *Eugénie Grandet*, Balzac seeks to change the role of the woman into that of an actor and not just a reactor. Like so many other *mères de famille* in *La Comédie humaine*, Mme Grandet is the classic reactor, and she suffers mostly in silence. Yet, the creation of Eugénie as almost a rival to her father is a revolutionary act. Both Eugénie and her father stand alone as independent actors: from the beginning, Grandet marks his own means of transmission, and if Eugénie is imprisoned for life, she will still, through her negation, abnegation, and *bonnes œuvres* at the end of the novel, determine a path for herself. The two of them stand in opposition to all other characters of the novel. As Sylvère Lotringer (486) states: "In the novel, the represented social sphere always appears, crossed by regular pulsations, incessant throbbings by which rites, feats, politeness, news, women, goods, wealth, everything is transferred and transmitted, from one to another [*de bouche à l'oreille*], from hand to hand, the movement itself pre-existing in a way the various substances carried in that manner." Against that preexisting movement, a version of what would now be called social construction, stand the two main characters of the novel who cohere as characters precisely because they outstrip the limitations of social construction: they are men.

The creation of Eugénie as the first woman in French realist fiction with some of the same rights to subjectivity as a man would have is Balzac's experiment in fiction. Eugénie is not masculine in the way in which Balzac will later invest Bette with masculine features, attitudes, and the general absence of feminine sensuality. Nor is she masculine in the way that Balzac's serving-class women are often without feminine charm. Eugénie is masculine in that she seeks to act, for herself, as if she had the independence of a man. But there is revolution in that action: Eugénie's position automatically brings alterity into the picture, precisely because it upsets the structures of dominance—feminine figurality joins the position of the subject. As Catherine Nesci (269) underlines the "strange and impure origins" of certain of Balzac's women characters, such as Esther, Asie, and Paquita, could that strangeness not be extended to Eugénie herself? Eugénie is a character whose representation involves a changed relation to semiosis and figurality; it will have echoes in the novel, because that change necessarily creates a modification of the dynamics of representation. The woman who had always been treated to some extent as the object of ekphrasis is both insisting on the revision of the model of bivalent opposition and destabilizing the gendered pattern. Balzac moves his narratives away from women's novels as such toward a different realm. As indicated in the introductory chapter, while the nineteenth century creates its various others, the woman is always already there both as the subject of novels and the writer of novels; she is and always has been represented, if sometimes only from an androcentric point of view.

Eugénie, however, is another kind of woman who rivals men's subjectivity and independence and thereby challenges the structuring of female textuality.[8] Eugénie moves from the realm of the typically feminine into the role of the active son who will eventually replace his/her father in the latter's business endeavors. Instead of being raised to be a potential rich spouse with an ample dowry, Eugénie is raised to be an heiress, to be the controlling figure of the money that will eventually be hers. Even the whole battle for her hand is subjected to Grandet's never saying yes or no. Suffice it to say for now that this endless deferral of definition on his part is reflected in the impossibility of deciding for Eugénie and the impossibility of deciding about Eugénie. She eventually assumes her role and fulfills her being economically without fulfilling her femininity (again, in the sense that androcentric textuality and ideology ascribe to her): she will be the heiress, but a wife in name only, and certainly not a mother perpetuating a bloodline.[9] Balzac moves his character from being reactive to active, though in this work, Balzac does not give Eugénie the ability to act until the background story is over. It is not without irony that Eugénie's behavior is in part due to the fact that Grandet has done much to raise Eugénie as if she were a son. If he expects her obedience to him and if he expects through his avarice always to control her money, he has also moved to make her an actor (though sometimes unbeknownst to her), as an heiress-in-training without full knowledge of who she is and what she has.

From the very beginning of this work and despite all appearances to the contrary, this novel is all about alterity: the construction of a woman as someone who can be subjected to men's laws just as a man can be and not as a victimized woman. It is, as Stendhal would say, "le premier pas." Balzac denaturalizes the woman from the role assigned to her as the "natural one" by eighteenth-century tradition: wife, mother, reactor, and subservient figure. So, in a process of distantiation, or what the Russian formalists called "defamiliarization," Balzac distances the woman from the roles assigned to her to make her a full player in his human comedy. For Balzac, the woman must be moved from her assigned role in the dyadic opposition to be the first of the others.[10]

Here, Balzac entirely reframes the structuring of the woman in the character of Eugénie. Balzac sets an impossible task of making Eugénie the feminine (but not effeminate), weak, or indolent son that Grandet never had. Eugénie incarnates the grounding of alterity in the known world, the construction of the other within the realm of the same, because she is constructed relative to laws of economic transmission and, ultimately, justice. Thus the question of alterity in the nineteenth-century novel is double. First, can there be a presentation of alterity within the narrative of the realist mode? In ranging ever more widely, the writing of the nineteenth century will seek to normalize otherness without giving up its own aesthetic imperative. Second, the introduction of the other, again as a figure in the Lyotardian sense, is nevertheless a disruption of the nomothetic laws, the structures of economy, local politics, and balance. With the introduction of the other, there is always a question of justice. Can there be just treatment of the other when the other has his/her own laws, when the other has a measure of the unknown? Even as the realist work seeks to include the other within the realm of that which is available for aesthetic consideration on its own terms, there is always the consideration that there is a disruptive element that may challenge the role, the locus, and the stance of the individual and that of the universal.

Balzac's own take on the construction of the feminine is related to the larger question of creating a character and limiting or delimiting the language of the character. For Balzac, the creation of a character in this world is an ekphrastic moment in which the pause that guarantees the construction is a safe, aesthetic position. That pause guarantees that the rhetorical moment of reading is one that safeguards narrative from the invasion of the other before proceeding safely to a continuation of the narrative. In *Eugénie Grandet*, the other is presented in the guise of Eugénie herself, but it is also through the introduction of the Parisian nephew, Charles, as other to the world in which Grandet operates.

It is easy to see Charles as being at first not only the outsider but also the Parisian contrast to the provincial cousins. Charles is a study in foppery and in acquired city polish:

Charles's manners, his gestures, the way in which he held his spectacles [*lorgnon*], his affected impertinence, his disdain for the box that had just given such pleasure to the rich heiress and which he obviously found either without value or ridiculous; finally, everything that shocked the Cruchots and the des Grassins pleased her so much that before falling asleep she must have dreamed for a long time about this phoenix of cousins. (1059)

If his uncle has the eye of a basilisk (1036) that fixes the gazer in his /her path, Charles is like another mythological creation, a phoenix born out of destruction and ashes. It is a fitting comparison both for the destruction Charles's father has gone through and for the prediction of Charles rising again reborn from that destruction. Charles will succeed: Balzac is already telling us as much; once he has removed all the signs that make him a Parisian, once he becomes his future by embracing an unsigned and unrepresentable alterity, Charles becomes the realization of his cousin's dream, the phoenix rising from its ashes. That dream will not be fulfilled as a dream but only as a figure, for the realization of a dream is part of the romantic baggage that Eugénie herself is saddled with as a *woman*; she will lose that as Charles loses his foppery. Both will become other and, by continuing, introduce that otherness into the realm of representation. Charles will inspire more than one dream in this novel: he is the peg on which many hopes are hung. What comes out of such a description is something far more basic: Charles is implicitly compared to his uncle. Like his uncle's, his manners are acquired: for the uncle's stammer there are suave city manners; both are said to be "affected" (1035 and 1059). Charles, too, is compared to a mythical beast, a phoenix, a bird born of fire that, rising up from its own ashes, is, as Borges puts it, "an heir to itself," is comparable to Grandet's basilisk, with its deadly look and poisonous gaze.

Turning from character to description informs us even more. The ekphrastic moment in Balzac is a moment at which development stops, in which he gives rein to a poetic, yet generally unironic, language and by which he haunts a space. Examples abound, including the famous description of the dining room in the Pension Vauquer of *Le Père Goriot* and that of the artist's studio in "Le Chef d'œuvre inconnu." In *Eugénie Grandet*, Balzac provides a set ekphrastic moment in the further description of the house. Whereas the first evocation of the house is a means by which he hints at a conclusion, the more developed description is charged with being a recipe for unreadability, a series of allegorical figures referring to everything and nothing, a mark of inscrutability. Like Grandet himself (1035), the house says neither "yes" nor "no":

Above the arch reigned a long bas-relief of sculpted hard rock representing the four seasons, whose figures were already eaten away and blackened. Atop this bas-relief a plinth jutted out on which there were several kinds of vegetation due to chance. . . . The door, in solid oak . . . was solidly maintained by the system of its rivets that made symmetrical designs. A square small grill, with closely spaced bars red with rust, occupied the middle of the medium-sized door, and served, so to speak, as a motif for a hammer attached to it by a rang and hit on the grimacing head of the main nail. This hammer, oblong in form, and of the sort that our ancestors called a Jack o' the clock [*jacquemart*] resembled a large exclamation point. Looking at it attentively, an antiques dealer would have found several hints of the essentially amusing figure it once represented and which long use had erased. (1039)

This ekphrastic moment bears some attention not only because it has been unjustly neglected but also because it provides one of the keys to the readability of the novel. Ekphrasis is a moment at which all reflexivity stops: a moment at which pure description takes over *qua* description to point the reader toward understanding description as meaning. At that point, the narrative is ostensibly heteroreferential, an instance of art being described with neither *mise-en-abyme* nor any other recurrent figure. The ekphrastic passage seems to sit outside the narrative line as forming a whole that can be reflected only as a thing in and of itself. It is not a moment of the Stendhalian mirror but a moment whose solidity is not even tempered by the merest transparence or translucence. Here, as elsewhere in his realist narratives, Balzac underlines that opacity with a set of figures that rhetorically push interpretation away: the figures form a symmetry, but no visible pattern; the figure was once readable but is no longer readable; the object or objects in question stand as mute remainders of that which can no longer be interpreted.

Put another way, the ekphrastic object in Balzac is that which defies reflection in all senses of the word. In *La Peau de chagrin*, the antique dealer's shop is described as a *capharnaum*, and the wild ass's skin can never be read properly: as much as the former is a jumble, the latter is an impossibility. It seems to be written in Arabic, but it is said to be written in Sanskrit. To read it, to accept what it says, is to reduce both oneself and what one is reading (Weber). Here it is not only the architectural motif but also the strange arrival of the outsider that becomes an odd moment like an ekphrastic moment, because in these cases, there is a defiance of readability.

If the door can no longer be read, neither Charles nor Grandet can be looked at directly within the parameters provided by the laws of realist narrative. Both are creatures of construction, but both defy the laws of representation in a fundamental way. Grandet's killing glance prevents any sort of equal exchange ever from taking place and therefore messes up any and every economy in which he participates. So, too, is it with Charles: he is, phoenix-like, his own heir. He does not need Eugénie to be his wife, for he can create his own future without her. Thus Balzac destabilizes the supposed anchor of white male dominance by making the figures thereof somewhat other in and of themselves.

Again, as a matter of prologue, Balzac manipulates situations to make his characters representative or exemplary individuals. In this case, in addition to the nuclear family of the Grandets and in addition to the outsider Charles whose very arrival is that which will provoke the resolution of the plot, Balzac limits the rest of the players quite severely: "Only six inhabitants had the right to enter this house" (1036). Just as the author has used poetic devices to multiply the means by which he gives narrative structure and depth, with this limitation of the *dramatis personae*, he helps the reader focus on what he (Balzac) considers to be the essentials of the story without any distractions from the tangential or accidental details that might otherwise have given a thickness to the reading. In that, Balzac is following the Stendhalian recommendations for streamlining a narrative, which, despite Stendhal's purported dependence on chance—"Between Julien and me, there is no signed contract, no notary; everything is heroic, everything the son of chance" (1:513)—are the watchword of his writing. The Stendhalian mirror (1:557) seems to offer a sharper image than that ordinarily held up to society. Balzac's means of reflecting society in *Eugénie Grandet* takes this position as well.

Balzac's processes, techniques, and ideological critiques are the means by which the narrative develops, the plot is formulated, chance is reduced, and dénouements are eventually enacted. All these are means that develop the narrative while ostensibly maintaining the readers' interests. In reading the first few pages, one might predict a dire outcome for the characters. Even aware readers of Balzac do not yet know how this singular development will occur or how Balzac's detours are cynical and ironic reflections. Such reflections are the basis for a critique of society that has turned its back on spiritual values, that has given voice both to the embourgeoisement of France—what Balzac terms "our mania for equality" (1032)—and to its niggardly negation in the character of a creation like Grandet. The rush for money instead of spirit is inappropriate in Balzac's eyes; yet the denial of basic human need is even more dastardly. Grandet's method of profiting from the bounty of the land that provides him with almost all his needs, seemingly a praise of the earth and of a system that precedes the capitalist model because there is little need for money when the earth provides all, is the means by which Balzac continues to criticize the avarice and stinginess of the character. Grandet gets all he needs from his tenant farmers, makes Nanon do the baking, and eats game only since his purchase of land with game on it (1034–35).

The details are sublime, yet this is not all, for even in maintaining both the laws of form and the parameters of realism Balzac challenges general laws by the needs of narrative, the vagaries of the plot, and his ideological ends. Some challenges rise above the level of the local *écart* to put the entire system into question. The move between the singular and the typical is homologous with the move from local to general, individual to universal. The generalized problematic can be rephrased as a decision on the universal: it can be resumed as a question of justice. Even if justice is perceived as a universal because it is fundamentally seen as such in the world in which Balzac sets his novel, a verisimilar one based on the universals of the Revolution (for example), justice is meted out in strange ways, ways that ultimately challenge the entire system at hand. But it is a question of *deux poids, deux mesures*: invoking the general and the universal brings to the fore the subject of this book—the other, and, specifically, the relation between the nonsubject and justice.

## II. Character

In what space, narrative or otherwise, can justice occur in this novel? But first, how can justice be represented? The laws of verisimilitude that enable a representation of justice as functioning with the same universal impact as in the world being represented are not, for all that, freestanding, independent laws. In part, they arise from the construction of the narrative itself, as it proposes its own paradigms for representation and, thus, as it finds itself creating—and bending—laws consonant with the author's goals, with the free play of the writing, the ideological structure, and the ambiguities of narrative itself.[11] The laws of verisimilitude for the Balzacian novel are affected by several factors. First, there are the internal constraints or limits of any verisimilar system: these may be internal contradictions, the impossibility of a perfect *mise-en-abyme*, or black holes and spaces of undecidability. Second, the laws of verisimilitude may be affected by other protocols: the gaze of the reader and the rhetoric used in the depiction of the reader; the discursive praxes that represent ideology both at a conscious level in the work and in the level of the novel's "unconscious"; and the ways in which chance and probability move the work in various directions that may or may not cohere with other constraints, parameters, and protocols. Moreover, classical thematic analyses and semiotic readings of any novel show the way in which "poetic" protocols affect the representational system and the manners in which the author's desire for an aesthetic product, affect, or result informs the laws of the particular universe.

The space in which the narrative occurs and the space that it establishes as the locus for verisimilar narration are crossed by the laws of form and the universals of the space already described. There is nothing new in saying this: the kind of verisimilar description favored by realist writing is not merely a description of the objects in the world, nor is it only an approach to a psychology recognized as a verisimilar one. As Le Huenen and Perron maintain, the role of the object in a realist novel is often as an echo, guarantee, criterion, point of origin, or terminus for the delivery of meaning (95). The objects themselves, as Claude Duchet has also shown in reference to *Madame Bovary*, form a system that is at times independent from or opposed to the literary system. Still, there is a material base from which both arise.

This world is therefore also one in which the laws governing the economic systems, family life, and various other institutions too numerous to mention are in agreement with those in the world described. Thus, Balzac puts a world in place that corresponds to that which he is seeking to represent. Certainly, there are *écarts* that are understandable as means of artistic expression. Most obvious in these areas are some of his descriptions, which have narrative and semiotic functions that deliver information to the reader. On the narrative level, "Balzac's lengthy, sometimes seemingly self-indulgent and excessively compendious, cataloguing 'bibliographical prefaces,' far from being just preliminaries to the action, are vital components as entrances to the realm of the fiction. They mark what Genette has called the 'frontière intérieure du récit'" (Furst 60).[12] In *Eugénie Grandet*, this description will help limit the world at hand to a stifling provincial town for which the realist methods of description and analysis are deemed adequate. As Smith-Di Biasio has remarked, the novel repeats "the very structure of the *Comédie*'s seminal fantasy whereby a microcosmic world exerts such a powerful hold on a subject as to make the 'real world' uninhabitable for her" (53). At the same time, there is the figure of escape that Balzac posits with the construction of this narrative prison: the impossibility of Eugénie's escape is contrasted with the necessity of Charles's departure, a means by which certain figures of otherness will be introduced into the novel. The evocation of the sad, almost pathetic poverty of the Montagne Ste. Geneviève at the beginning of *Le Père Goriot* and the creation of a melancholic provincial town on the first pages of *Eugénie Grandet* relate to the creation of an atmosphere in which what one might otherwise call photographic description is troped by the author's desire to instill a set of subjective emotions in the scene, impart them to the reader, and, therefore, provide a local momentary irony on which the reader can meditate. Consider the opening of *Eugénie Grandet*:

In certain provincial cities there are houses the view of which inspires a melancholy equal to that provoked by the most somber cloisters, the darkest heaths/moors [*landes*], or the saddest ruins. Perhaps in these houses there is the silence of the cloister, the dryness of the heaths, and the remains [*ossements*] of ruins. (3:1026)

Balzac is preparing the reader by troping the description with an overlay of several semantic fields. The provincial house he has evoked will be one in which people live a monastic life—a description reinforced a few lines later by the mention of a person whose face is "half monastic." This is quite obviously not only the life of spare pleasures and reduced luxury to which Eugénie will be treated, despite her father's extensive wealth, but also the prediction of a future for her that will not be a happily married one. At a more metaphoric level, relating the house to a sort of wasteland of dry heaths underscores the aridity of the life within, the stifling of desire, and the squelching of all light and life. The description predicts a sterile future with nothing but ruins and the bones of its erstwhile inhabitants lying around as remains and reminders.[13]

That same description also begins to challenge the notion of pure subjectivity equivalent to the independent subject. One individual flows into another. An independent subject for transactions becomes one with her past, her future, her speech, and her silence. The implied reader is also supposed to figure melancholy within his or her silence and a tacit acceptance of the situation. The novel is already in a state of mourning, understood as that figuration of the other never wholly seizable or ever completely dismissed. The realist novel is already the work in which the representations, albeit of the present and its avatars of presence, endlessly remind the readers of the "remains of ruins."

There is thus no surprise here: Balzac almost undercuts his developing irony by the straightforwardness of this prediction. He is preparing a trip to a world in which the potential for success is ever present but in which, sooner or later, the characters—and, one would venture, the title character in particular—will not be able to live a life of happiness, light, and pleasure. Balzac uses descriptions such as this, or descriptions of a character, to provide an insight, a prediction of the future, or a resurrection of the past: an insight into the psychological that shows, through poetic language, what might otherwise take dry, lengthy disquisitions to show in a purely verisimilar narrative. Thus a few words of comparison with real and imaginary animals are all Balzac needs to show Grandet's inner nature: through the comparisons of Grandet to a boa constrictor and a tiger (1033) and a prelude to the longer physical description of the man, whose "eyes had the calm, devouring expression that the people say is that of the basilisk" (1036). Grandet is a beast of prey, with neither pity nor mercy; he is a carnivore, if not to say a cannibal, who will stop at nothing to accomplish his business goals; he has a magical power to fix people dead in their tracks. It is not a long path, but only a short metonymical displacement, from the eyes of the basilisk to the investment, in something completely anodyne, of this same generalized feeling: people feel that the wen on his nose is "full of malice" (1036).

Such descriptions are a local detour of the laws of representation that do not necessarily have a consequence beyond the local level. The use of poetic language, the comparisons evoked, and the metaphoricity of the Balzacian narrative remain consonant with the universal laws of verisimilitude and realism. In fact, Balzac quite often seizes a local manifestation such as this and raises the local to the level of the universal: the people's perception of the malicious nature of Grandet's wen is said to be "not without reason." In that, this unprovoked and unsubstantiated insight is consonant with Balzac's own set of descriptions, it is considered to have a more universal value and is an illustration of the importance of the *vox populi* for Balzac.

Recent critics have often discussed the relation between Balzac's narratives and what one might call master signifiers such as money, capitalism, and society as a whole. Balzac's novels occur as discourses within and against the structures of bourgeois society and its economies of meaning and value. Is there a space, within all that, within the ideological and semiotic structures of the narratives, in which there can be justice? Furthermore, what would justice (or justness) be? To be just means applying a universal law (in the Kantian sense) to a situation, but it also may mean applying a more local law that may contradict a universal or general truth. There is a general disruption of representation with Eugénie's status; it becomes necessary to decide whether there are consequences, and perhaps the most telling way of doing so is to look at the perception of the subject as a subject of the law.

More to the point, the impetus necessary to the development of narrative may preclude the possibility of there being justice. A case in point would be the second part of *Illusions perdues*, "Un Grand Homme de province à Paris," where, for the development of narrative, Balzac must necessarily set Lucien de Rubempré up for a fall. Thus, despite Balzac's own espousal of universal principles that determine right and wrong, to wit, the transcendental figures of "the throne and the altar," fictional needs outstrip any sense of justice. Again, on a different level, the necessity for the ironic apotheosis of Vautrin in *Illusions perdues* and *Splendeurs et misères* makes any sense of justice impossible. If Vautrin is justly caught in the earlier *Père Goriot*, the eventual turns taken by the character show that capture to have been more a fulfillment of the law than a "carriage" of justice.

In other works, including pieces as disparate as "L'Auberge rouge," "Les Marana," "Le Requisitionnaire," "El Verdugo," and "Un Épisode sous la terreur," a local sense of justice—local in time and/or in space—may come into conflict with a greater good, a transcendental ideal, or a universal. In such cases, the weight of the universal is countered by an appeal to the political or the philosophical schemas that are temporal responses to a problem of justice. A third kind of matter relating to justice can be seen in a work such as the unjustly forgotten *Pierrette*, in which the law of the family and its personal sense of justice conflict both with honor and the economy of society as a whole. The contradictions embodied in the opposition are all visited on the poor title character, whose personal calvary can be seen as the complete antithesis of the actions of justice in narrative. In all cases, the narrative must contain and integrate arguments and ideologies of justice, politics, and philosophy.

Balzac's depiction of individuals always depends on a rendering of characters that moves between singularity and typicality. There is a play between the delineation of a character as an individual and the greater scientific project of illustrating a type, part of the human zoography. There is a second dynamic at work that depends on the readability or the impenetrability of characters. Rather than explain everything, Balzac will leave secret, silent corners, be they emotional ones, as in the case of numerous female characters, or, to take the most notable example, Vautrin's unreadability that becomes readable only when he is stripped. Here rendering of justice to a character (or by a character) depends on the delineation of an individual.

In *Eugénie Grandet*, the rules of justice, while not as capricious as a *sort virgilien* illustrated by Sartre's "reading" of the novel, are still somewhat less than the absolute Kantian conception of justice for all. There are at least two systems of justice, one operated by Grandet, a male system that depends on the accumulation of gold, both as the transcendental signifier and as the transcendental signified: the one with the most toys at the end of the game *does* win. The second is women's justice or the lack thereof: the impossibility of women to speak for themselves, to read and write for themselves, or to control their own destinies. Grandet will not allow his daughter to read, to calculate for herself, or, to use the fortuitous etymology that French offers, to *chiffrer* and to *déchiffrer*. He will not render her justice, will not be just with his daughter until it is too late, just as he will not be just with his wife: "Mme Grandet was a dry, thin woman, yellow like a quince, clumsy, slow; one of those women who seem made to be tyrannized" (1046).[14]

It all seems so simple then: there are women made to be tyrannized and men made to tyrannize them; there are women meant not to have justice in this world, women meant to be innocent victims; there are men made to do the dirty work. Is it certain that these categories are so clearly defined? If it were clear who the men and the women were, it could be determined how justice is meted out to one and all. A difference between making and being: women are *made*, as Simone de Beauvoir puts it. Instead of an eternal opposition that arises from nature, the women in this novel, and specifically Eugénie,

show the marks of having been constructed. As such, they are considered to be fungible goods. Of the servant-woman, Nanon, Balzac
writes: "her face would have been most admired on the shoulders of
a grenadier in the guard . . . a female creature with the shape of Her-
cules" (1042). Eugénie is equally heroic, but again, in the masculine:

> She had an enormous head, with the masculine but delicate forehead of
> Phidias's Zeus and gray eyes on which her chaste life, completely borne
> there, printed a startling light. The features of her round face, formerly fresh
> and pink, had been enlarged by a case of smallpox that had been mild
> enough not to leave traces but which had destroyed the smoothness of her
> skin, nevertheless still so soft and fine that her mother's pure kiss traced a
> transitory red mark on it. (1075)

Balzac's description of Eugénie sets the tone for reading the character. Although the daughter steeped in femininity, she has a masculine
strength like that of Zeus. Even if the gray eyes are a reference to
Athena, that connection is implicit at best here; Athena was, nonetheless, born through a particular form of male parthenogenesis. In
any case, all comes under the aegis of Zeus, the figure of paternity
that thoroughly marks Eugénie. In several phrases, Balzac insists on
the manner in which Eugénie has been imprinted, once by light that
reflects her chaste life, a second time by a mild case of smallpox, and
a third time, in a more ephemeral fashion, by her mother's kiss.
Eugénie is marked and remarked by each of these writings/events, as
if she were a paper to be read, a gold coin that glistened, or a writ to
be executed. The construction of the masculinity of the character is
thus tempered, not directly by femininity but by various means of inscription of forces of nature, natural law, and emotional bonds.

    Likened to gold, Eugénie is set not in opposition to the masculine
as its bivalent opposite but as some product of Grandet and his possessions. At the same time, it is as if she were one of his possessions,
the material correlative of the gold or the living tribute to what he
has accomplished. Capable of being marked, yet retaining her
chastity, Eugénie is already cast into a situation that will not see her
fulfill a woman's traditional role. The figure cut by the feminine in
the person of Eugénie reorchestrates the opposition and introduces
a measure of otherness, precisely because the feminine is no longer
the opposite of the masculine. In this material novel, the role given

to the feminine is that of a hybrid construct that refigures the sets of oppositions. The construction of Eugénie will itself contribute to a reconsideration of masculinity in the novel and to the roles of the more exotic others.

The description of Eugénie is a point of indeterminacy in the plot. Will she, like a son, be entrusted with the mantle of her father? Will she get to carry on the family name and honor? Or will she, like a daughter, accept her lot, her fate at being handed over to another, the heiress who will marry and, like chattel, be handed over to her new husband? Two laws, two systems of justice, two ways of behaving. Eugénie is not the only one to suffer from such ambiguity, for a reading of an interaction between Nanon and Charles shows how Balzac makes his characters don a veil of irony. Quite literally, it is a question of clothing.

Clothing is a heavily coded, polarized language. Clothing should tell us all, and yet Balzac continues to confound his readers. When Grandet's Parisian nephew, Charles, comes to stay in the Grandet household, it is an event that unleashes all the forces at work in the novel. Grandet does not like such young fops as this sensitive nephew: such Parisian young men are "almost like girls to be married" (1078). His masculinity, like that of all such men of his class, is in doubt; they are sensitive, effeminate creatures, a fact that the good-hearted servant, Nanon, has already noticed: "'This gentleman is truly cute/tender [*mignon*] like a woman'" (1071). One does not need to be as knowledgeable as the wily Grandet to see that there is an improper signing; even an illiterate servant, unaware of the ways of the world, knows this. Even the narrator may be inclined to agree: "it is true that Charles, raised by a gracious mother, perfected by a stylish woman, had coquettish, elegant, dainty movements like those of a sweet mistress" (1088). There seems to have been an exchange then, for just as Eugénie has been constructed to be her father's son, although with the maintenance of her servility as a daughter, Charles has been constructed by women. Charles's gender then is a derivative construction from within the category of femininity; it is at one remove from "true" masculinity.

Balzac establishes a dynamic of stereotypical behavior. Everyone knows that a man is a man and that a woman is a woman, yet there are affronts to the categories inflicted by Parisian dandies, for example, that show the improprieties. Grandet and Nanon represent the essentialist tradition that knows the truth of sexuality and gender and knows that such a truth cannot be masked by signs and that the improprieties are visible for all to see. With essentialism figured into the novel, the ideological position allotted to these characters reinforces a whole conservative strategy of interpretation by which meaning is denotative and where connotation and the freeplay of the sign are reduced to a narrow scale of possibilities. The essentialist strategy is thus consonant with the Balzacian picture of the ekphrastic moment that makes the figure subject to the set of acceptable meanings allotted to interpretation within the ideological framework.

Figurally, the essentialist position is opposed to a different set of possibilities that lead us to believe that there is already a possibility of sexual identity and gender being related to situation and sign instead of to essence. In this scenario, imported by Charles from Paris to the provincial town, gender is at least in part a matter of social construction. One is who one is signed to be. In this case, Charles figures in a chiasmatic reversal: if Charles is not a real man in his uncle's eyes, it is because Charles is betraying the essence of masculinity. But for Charles, Nanon could be a man, not because she is not feminine but because she fulfills a role allotted to a man; she performs masculinity. Moreover, these positions are not constant. In his world, he can still be a man, yet effeminate—be a dandy. What Nanon is, and whether servants even have a gender, remains to be seen.

Nanon kindheartedly offers to help Charles unpack his bags, an offer that Charles accepts in the following terms: "Upon my word, of course, you old trooper. Didn't you serve in the navy of the royal guard?" (1071). Laughing, Nanon can't believe her ears: "What's that then, the navy of the guard? Ain't it salty? Don't it go on water? [Quoi que c'est que ça, les marins de la garde? C'est-y salé? Ça va-t-il sur l'eau?]" (1071). Why should she be taken for a man? She knows she is a woman, her signs are appropriate, and it should matter little that she is big and strong, for that is how servants should be. The essentialist servant is confounded by Charles's discourse, for she has never been treated as an object by the Parisian social constructivist that Charles is. In contradistinction to his uncle, Charles knows that he is stereotypically Parisian, a construct of foppery and frippery, of dandyism that is, for him, the proper socially constructed sign of his performance of his masculinity. It would never occur to Charles to see himself as anything but a masculine man.

As befits his habits, Charles must change into his *robe de chambre*, a luxurious piece of clothing "in green silk with golden flowers and antique designs" (1072). Having already had her sense of hearing fail her when Charles jokingly took her for a navy man, Nanon now cannot believe her eyes. This is no housecoat but something that should be the cover for the altar of the church: something not for men or women but for others. Charles generously offers her the robe to do what she will after his departure: "you may do with it what you will" (1072). Nanon muses as she leaves Charles to his bedtime rituals: "'To give me this fine frock [*atour*],' she said as she left. 'The gentleman is already dreaming'" (1072). But it does not take Nanon, the die-hard essentialist, very long to change her colors: "'I'd have this golden robe,' Nanon was saying, as she fell asleep clad in her altar cloth, and she dreamt of flowers, of watered silk [*tabis*], of damask, for the first time in her life just as Eugénie was dreaming of love" (1073). Love makes Eugénie a real woman: "The very sight of her cousin had awakened in her the natural inclinations of the woman" (1077).

It takes an improper Parisian fop to convert the essentialist Nanon to social constructivism, but at the same time he makes her a woman. She who has never thought as a woman thinks, is now, in her mind, dressed as a woman. What was initially promised to the altar is now wrapping her body. Transformed from a navy man into a sublimely dressed woman, she dreams, finally, in the feminine. That must mean that she, too, was initially other, neither of one sex nor the other, neither man nor woman, until she donned the signs of femininity offered her by a man, whose signs they once were, signs of his impropriety as a man, signs of his effeminacy. To coin a phrase, clothes make the woman.

The opposition is not merely between an already established man and his other, the woman constructed as opposite and secondary, a safe figure who neither threatens nor revolts. The opposition is between a position that sees, on the one hand, the signs of the feminine as being intrinsically related to the essence that they are supposed to describe and, on the other hand, signs that do not necessarily signify anything but participation in a sign system. For Grandet, signs must be returned to what they signify: his stammering is a means of avoiding saying whether a sign is proper or not, whether a value is right or wrong, or whether a deal is good or not. For the position represented by Charles, the possibility of signs forming their own figures without any necessary reference to some atemporal essence is the foundation of a position that will be the means by which the other finds a proper ground.

If some signs can be represented within the limits imposed by the discourse, the other can be introduced as a viable mechanism. There is no need to have a radical requestioning of the essence, heart, or self, and in this phenomenological semiotics, that is beside the point. Balzac can turn the unrepresented into the represented, not by questioning the proper nature of the sign, because the question of property or propriety has been emptied of its meaning. He can do this by developing a language or a semiosis consistent with the means of representation that realism has to offer. It is no longer necessary to have recourse to the system, and the zoography of the human species depends more on the graphic impulse than on the zoological one. Second, the very troping movement itself that is the move to a set of descriptions is a means of preempting any essentialism of its dominance. Balzac is able to gather all "others"—and not only sexual or gender others—in his categories of difference and allot to them a vocabulary that will eventually be able to bring them into the fold.

This is not to say that Balzac becomes a social constructivist *avant la lettre*. Far from it. He believes in the *Ewig-weibliche*, in the priority of the male, and in the hierarchy of values ordered by the system founded on transcendental values of church and kingdom. The mechanism he is using is valid whether or not the observer has knowledge of an ontological identity beyond the semiosis. Whether a woman is born or made, or whether Vautrin's homosexuality is due to nature or nurture, is completely beside the point. Whether the other is really, truly, or fundamentally other, or whether he, she, or it is merely unknown is now moot. Balzac moves his sense of textuality from the unrepresentable to the unrepresented. What is unrepresented is always potentially representable in some future writing. Balzac actualizes Stendhal's model, not only of a mirror walking along a roadway but also of ideal readership who will understand him some time in the future. The potential existence of that reader makes the writing of the other always potential, but impossible. It will remain only the essence, endlessly deferred: the absolute that is never findable, that remains elusive.

## III. *The Writing on the Wall*

Potentially then, any figure can become a subject in *La Comédie humaine*, and it is in *Eugénie Grandet* that Balzac first realizes this by putting into question the very construction of the other in the form of the woman. But to move from there to a universal concept of alterity becoming subjectivity is not so easy, and that is where the system has a problem. The normalization of the other—here Eugénie, elsewhere Vautrin, la Zambinella, Gobseck, Esther, and numerous others—means the granting of some status of subjectivity to that other. The other is not yet devoid of its figurality—that which renders it always other. The presence of that figurality, in this case, Eugénie's femininity, is what impedes the universalization of the subject as subject. Even if the other is brought toward the normal and even if the normal is opened up to include alterity, the figure of difference remains. The game takes place in that vacillation between same and other.

A convenient way to think about this question of the subject is in terms of the function or the representation of justice in the novel. If justice is understood as an abstract of what is mete, fair, or good, then it relates intimately to the definition of the subject. A subject is not only a subject of action and/or a subject of enunciation. A subject is also a subject before the law, a subject of justice. Whether in a local system of laws or a general one, subjects should, under the concept of the universal, be treated the same way relative to the law. Justice is given in the law and in laws and in writing, so any understanding of the structuring of justice relative to the insistent otherness of the characters has to relate to the construction of writing within the novel. Balzac infuses various motifs—the description of the house and town, the description of Eugénie herself—with words relating to writing (Mortimer). Beyond that, writing proper figures in the novel as the means by which the plot is engaged but, more specifically, as the means by which the radical otherness of the characters is constructed.

Writing is first of all official and authorized writing, which are not necessarily the same, although their figures coalesce with each other. They are the embodiment of reason, of ideology, of the law. Sanctioned by power, official discourse marks the subjects as subjugated to and determined by it. The clearest example of official discourse in *Eugénie Grandet* is the newspaper article relative to the death of Grandet's brother. While hinting at some of the causes of the suicide, the official necrology (1083) suggests only that he might have found a way out of his financial troubles. The article is consonant with a policy of bourgeois self-enrichment, one Balzac himself found distasteful, but such was the watchword of the era, canonized under Louis-Philippe as the imperative, "Enrichissez-vous."

The valuation of self-enrichment subjugates the individual to the value incarnate in the writs, in writing, in money, and in the law itself: to be a good subject, one must profit. These are Grandet's own desires and wishes. If he is eventually seen to have an unhealthy relation to the money he avariciously hoards, it is not because he is in violation of the laws of the era but because he is in violation of what Balzac believes to be a higher set of laws. In letting her heart speak over her mind, Eugénie violates the model of the economy of the law. Writing therefore, consonant with the law and with money, is a universal equivalent and the metonymy of universal power to which all are subjected.

It is no accident then, in consonance with the structuring of this novel, that the ekphrastic, stand-alone figuration of writing will have supreme importance. Sartre's image of *Eugénie Grandet* is matched by another kind of bibliomancy, or a kind of writing taken as prediction of meaning, value, and justice. If Sartre chooses to illustrate what is wrong with the nineteenth century and the nineteenth-century novel by picking up on the over- and undervaluation of life and liberty, Balzac himself chooses a far more lofty example, a reference to the Book of Daniel. In the Book of Daniel, Nebuchadnezzar's son, Belshazzar gives a great feast to more than a thousand guests. Suddenly a finger appears, writing on the wall. The words given, known to all, are always quoted in the original language and then translated: "Mene, Mene, Tekel, Upharsin," or in French, "Mane-Tekel-Phares." In either case, "the writing is on the wall." Puzzled by what he sees, Belshazzar invites his father's seer Daniel to interpret the message. Daniel tells the king that the meaning is clear: You have been counted, you have been weighed and found wanting, your lands will be divided up among the Medes and the Persians.

The phrase is itself cause for reflection about justice and honor; its metaphor is of gold, of money; there will be retribution to pay for having come up short. Human and economic values are inextricably intertwined: the lack of value in an individual will be compensated by a redistribution of earthly possessions. The story is an allegory about earthly greed, about human value and honesty, and about possessions, gold, and the properties of inheritance. The writing on the wall is an accusation, an investigation, a judgment, and a sentence.

In this novel about avarice, a reference to this exemplary scene is not unexpected. For after all, Balzac's book seems almost formulaically to illustrate the various mythemes of the story of Belshazzar's feast: the accumulation of money for no other end but wealth itself, the deformations of the human spirit operated by greed, and the display of wealth. If Belshazzar overvalues conspicuous consumption, Grandet undervalues it by turning comfort into penury and modesty into deprivation. Structurally these *écarts* are the same. In the general scheme of things, in the development of the plot and in the moral of the story, Belshazzar's feast is the operative concept: Grandet's brother has been counted and found wanting, and his son does not inherit from him. Grandet endlessly counts and weighs his gold, which he believes includes his own hoard plus that which he has given Eugénie. When it is found wanting because she has given it to her cousin Charles for his trip, as she feels, unlike her father, that it is hers and therefore hers to give, she no longer inherits from her father: not his gold but the ever-renewed and uncountable gift of his love and affection.

The image of Belshazzar's feast makes sense in this value-laden novel in which all characters seem to come up short. They lose their money, the love of others, or their economic or emotional inheritance. And many of the characters seem to overvalue or undervalue money or love. Belshazzar's feast does appear, but not where and how it would have been expected, as an emblematic warning to the abuse of Grandet himself; rather, it is undercut, reversed, or erased. Is Balzac, who has produced this most normative novel, just taunting his readers with an extraneous reference? Or is he doing something deeper and darker? Grandet's nephew Charles, now an orphan because of the suicide of his father (from shame), finds himself in his uncle's house. Eugénie, Grandet's daughter and Charles's cousin, suggests helping out the poor family member. After all, Eugénie suspects that her family is well-to-do, even if she does not know the extent of that wealth, even if they live under the rule of an avaricious, if not to say cheap, head of household. When Eugénie suggests that Grandet can easily help Charles, her father reacts in biblical proportions: "The astonishment, the anger, the stupefaction of Belshazzar seeing the writing on the wall [*Mane-Tekel-Pharès*] could not be compared to the cold ire of Grandet" (1099). Thus there is a displacement of the emphasis of the scene from the meaning of the words (which Belshazzar would have understood) to the indignant reaction of the protagonist, as the author moves from meaning to anger.

Is this exaggeration on Balzac's part? Is it merely a novelist's trick to suggest the extent of Grandet's emotion? There is a difference between readers' expectations and Balzac's twist on the realization: Grandet's Belshazzar-like ire should have appeared much later, when Grandet learns that Eugénie has given her money to Charles. At that point in the novel, some fifty pages later in the Pléiade edition, Grandet does the ironic thing, he chooses to lose one more possession, his daughter. She admits to her father that she no longer has *her* gold (1153). Beaten by her logic—i.e, that she is an adult and allowed to do what she will with her money—he damns (1155) and disowns her: "she no longer has a father" (1156). No, the reference to Belshazzar comes much earlier, when Eugénie merely suggests some Christian and familial charity, help, or succor. Nothing, in short, necessitating the grand and miraculous gesture of divine intervention or an equally large reaction thereto.

Grandet's ire cannot be measured, even by the weight of biblical example, even by the writing on the wall, or even (implicitly) by the hand of God. Grandet is without parallel, without reflection, and without similitude. No writing on the wall can measure up to his own sense of value of self and other. Grandet lives in a universe of absolutes, where goods and values are accumulated, and where every exchange that is not materially to his benefit cannot exist. Moreover, he will not accept the writing on the wall: no one will weigh him, no one will find him wanting, and no one will divide up his kingdom among the Medes and Persians (or between the Cruchots and the Grassins). No one, not even his daughter, who is the apple of his eye and his unique heir after his death and that of his wife. When it comes to the law, justice, and judgment, Grandet becomes, at least for a time of great critical tension in the novel, the very wall on which the hand of God writes: "The most complete forgetting of his daughter seemed to be engraved on his forehead of clay, his tight lips" (1161–62). He is God, judge, jury, scales of justice, and sentence all in one.

One could say that he is doing this for her, that his sense of honor, duty, and paternity is for her, and even if she cannot apply the most severe set of rules and laws to the conservation of her goods, he will do it for her. If she is going to be so foolish as to spend a few sous on butter, cream, or sugar, or if she is going to be so foolish as to try to help the unfortunate Charles with some untold sums, it is all the same to Grandet: neither is an acceptable use of money. Money is to be kept, hoarded, always weighed, and never found wanting. Consider the image of Grandet's office/study: "There, undoubtedly, a hiding place had been handily set up, there were stored the titles for property, there hung the scales for weighing *louis*, there, nightly and in secret, the receipts and calculations were done—so that businessmen, seeing Grandet always ready for anything, might imagine that he had a fairy or a demon at his beck and call" (1070). What in fact does he do there? Balzac waxes poetic. When everyone else was asleep, "the old cooper would come to fondle, caress, gaze upon, ferment, pile up his gold [*choyer, caresser, couver, cuver, cercler son or*]" (1070). As the narrator uses verbs that usually are employed for describing intimate behavior between people, the gold receives the attention and love that Grandet cannot give another person.

Grandet's ire cannot be measured or reflected, for no one can know what he has, what he counts, weighs, multiplies, and divides. But his ire also means that justice cannot be served: Grandet has one law, his law, a law of gold and a law of order, a law that increases his holdings: "Financially speaking, M. Grandet had the traits of a tiger and a boa: he knew how to lie in wait, eclipse himself, face his prey for a long time, and pounce on him; he opened the mouth of his purse [*la gueule de sa bourse*], gulped down a load of *écus*, and lay down quietly, like the snake digesting his food, impassible, cold, methodical"

(1033). Nothing can come against that law: not the age of majority of his daughter who believes (wrongly according to him) that as an adult she can decide what to do with what is hers, not familial ties, not love.

For there to be justice, there must be reflection: the law must reflect the good of all of the commonweal, singularly and in community; for there to be justice, their behavior must reflect that law, and difference from it must be remarked, if not to say punished. Sometimes the punishment is self-inflicted: having failed—at life or at finance—Grandet's brother commits suicide, as he holds himself accountable for his failings, and as he pays what he believes to be the ultimate sacrifice. His brother would probably see the loss of monies as the ultimate sacrifice, rather than his life itself. But here, in *Eugénie Grandet*, there is no reflection, at least in Saumur, the provincial town where much of the story takes place. In Paris are honor, representation, reason, and reflection. In Saumur, there is a gulf opened up, a gulf of meaning and representation in which justice slides after the deconstruction of the individual.

Saumur is a singularity in the Balzacian universe, a locus in which the distinctness of the individual is lost in a gulf between a reflective system and one that allows no reflections. In Saumur, meaning is emblematically lost in favor of a meaningless sign whose value is its presence as sign of the past and whose value is determined by the presence of the sign. Describing the houses in Saumur, the narrator writes: "Further on, there are ports studded with enormous nails where our ancestors' genius traced domestic hieroglyphs whose meaning will never be rediscovered" (1028). Here, in these daunting facades, no one can read, no one can say yes or no, yet all can attest to their value.

Saying yes or no would determine fixed meaning: it means avoiding speculation and accepting commitment. Saumur is exemplified by Grandet himself, the repository of the society's meanings and value systems, that unique world in which no mirror image can be given: "M. Grandet enjoyed a reputation in Saumur whose causes and effects will not be fully understood by people who have not more or less lived in the provinces" (1030). Master figure of this universe, Grandet is the quintessential reduction of his less talented fellow citizens, who themselves can see no intrinsic value but who value what they believe they can read, see, or understand. Grandet buys low and sells high: he bought vineyards "for a song [*pour un morceau de pain*] legally, if not legitimately" (1030), which became considered as first growth [*la tête du pays*] through his care (1031). The citizens do the same: they seek to traffic not in bottles of wine but in chattel. For them the greatest prize is not first-growth vineyards but Eugénie herself: "The secret combat between the Cruchots and the Grassins, in which the prize was the hand of Eugénie Grandet" (1037).

Grandet mastered the sign system—in 1789, Grandet was a cooper who knew how to read, write, and cipher (1030)—but far be it from him to let his signs be read by others, be reflected on by others: "he never said yes or no and wrote nothing" (1035). What is written is damning, because it is definitive; it is useful only if it can no longer be read as writing, if it cannot be interpreted as a just or moral sign. Just as it is with the hieroglyphic facades of the houses of the town, it is the same with the moral lessons inscribed particularly in the Grandets' dining room: "The old-fashioned seats were adorned with tapestries representing La Fontaine's fables; but one had to know in order to recognize the subjects" (1040). Certainly that dining room, somewhat like the dining room of Mme Vauquer, is meant to suggest poverty, false in one case, somewhat true in the other. But the signs, in their unreadability, also attest emblematically to the impossibility of reading the "neither yes nor no" strategy of Grandet and finally, or summarily, the impossibility of interpreting a moral or ethical statement, the moral of a La Fontaine fable. Who will determine legitimacy (if not legality) if the moral of the story cannot be read, if the writing on the wall is so smudged as to be unreadable?

Reflecting silently in thought, but not letting oneself be reflected, this is how Grandet operates, this is how he can open up the gulf between the legal and the legitimate.[15] This is where the others can fall in, taken in by a trap, a game, a hum between reflection and nonreflection; they are trapped by his stammer, the singular mark of his speech pattern (1035). The narrator mentions the stammer almost at the very beginning of the novel. At first, it is a means of attaching a singular feature to the character:

He stammered in a tiresome way as soon as he had to talk at length or to keep up a discussion. This muttering, the incoherence of his words, the flow of words in which he drowned his thought, his apparent lack of logic all attributed to a lack of education were affected and will be sufficiently explained by the events of this story. (1035)

The description of this stammer, like that of the house, is meant to give a depth to the novel or to the tic that it otherwise would not have. By drowning his thoughts in a sea of words, Grandet may make the better deals, but he kills the thoughts in the process. This effective means of trumping his interlocutor, by making a deal in words of which the other has no comprehension, is useful in the business world. Unwilling to say yes or no, incapable of signing his name as an affirmation of who he is, he uses the same technique at home, where the words should be honest and forthright and where they should be able to convey relation and emotion. Grandet invests in a *langue de bois*, a language as far removed from justice as it is from human kindness, and it is that untempered language that always already drowns its contents that will help to be his undoing.

The stammer has an effect now and an origin, a false origin that marks it as a figure. Its effect is in its deal-making qualities, a trick of the tongue that catches the other. There is perhaps a deeper meaning in the present. Dufour maintains that Grandet's slowed voice puts language "under the sign of a lost plenitude" (45), which may be the case. That voice marks absences and silences unfilled by any words, yet, because of the attenuated continuity, they leave no place for filling in what might not be in his discourse. Dufour remarks that if "Grandet stammers, it is that the other listens" (45). This other is the other of public opinion, the collective that is the chorus of voices of Saumur. The stammer marks even more palpably a point at which he, Grandet did not listen and listened only after the fact to what he had or had not heard.

The stammer is not "natural," to repeat Balzac's description of Grandet's acquisitions, for it is one more acquisition; it is legal but not legitimate. Years before, he was duped by a Jew who faked being hard of hearing and who seemed incapable of finding the right words (1110–11). Caught by the Jew's stammer, Grandet found himself trapped in what he believed to be the words of the other, offered what he thought were the other's thoughts, words, and ideas:

Long ago, despite all his finesse, he had been duped by a Jew who, in the discussion, put his hand to his ear like an ear-trumpet, on the pretext of hearing better, and talked broken French so well as he looked for his words [*baragouinait si bien en cherchant ses mots*], that Grandet, victim of his humanity, though himself obliged to suggest to this wily Jew the words and ideas that the Jew seemed to be searching, to finish the arguments of the said Jew, to speak as the damned Jew would speak, to be, in the end, the Jew instead of Grandet. (1110–11)

Although the Jew bests him in the deal, Grandet winds up blessing the one "who had taught him the art of making his business adversary impatient" (1111). If this is the only business deal Grandet ever loses, he has learned something in return: how to stammer and how to open up the gulf while seemingly bridging the gap between representation and its falsity. He learns the difference between the legal and the legitimate and aims to stay within the letter, if not the spirit, of the law.

Grandet, this singularly avaricious and linguistically abstemious individual, would seem the least likely figure of the narrator in the novel. But it is a hypothesis worth considering. In the earlier novel, *Le Père Goriot*, it is arguable that for all his moral shortcomings, Vautrin serves as a kind of figure for the Balzacian narrator: able to sneak in surreptitiously, able to know what others are thinking (a trait that will be reinforced in the later works in the Vautrin series until he reaches the apotheosis of narratorhood as the head of the secret police), able to divine motives, and subject to being unmasked only when people play unfairly. Here, Grandet, the least charitable and most stingy of characters, also seems to be a poor choice for being a figure of the narrator. But certain of the processes are remarkably akin to those involved in Balzacian narration. Grandet is able to amass capital and gather things together, and in so doing he knows their value. He introduces the foreign (the other kinds of gold) into the realm of the safe haven of the home, the self, and the identical, yet he knows what each one means and what each one is worth. Parsimonious with language, Grandet is also able to read the minds of others and complete their thoughts, much as the Jew did for him. Grandet is the one who determines who is in and who is out, who is a worthy subject for inclusion in his own material, if not textual, economy and who must remain outside the fold. If not the exact figure of the benevolent narrator, Grandet (like Vautrin) is certainly his persona, his animus, and his darker side.

Legitimate representation and justice depend on "yes" being "yes," and on "no" being "no." But Grandet's stammer leaves all in an eternal middle ground: a hum of sounds, broken French, broken promises, and broken thoughts. For there to be true, legitimate representation and for there to be reflection, there must be the spirit of the law: representation must be haunted.

But by what? Representation must be haunted by a spirit of identity: in this novel of exchanged clothes and exchanged sex roles, is it any wonder that Grandet can become a Jew at the drop of a hat? That he can shed his own clothes for those of a Fagin-like or Shylock-like Jew? That he can circumcise himself and uncircumcise himself at will to make a deal? By impersonating this wily Jew, by learning to stammer, Grandet thus remarks the covenant, remarks the ritual circumcision, remarks the unrepeatable and unrepresentable act, which is the removal of the signifier of the foreskin. But Grandet fakes it: his stammer is a sign of getting around an agreement, a covenant, and an incarnation. To be blunt and vulgar, one has to have balls to succeed in this world, *quibiscum viis*. As Balzac writes in the preface to the novel: "the virile act [of creating a drama] would provoke riots in a republic in which, for a long time, it has been forbidden, by eunuchs' criticism, to invent a form, a genre, any sort of action" ("Préface" [to the first edition] 1026).

Grandet's stammer then is the mark of his faked anticovenant, not with some god of the Old Testament but with the god of lucre, a means of splitting hairs (if not skins), of transforming all he touches into gold: Grandet's stammer is the Midas touch. But his stammer is also the means by which he can remain free from judgment and justice; he stays within the legal bounds of a system but on the margins of legitimate behavior. Unjust toward his own nephew and all his flesh and blood, Grandet can be just only toward what he has amassed, the gold that he has gathered, the poetics of which can be heard in the exemplary catalog of the gifts he has given Eugénie, a veritable miscellany of names for gold: "vingt portugaises . . . cinq génovines . . . trois quadruples d'or espagnols . . . cent ducats de Hollande" (1127–28). In this naming, is there a not so subtle hint at the purported cosmopolitanism of Jews that Grandet may have adopted with the stammer? For, generally, Balzac gives all high prices only in *livres* or *louis d'or*. Here, it is not only, or even, the value being remarked but the material existence of the coins themselves. Balzac goes on to make a point about the readability:

This treasure contained new, virgin coins, veritable pieces of art about which Father Grandet inquired from time to time and which he wished to see again, in order to explain in detail to his daughter the intrinsic virtues, like the beauty of the milled edge [*cordon*], the clarity of the face, the richness of the letters whose high relief [*vives arêtes*] had not yet been marked. (1128)

In mint or uncirculated condition, the coins are virgin, a virginity whose metonymy, the virginity of Eugénie herself, is relevant from one end of the book to the other. At the end of the novel, because she has "neither husband, nor children, nor family," she is still called, even in her widowhood, "mademoiselle" (1198). The coins' virginity also corresponds to the magic stammer of Grandet, his verbal circumcision, his remarking of the foreskin as *parois*, as *tympanum*, as *hymen*, not reproducible, not justifiable by any but him, not reflectible in any mirror, language system, or economy of exchange. Even the readability of the money is part and parcel of the game: like the houses of Saumur, like the stammer of Grandet, like the worn La Fontaine fables on the upholstery of the chairs, the coins can be read only by those who know and who have not forgotten.

It is clear what is just, right, and appropriate to Grandet: reading the other, profiting from the other, and amassing the gold that *should* circulate but does not. The gold must remain virgin, just as his daughter must remain virgin until he says it is all right for her not to be. He is the master of her gold and her fate. He will decide who is to have her hand, her hymen, and her gold. What is unjust to him is a disruption of the system. On his daughter's question what going bankrupt means, Grandet says that "going bankrupt . . . is committing the action that is the most dishonorable among all those that can dishonor man" (1094).

## IV. Women's Justice?

Eugénie naturally thinks otherwise. She believes herself to be an adult, her own mistress, and owner of all she possesses. Justice for her is doing the honorable thing; justice for her is illustrating the activities of the devout Christian, taking care of her family, and being trustworthy, honest, and forthright. Like her mother, Eugénie believes in a virtue that extends to the entirety of the family, including her cousin Charles, whose intrusion in her life is so upsetting that she completely forgets her manners and violates his personal, private space. It is a violation she refuses her father in their ultimate showdown, but here and now, as her love grows for her cousin, she hesitates but finally gives in to a violation of his privacy. The same strands reappear that intertwine love, gold, and reading. Eugénie hesitates but finally reads Charles's letter to Annette. "Dear Annette" were words "she read everywhere, even on the tiles, written in flames" (1121) . . . "a demon screamed the two words in her ear" (1122). Having read the letter, Eugénie decides that she will give him her gold. She reads his interrupted answer, and ignores his coldness because of her own innocence (1124), and then reads a letter Charles has written to a friend (1126).[16]

Eugénie's sense of what is right is essentially Judeo-Christian, and action demands reflection, thought, and representation. It is tied up with her ability to read into the heart and soul of Charles (so she believes), and writing itself. Whereas Grandet, having long ago wrongly believed that he could read the mind, if not to say the heart, of a wily Jew, steadfastly espouses a strategy that denies the possibility of reflective representation, his daughter does the contrary. She pries into Charles's affairs (his letters) to read his heart and misreads his emotions because she truly believes in his virtue and her own. She is thus, unbeknownst to her, repeating her father's action of long ago: reading the mind/heart of the other and doing it wrong. Nevertheless, she maintains her illusion, the illusion of love. This is not to say that she is wrong to do what she does; for improperly reading or not, she believes in a higher moral order that tells her to give help to her family. In her own view, she is doing the right thing, she has done the right thing, regardless of the consequences, even if it ultimately provokes the death of her mother from chagrin, even if it means blaming herself for that death, for Eugénie sees herself as the "innocent cause of the cruel, slow illness devouring her" (1161).

Balzac emblematically insists on Eugénie's belief in the reflection accorded to the representation of the world in his description of

Eugénie's sympathetic following of her cousin, for Eugénie gets a map of the world that she hangs up next to her mirror to follow Charles's peregrinations (1147). But why is it so important to be able to see representation as a reflection of the world in order to have a sense of justice? To relate signifying discourses and representational systems is to see a possible exchange of meaning, but it is also to establish the possibility of the exchangeability of positions: anyone can stand in for another. To believe in the possibility of the representational system indicating the world or part of it means that the position of the subject—receiving or rendering justice—can be replaced by the sign of that position. The possibility of representation is the *sine qua non* of the universality of justice. Otherwise each position is local, each position is subject to its own local laws, and there can be no generalized notion of justice.

By stammering, Grandet scrupulously avoids that representability by making sure his language does not commit, by making sure his transcendental signifiers are visible (meaningful) only to him, by alternately possessing and alienating his property (body, daughter, gifts) as it suits him. Grandet assures that no one will read him and that no one will interpret for him except in a false interpretation of the law that is his law. No one will stand in his stead before the law. In contrast, Eugénie reaches out, sympathizes, empathizes, and identifies with the other, first in the character of Charles and then later in the closure of the novel, as she is the benevolent benefactress of the community: "The hand of this woman heals the secret wounds of all families" (1198). Her hand repeats and replaces the handwriting at Belshazzar's feast as she corrects that which has been weighed and found wanting. Eugénie attempts to right wrongs and heal moral wounds with the help of her material wealth: "pious and charitable foundations, a hospice for the elderly and Christian schools for children, a well-endowed public library" (1198).

## V. His Uncle's Nephew

Poor Charles, literally and figuratively, poor Charles. He cannot be a man, become a man once he is torn from the socially constructed world of the big city. Informed of his father's death, he cries like a baby—or, more accurately, he cries like a woman. With the news of the ignominious death spread through the household, one could hear the crying and sobs of three women; Charles, face down on his bed, is crying as well (1093). To make him a man, he must be torn from all his earthly trappings and be reduced to zero. He gets his manhood at the price of what he possesses. But what manhood does he get?

Balzac tells us that as Grandet gets older, he becomes more and more fixed in his obsessions. Speaking of Grandet's increasing avarice, the narrator writes that "The sight of gold, the possession of gold had become his monomania" (1167). As is the case with some other Balzacian characters, such as Balthasar Claës in *La Recherche de l'absolu*, Grandet ironically becomes possessed by what he once possessed; he becomes a slave to his obsession. It is different with Charles, sent abroad, where there is no justice and no law. If Grandet becomes the ironic slave and victim of his own thought and success, Balzac offers two solutions, two possible incarnations of a solution to that dead end. One is Eugénie's sense of justice: her Christian charity, exhibited after her father's death. The other solution is that of Charles, the dark fulfillment of what Grandet would have done, had he only been able.

For Grandet is subject to some laws and some sense of justice. Sent into exile by his uncle and with his uncle's funds, Charles is the investment in a world in which no one need heed a sense of justice, law, liberty, or dignity. The sponsoring of the trip starts out small but then is fully supported in exchange for Charles's last worldly goods. Grandet tells Eugénie that he will pay Charles's trip to Nantes (1095). Later (1138), having received Charles's jewels, he offers to pay Charles's trip to the Indies. The uncle invests in the nephew and gives him free rein to die or to succeed unhampered by a system that insists on human value. Charles will become worse than the Jew, worse than the stammering Grandet. For this most selfless of individuals, nothing is barred: Charles takes a pseudonym, Carl Sepherd. Indeed, it is tempting to speculate on the onomastics of this pseudonym. While Carl is close to Charles (and while it precedes Vautrin's metamorphosis into Carlos Herrera), the last name seems to suggest that Charles becomes "sépharade," that is to say, Jewish, like his uncle.

Charles is ultimately the incarnation of all the social constructs of

Paris: there is nothing there, no sense, no honor, and no heart, just a collection of behaviors. Little does it matter what path he takes as long as he is marked with success. Whatever means is available is the one to be used. The newly named Carl Sepherd "resolved to make his fortune *quibiscum viis*" (1182). Shorn of his birthright and his name, he sets out to make his fortune. If Balzac ultimately ironizes his eventual success, by moralizing that he would have been better off by being faithful to the one who loved him (Eugénie) for she winds up far richer than he, so be it. He still works toward his success by any and all means available.

What paths does he take? He turns his back on the West and its laws, or more accurately on what the West says its universal laws are, laws that are in fact only fully applied to white males. Everyone else is fair game, and Charles makes the most of a system of justice that allows injustice at every turn. His success is built on the slave trade, on the possession of others, and on human degradation. Once he is in the Indies, Charles "realizes that the best way of making one's fortune, in these intertropical regions as in Europe, was buying and selling men" (1181). He trades slaves and joins "to his commerce of men, that of the most advantageous merchandise to trade in the various markets that his interests led him to" (1181). People, objects, and chattel are all things to be moved, to be bought low and sold high. He has learned his uncle's lesson well and applied it in a world where from the view of a parochial west, there is neither the legal nor the legitimate.

The slave trade, the rape of colonies, and the complete reduction of humans to objects are Charles's stock-in-trade: Charles "sold Chinese, negroes, swallows' nests, children, artists" (1181).[17] Charles even takes the ultimate step, in participating in that most heinous of acts, *la traite des blanches*, with white women reduced to being one group among other commodities. Long before Flaubert's descriptions of the variegated group of soldiers fighting for Carthage in his *Salammbô*, Balzac offers us a thumbnail sketch that mixes groups into a giant commerce of human bodies bought and sold. Charles has lots of exotic women, but Balzac's arrangement of the catalog results in making white women as exotic as the others: "Negresses, Mulatto Women, White Women, Javanese Women, Egyptian Dancing-Girls [*Almées*], orgies in all the colors of the rainbow" (1181). Possession, purchase, sale, it little matters when these lives are nothing but a series of empty signs for the procurer, purchaser, or purveyor.

What of Eugénie in all that? She is condemned to her *bonnes œuvres*, condemned never to be a full, complete woman, condemned, in a way, to be the *alter ego* of Vautrin, the good angel corresponding to his devil. More radically, does Eugénie become a figure of homosexuality, male homosexuality in specific? At one remove, Eugénie winds up being the origin of Charles's slave trade; she performs thereby what Vautrin could not do in the southern United States and presages what Vautrin will do as he becomes head of the secret police, a position in which he controls all others. It is a reversal of the original system in which the individual male was seen to function as an independent subject. Vautrin will control not so much those independent subjects, if any are left, but the others all subsumed under the system. By not assuming any real role as a wife, or any role as a mother, Eugénie does not fulfill her destiny as a woman; she has become another man, an alternately gendered son to a father who understood nothing.

Balzacian justice? Hardly an operative concept in this most normative of Balzacian novels. Through an insistence on detail that is often rare in the work of an author accused of sloppiness, through an unconscious construction of a scenario that precludes closure, Balzac offers the reader a world in which no justice can occur, for the abyss is too deep. Balzac's disillusion starts far earlier than was once thought.

## VI. The Bridge to Cynicism

By the late 1830s, having invented the continuous and polyphonic narratives of the *Comédie humaine*, having introduced (but not having invented) the recurring character, and having fulfilled a certain will to exploit his own philosophical interests in the *Études philosophiques*, Balzac focuses more and more intently on the singularities of the human zoography he describes in the "Avant-propos." Having constructed a world against which and into which each new narrative is integrated (though some less intrinsically than others) and all new characters are set, Balzac begins to write the novels of disillusionment, in which the individual character is ultimately (and eventually initially) dis-integrated from society. The turning point, in terms of the *summum* of narrative complexity and complicity, is the dis-integration of Lucien de Rubempré in the second part of *Illusions perdues* followed by the extraordinary second life of Lucien under the tutelage of Carlos Herrera, also known as Vautrin.

It is true that Balzac wrote the first part of *Splendeurs et misères des courtisanes* before he wrote the encounter between Vautrin and Rubempré when the former saves the latter and prevents his suicide. Thus the meeting has something artificial in it, in that it is a bridge created for the purposes of implying a seamless continuity, a fiction within a fiction, not at the level of contents, as a story within a story, but at the level of narrative itself. The meeting between the two thus becomes a narrative bridge created for the purpose of underlining the continuity and the interconnectedness of *La Comédie humaine*, but the narrative, in truth, does not connect to anything but a previous incarnation of narrative complexity. This meeting connects to a narrative in which Balzac has given us a more traditional approach to and meditation on the human comedy than that which the bridge itself presents. The first part of *Splendeurs et misères* connects Lucien and Esther melodramatically to other mainline narratives in the collection and relates the readers to concerns and values, including the centrality of money and *arrivisme*, that are the focus of Balzac's writing from *Le Père Goriot* on, through the end of the thirties. Esther is Gobseck's granddaughter and is involved with the Baron de Nucingen in a pessimistic, cynical *mise-en-scène* that allows Balzac to use one of his favorite devices, the transcription of accents, in almost an abusive fashion, in the many scenes in which the Baron de Nucingen appears. It also allows Balzac, again cynically, to depict Lucien in the role of pimp, in a singular debasement of a character who had once been an idealist and poet. Ostensibly, Lucien's behavior and his loss of illusions can be attributed to Vautrin's influence, the amoral behavior of the former condemned prisoner whose own *arrivisme*, by less than orthodox means, is accomplished by violating as many of the ten commandments as possible. Lucien thus cedes his morality to Vautrin's seductive explanations for a bright, successful, and rich future. Lucien abandons his ideals for the success promised by Vautrin in the material world, a world in which victory is exacted at any price.

Wholly distinct from narratives like the first part of *Splendeurs et misères* are the far more complicated narratives of the 1840s, including the masterpieces of *Les Parents pauvres*, such as *La Cousine Bette* and *Le Cousin Pons*. Comparable to late Beethoven, striking out on a new path, Balzac is both reductive and expansive in his approach to writing, to the constitution of characters and the representation of desire, and to the construction of the social world in which they fit. Late Balzac, including "La Dernière Incarnation de Vautrin," consists of characters who are profoundly alone and who need to structure social universes. No longer in a world of brothers and sisters, wives and husbands, parents and children, or lovers, these narratives emphasize the tenuous nature of human relations, the construction of the social relation, and the naturalization of the bond with the other. In *Le Père Goriot*, Rastignac can call on Mme de Beauséant to ask for a favor: this request uses the family relation, but not parasitically. Even if Eugène and Mme de Beauséant are part of the same extended family, she has no intrinsic (i.e., nonnarrative) reason to do him a favor. The *cri du sang* brings cousins together, reduces the distance of the relation, and makes them family in a more immediate sense. Eugène uses this contact and profits from it, but neither at the expense of Mme de Beauséant nor to her detriment. If they are "quelque peu parent," this distance or indefinite/imprecise quantification of bloodlines collapses. This collapse seems to make the bestowal of a favor something that naturally relates to the importance of family and thus to the reduction of the relation of distant cousin to something more intimate like aunt and nephew. In contrast, the relations that develop in late Balzac emphasize the distance, the abuse that comes with that distance, and the need to construct a viable relation outside the family unit. So Bette's cousinhood and that of Pons are remarkable because they are solidly opposed to the construction of familial obligation in earlier works. Bette abuses her family; Pons is abused by his.

Perhaps the most striking example of the abusive and distant family relationship is that of *Pierrette* in which the baroque constructions of bloodlines among the protagonists leads to the hellish coexistence under one roof of characters whose concept of the family relation is on the one hand sadomasochistic and on the other almost incestuous. Rogron and Sylvie, incarnations of the evil stepmother and stepsisters

of the Cinderella story, turn their "cousin" Pierrette into an indentured servant, mark her as an enslaved other to be abused, and ultimately kill her through their actions. In opposition, in what Lévi-
Strauss would have considered an overvaluation of the family, both
Rogron and Sylvie form an incestuous couple, not literally (sexually)
but certainly emotionally. They act as a pair as they develop, work,
plot, act, and respond to the actions of others.

This novel is perhaps underappreciated because of the very complicated and very extended background that Balzac needs to give to
the drama (as he puts it in the earlier *Le Père Goriot*) and partly because of the levels of violence and abuse to which the actions of the
novel rise. This work both defines and illustrates abuse; it is a novel,
some of whose scenes rise to the level of melodrama surpassing that
of "La Fille aux yeux d'or," for the violence of that story is more off
stage than on, as is recommended by *bienséance*. The results of that violence are represented as Madame de San Réal stands there with the
dead, bloodied body lying on the ground. In *Pierrette*, the violence is
on stage, with a fight between Sylvie and Pierrette, provoked and
forced by the former, that ultimately leads to the death of the latter.

*Pierrette* remains an interesting work on a theoretical level, and a
work far more indicative of late Balzac than the better known beginning of *Splendeurs et misères*, yet it unfortunately remains mostly unread by a general readership and even by a more focused readership
of Balzac specialists. In the context of this book and in light of the
figurality of the other in nineteenth-century literature, both the encounter between Vautrin and Lucien and the singular preface to
*Pierrette* augur late Balzac. Both works are meditations on the construction of identity, on the construction of the relation between subjects, and on the figure of otherness involved for him in any identification of the self. Moreover, though this is neither necessary nor
intrinsic to the argument, the relative slowing down in production in
Balzac's life in the 1840s relates not only to external exigencies, including the publication of the Furne edition of his collected works
and thus the sanctification of the *La Comédie humaine* as *œuvre*, the
time spent in making that edition the last word and the last incarnation of his textuality, but also to the aridity of the author's changing
conception of self and alterity as seen in his works of this era.

The preface to the first edition of *Pierrette* is adamant, polemical, and vitriolic. Untempered in its first pages, these prefatory remarks set out a stark contrast between society as a whole and the bachelor, who seems to be immediately castigated as being both antisocial and frankly *contra naturam*. Balzac starts by pulling no punches: "The status of the Bachelor is contrary to society" (4:21). For Balzac, the construction of the social system has been one in which its flowering depends on its very "natural" nature. If he writes with the light that comes from the altar and the throne, he also writes a zoography, a textual representation of the human world analogous to the Linnean system of naming and thus to the biosphere in which there is a logic, in which form follows function, and in which the links serve to form a rich variety of related but differentiated species. Balzac offers the reader his writing as something analogous, if not to say homologous, to the natural world, but his writing, the natural world, and the social world are completely aligned: his natural writing corresponds to the biological model, as does the social world. Parenthetically, this means that his writing is worthy of describing that social world because the three systems of nature, social structures, and the realist narrative are in alignment.

The bachelor stands alone, much as a sterile animal or plant cannot reproduce, much as an isolated sentence itself cannot form a real narratological structure. To say that the bachelor has a civil status contrary to society is to say that he does not enter into a foundational human relation with another member of society. Significantly, with very few exceptions, the bachelor is male. In his list of bachelors, Balzac includes only one explicitly named bachelorette, Mlle Michonneau of *Le Père Goriot* (4:21). Implicitly, especially because Balzac is using this work as the preface to *Pierrette*, the unnamed Sylvie Rogron should be understood as the second bachelorette. But if the model is a natural one, the state of bachelorhood is, by and large, male.

The bachelor then is doubly at fault, for this man of action, as befits the structuring of the male as the one who acts, moves, and changes, commits a sin (or an act of *lèse-société*) by not taking a wife. He thus, implicitly, prevents marriage, which is the only suitable state for a woman because it keeps her in her place; he also does not legitimately reproduce, and, most extremely, he maintains the virginity, the unbroken hymeneal nature of some unknown other. The state of the bachelor is thus against society because it maintains the

virginity of someone who is thus consigned—if love is in the stars—
to being an old maid, to becoming the unfeminine dragon of characters like Mlle Michonneau and, eventually, Bette. Against society and
against nature, the bachelor refuses the simplest of human bonds.
Tellingly, this bond, which is the very figure of Balzacian sociality, is
both singular and nonreciprocal in nature: the bond that defines the
most minimal social contact is that of a man and a hymen to be broken. The female character is always secondary to her function, and
even the seemingly irreducible bond of mother and child depends
not on some intrinsic essential human relation but on the mother's
hymen once having been broken, so that, fertile and fertilized, she
could become a mother.

The basic relation is unnameable, and it depends not on the existence of the other as some whole being or as some partial object but
on the disappearance of that other. Balzac thus predicates the basic
quality of the nature of the relations of human existence on the relation between the male and the imaginary. One could argue that the
male himself is merely an incarnation of some phallic power, and
thus the relation is between two imaginary (or symbolic) figures of
phallus and hymen. But Balzac gives us the man, the bachelor who,
even if he were married, would not change in nature. No, the difference is external to him; it is in the relation that he does or does not
establish with a woman for the purpose of reproduction of life and of
possessions. It is not for nought that, after having made this oppositional statement, Balzac immediately changes modes and moves to
finance. While generally critical of the Revolution and what it has
brought to France, Balzac buys into an idea of the Convention that
saw fit to envision the possibility of taxing the unmarried at a rate
twice that of married people. For Balzac, "[i]t had had the most eq-
uitable of all fiscal thoughts and the easiest to execute" (4:20). Balzac
makes allowances for history in his version as he accepts widowhood
as a noble state equivalent fiscally to marriage: "Direct contributions
of all sorts will be doubled when the contributor is not or has not
been married" (4:20). So the physical reproduction of children is not
as necessary to the stability of the system as is the possibility of having or having had legitimate children, as the certainty of a broken
hymen.

This is, Balzac tells us, consonant with a basic principle, "the author's deep hatred of any unproductive being, of bachelors, old maids and unmarried old men, those drones of the hive" (4:20). The natural metaphor of bees, and specifically drones, in a hive is not misplaced, because it reassociates the social structure of the human zoography with a natural context. The metaphor cannot go far: as much as Balzac may believe in the Monarchy, the metaphor of one queen with workers and drones does not match Balzac's own panoramic conception of society. Still, the figure returns us to a collusion or a conflation of social and natural in the Balzacian conception of both his project and human relations.

At the same time, the foundation of the relation is a negativity: hatred. This subject he hates, the bachelor, will be the focus of much of the important writings of the years to come. The category is mitigated with certain notable, noble examples: the priest, the soldier, and "several rare devotions" (4:22). The first two categories correspond quite simply and directly to a feudal system in which the law of primogeniture and succession determined the roles for second and third sons after the first inherited lands, title, and chattel. As far as the rare devotions are concerned, certain traditionally defined feminine behaviors, like those of caretakers, nurses or nursemaids, and even devoted servants (though it is not clear if Balzac speaks of anyone outside the upper and middle classes here), fall into this category. It remains to be seen whether there is the possibility of a male relation that fits under this category: the test example is the relation between Vautrin (Carlos Herrera) and Lucien. The other test example will be the possibility of a totally different relation, such as that not yet written between Pons and Schmucke in *Le Cousin Pons*.

Aside from those exceptions, which seem to radiate their own goodness, there seems still to be a force compelling the author to write about something he hates: "Thus, in the long, complete portrayal of mores, figures, actions, and movements of modern society, it has been resolved to pursue the bachelor" (4:22). This is a logical movement for him, from hatred to a compulsion to write, yet the hatred itself is put into question shortly thereafter in a passage written with typical Balzacian brio:

Do not accuse the author either of malice aforethought and the intention to bite people as would mad dogs: he is not a bachelorophobe [*il n'est pas célibatairophobe*]. One of the most hateful, invidious, and ridiculous stupidities among all those of which he is the object or butt of the joke is to make believe that he has absolute ideas, a constant, indivisible hatred of certain social classes, of notaries, merchants, userers, the middle classes, owners, journalists, bankers, etc. (4:24)

Few are left out of this picture, or at least few men, and the list would include most of Balzac's male characters. Arguing against his rhetorical accusers, Balzac says that he is not at all like that. His hatred is not constant, his objects are not treated with an absolute imperiousness but with, one would suppose, a measure of *caritas*. He has just said that his principle is the hatred of bachelors.

Hatred and fear are not the same: he hates bachelors (among others), though this hatred is neither unrelenting nor bereft of the Christian love that guides him, the sentiments of *noblesse oblige* that marks all his endeavors. Certainly he does not fear bachelors. Why should he? With a few noble exceptions for devoted friends filled with human kindness, along with soldiers and priests giving their lives for a greater good, these men are not pillars of society. They are the men who bring discord to marriage, who father illegitimate children among married wives, who are generally social parasites, and/or who are ultimately sterile because they do not reproduce appropriately. There is no contradiction here: illegitimate reproduction and virginal sterility are on one side of the line; on the other, legitimate fatherhood and a barren marriage, plus the transcendence of soldiers and priests, married to the state and to religion. So there is no need to fear, because these men are not worthy of fear; again the example of Vautrin begs the question somewhat, for even if he is disguised as a priest he is not one and should therefore come under the category of bachelor, while remaining the most fear-inspiring man in Paris.

In this introduction, Balzac notes that "one of our most terrible bachelors, Maxime de Trailles, is getting married" (4:22) and though the male protagonist of "La Fille aux yeux d'or" seems to have remained a bachelor, he served his country as a politician, if not as a priest or soldier. Similarly, the author takes pain to note that Rastignac, too, has finally gotten married to Mlle de Nucingen (4:23), the daughter of his former mistress. But one would argue that Rastignac, though it took him a while and though there is an age difference, was never a confirmed bachelor in the same way that someone like Poiret is. Again, though Rastignac remains unmarried for a long time, in *Le Père Goriot*, he totally fits Balzac's allowable category for bachelorhood: "If we meet bachelors in the world of the *études de mœurs*, attribute them to the necessity that we have all obeyed to be twenty years old" (4:24). Rastignac's bachelorhood is not essential to his being, for his *telos* is as a productive member of society, productive in the Balzacian sense of contributing to material gain, the reproduction of children, and capital.

Where the question of bachelorhood becomes problematic, where the very contradictions about hatred and phobia become palpable is precisely where the bachelorhood becomes an essential part of the character, in what Balzac calls "seriously bachelored bachelors [*célibataires sérieusement célibataires*]" (4:24). The status of bachelorhood is not even itself intrinsic to being an inveterate bachelor: "*Pierrette* is thus the second picture in which bachelors are the main figures, for if Rogron marries, his marriage should not be considered a dénouement; he remains Rogron; he does not have long to live; marriage kills him" (4:26). This means that the incompleteness of the minimal human relation as defined above becomes internal to the construction of the character. Or, to put it another way, the construction of a character such as this is always already flawed because the character can never be complete, having as it does a gap within, an impossibility without. Heretofore, the characters have not been the central characters of the novels: "they have not been main figures" (4:22).

Even beyond that, the characters that the author has drawn heretofore who are inveterate bachelors have been secondary, easy foils against whom the protagonists can be set. Whereas the former are two-dimensional, the latter have been "people whose brows are marked with a social or philosophical meaning [*types portant au front un sens social ou philosophique*]" (4:22). The contrast is palpable because it takes place on two different registers. The essential bachelor has a gap, a *manque* at the very core of his being, a gap that, at least heretofore, has not been described except by negation. The essential bachelor is incomplete in his/her basic human relation, for in the Balzacian world, the individual is complete only if he or she extends beyond himself or herself toward the other. The basic human relation is an extension of self, an expansion of self beyond the individual. On the other register is the fact that a protagonist is by definition a marked character, bearing, like Eugénie and so many others, a sign, be it readable or not, on the forehead. The sign, too, is an extension beyond the individual, beyond the monad. In a nutshell, both the source of Balzacian representation and the source of his irony are in the freeplay between these signs, as they relate to a generalized semiotics and the extension of the human relation itself beyond the individual.

The confusion about hatred, the admission of hatred, and the denial of fear begin to make sense if this introduction is less a commentary on *Pierrette* than as the announcement of a project. In *Pierrette*, Balzac distends the familial relation so extensively as to make it the merest and most insignificant minimum. It is a means of testing the waters by moving the bachelor brother and sister away from any legitimate family relation other than the self-evident siblinghood and toward being prototypes for protagonists. The problem with *Pierrette*, aside from the complications of the plot necessitated by the means needed to throw these characters together in their own personal hell, is that the titular protagonist is the innocent victim of her distant cousin(s). The power of the work is thus divided between bachelor actor(s) and their victim, and the power of representation is thus diffused by this division. In terms of the representational mechanism, the key to the modification of the representational system will be to find the means of having a correspondence between the mark or sign that Balzac reads, and the absence of external relation to an other, that extension of self that guarantees the integral nature of the unit.

## VII.  Homosexual Rebirth

Lucien de Rubempré's rebirth into a life that has already been written, which is the first part of *Splendeurs et misères*, starts belatedly, toward the end of *Illusions perdues*, in a scene written later. The scene is the bridge, artificial at that, between two sets of events. The assiduous reader of *La Comédie humaine* knows that Lucien does not commit suicide, here and now, and this despite the despondency and bleak future associated with the character. For that reader is already familiar with what will become the first part of *Splendeurs et misères*, in which Lucien's new life will be described. Paired with, though independent from, the story of Lucien is that of the phoenix-like rebirth of Vautrin as the false abbé Carlos Herrera. This chance meeting will lead somewhere. On the far side of this event will be a shared history for a while, and then a parting of the ways: Lucien's suicide and Vautrin's metaphysical reincarnation, in what Balzac calls "La Dernière Incarnation de Vautrin," the last part of *Splendeurs et misères*, in which he becomes the head of the secret police.

Arguably then, the construction of this narratively logical bridge to a preexisting "prequel" serves several purposes. On the level of surface logic, the pages serve as a means to get the two characters (Vautrin and Lucien) to meet and to explain their subsequent adventures. Balzac thus justifies the encounter of his characters for which he had not previously given a reason. This becomes all the more necessary given the fact that Lucien is not going to commit suicide at the end of *Illusions perdues*. The author is thus able to satisfy the inquiring logical minds of readers, who otherwise would have perceived a logical inconsistency between the two tales. The encounter is also the means by which Balzac introduces a homosexual element into the relationship and justifies the attention given to Lucien by Vautrin in "La Torpille" and the concern and melodrama in the pages that will be associated with their double arrest and Lucien's death. The encounter between Lucien and Vautrin is thus the preliminary justification for marking future adventures of Lucien (including the one already written) with a homosexual overcast. Finally, the bridge is a justification for what will happen to Vautrin himself after Lucien's death, after the loss of the one he will have loved the best. But the passage, along with the introduction to *Pierrette*, is also, most importantly, the key to Balzac's new attempt to defining the minimum quality of the human relation by reducing the effect of the family unit and the bourgeois marriage. Balzac attempts to define that minimum human contact, unnamed and unnameable; it is something that, for him, since all chosen relations are motivated, lies between altruistic friendship and elective affinities.

For Balzac, there is generally an obligation, often redoubled by love, in the family relation defined by bloodlines. Thus a mother is devoted to her children, altruistically and even sacrificially. The father, too, has an obligation, though most often it is more distant than that of the mother, and even when taken to excess, as is the case with Goriot, it is mediated more by money than by directly expressed affection. Thus the father provides materially, whether it means sell-ing his belongings to pay for the needs of his daughters caught in problematic marriages, as is the case for Goriot and his two daugh-ters, or whether it is simply providing a dowry or the wealth associ-ated with an heiress, as is the case for Grandet and Éugenie.

Depending on obligation and serving as one of the basic building blocks of the human condition, the family relation is not the pure re-lation that Balzac is seeking to understand for the individual. It is his or her extension of self beyond the corpus, the social, and the be-havioral. This extension has no name, but it underlies all human re-lations apart from those for which there is a divine or ethical imper-ative. As Balzac notes in the introduction to *Pierrette*, there are examples of pure Christianity and not just concupiscence. Few fall into this category of living saint. In most cases, there is a selfish mo-tivation that individuals have: self-interest, a desire for success, or a desire to arrive.

Certainly the way in which the arrival is envisaged is related to a semiotics of presenting, a semiotics of traits, characteristics, emo-tions, and feelings, a range of beliefs, and an attribution of morality and ethics. Such attributions or pairings of means and semiotics strike an artificial note because certain things are not taken into con-sideration: a negative desire or a desire not so much for success of self as for the failure of others (such as what the author will describe in *La Cousine Bette*); an unmotivated friendship or relation (such as what he will describe in *Le Cousin Pons*); and finally, and perhaps most radically, the behavior of both Vautrin and Lucien in their last incar-nations. The most problematic of all these is found in this bridge narrative in which Balzac has to make an encounter happen and in which he must create interest: an interest in each of the characters for the other, in what amounts to a relation for which society has no name; an interest like Vautrin's eventual investment in Lucien's het-erosexual success; an interest on the part of the reader in the en-counter of these two characters and functions.

For the characters are not just any two chosen haphazardly from among the many in the *Comédie humaine*; they are unique individu-als, one of whom has already served as a protagonist and who is, *par dessus le marché*, a writer, and therefore, by implication, at least some-how a figure of the author. Lucien is a negative figure who will fail where the author succeeds and who, despite all his *arrivisme* and his incarnation of many of Balzac's own preoccupations with status, the *particule*, money, and success as an author, will serve as a moral to those who cannot succeed. The other is a unique character in his own right who serves in a secondary but riveting role in *Le Père Goriot* and who is from first to last, because of his outlaw status, because of his homosexuality, and because of his incarnation of power, the focus of attention. To understand the encounter of the two characters and the way in which Balzac is using the encounter to redefine the human relation, they must be examined individually. For it is in this encounter between the one who writes and the one who cannot be read that everything will be played out, including the strangely told tale that takes its place along with the tale of la Zambinella told in "Sarrasine" and the posited undecidability of "L'Auberge rouge," one of the strangest in all *La Comédie humaine*.

Vautrin is given to the reader as the master semiotician within the novels. Starting from the pages of *Le Père Goriot*, Vautrin serves as the figure of the powerful reader. Capable of discerning others' innermost thoughts, Vautrin makes his power known to Rastignac, for example, with cynical lessons on how to read society, as he offers the insidious version of what Madame de Beauséant offers in a more worldly way. Significantly, each of those master readers has a fate that corresponds to reading. Madame de Beauséant, having misread her lover's actions (and going on, in "La Femme abandonée," to misread again), marks her vulnerability with the note she writes, as it finds its proper *destinataire* and thereby undoes the writer. Where she has once been strong and able to sign with a simple "C" for "Claire de Bourgogne," she is now undone by the note that reveals her, marks her vulnerability, and sends her into exile.

Vautrin is also undone by reading in his first incarnation. Escaping being read up to the moment of his recapture, he can give false clues so that others misread him and draw inaccurate conclusions about who he is. At the moment of discovery, his shirt having been removed, all can read the two "fatal letters" of "T. F.," for "travaux forcés," marked on his back. Thus is the most powerful man in all of Paris laid low by Mlle Michonneau working in collusion with the police. Balzac's construction of the reading of Vautrin is effectively done with the letters on Vautrin's back fulfilling themselves in an act of presence, a self-presence in which representation (writing) truly becomes re-presentation, as signifier and signified "appear" manifestly, immanently, and perfectly on his back.

Balzac will take great pains to disfigure Vautrin as he transforms this figure into the false Abbé Herrera. One of the most important acts will be the scarification of Vautrin's body, by which the two fatal letters can no longer appear. When the moment of identification comes around again, as it must, Vautrin cannot be read in the same way as he is in *Le Père Goriot*. In this new incarnation, Vautrin is perhaps even more powerful than he is in the earlier novel. Completely unreadable, for example, in his disguise at a masked ball at which he appears to Rastignac, dressed all in black, *en domino*, he is nonetheless able to read Rastignac so well that he can even read the latter's mind (6:434).

If Vautrin is the great reader of *La Comédie humaine*, and the last of the great readers, for the final books will be concerned with misreading, Lucien is the great writer. Not that he is a great author: his Paris experiences are a great disappointment, and his poems remain unread by editors. He winds up earning his living in the harsh world of Paris as a parasitic writer for newspapers, writing columns and countercolumns, flirting with the theater, becoming the master of the palinode, and generally living off writing plied as something less than an art form. Lucien is the opposite of Balzac and Vautrin, the superreaders. But he is, at least initially, a writer, one of the benighted and idealistic figures whom Balzac posits as searching for an absolute in art, music, chemistry, money, or literature. If he fails, if he loses his illusions, he loses the innocence and purity of his writing, too. It is fitting that the volume of poems, *Les Marguerites*, remains unread. For dramatic effect, Lucien is cast at the other pole, that of the base journalist who writes for newspapers and does no more than that. This is not to imply that Balzac, who himself wrote for newspapers and who published numerous works in serial form in the press of his time, found journalistic writing merely vulgar. But he does destroy Lucien's illusions by casting him into the pit of daily journalism, where writing is ephemeral and vapid. Lucien is also a bad reader, misreading the signs given him by others and not really learning from his mistakes. It is there that he differs from Rastignac: Lucien goes from abuse to abuse, never quite becoming the better reader he should and therefore never quite becoming the better observer or the better writer.

Thus, the encounter between Lucien and Herrera is also the meeting between two characters defined by a dynamic of reading and writing. Not coincidentally, this episode is framed by writing and crisscrossed with the strange story of an eater of paper. Lucien's last act before leaving his sister's house is to leave her a letter equivalent to a suicide note: "Goodbye forever" (5:688). At the other end of the episode, the letter is found: "At the moment that Lucien was getting into the carriage with the false Spanish diplomat, Ève was getting up to give her son something to drink; she found the fatal letter and read it" (5:709). Quoting his own marking of Vautrin with the expression "fatal letter," Balzac associates writing once again with the finality of death, determination, and the fulfillment of a determined destiny. Writing is fate, *habent sua fata libelli*; writing marks the character as readable, as masterable, as dead. At the same time, Balzac is careful to underline the strange dramatic nature of this episode: nothing else is going on. Significantly, nothing is happening in the world between the time that Lucien leaves the letter and the time he gets into the carriage or the time at which his sister reads it. Nothing except this encounter: nothing to deter, detract, or frame this. These characters—Herrera and Lucien—are alone in the world with no one to see them, no other action going on, and nothing in counterpoint. There is nothing but this encounter and the telling of a tale.

One action is precluded and two are offered in its stead. Lucien cannot and will not commit suicide, and thus all the indications of that suicide, from his writing of a farewell letter to the musings about a world bereft of his presence, are inherently or essentially false leads, fakeouts, or misdirections, or would be, if only the reader, rhetorical or real, were able to be gulled. But this is not the case: the rhetorical or real reader is always already aware that the suicide will not occur. Instead of suicide: an encounter and a telling of a tale. A telling of a tale, in specific, in which there is a strong element of the homoerotic, in which there is a use and a misuse of writing, paper, reading, and in which death, too, is subtly avoided. But the avoidance of death within the tale told is not predictable. Where there is no moment of suspense in Lucien's story, which now serves as a frame tale for Herrera's tale, the suspense in the latter is carried off until the very end.

This double introduction of the unpredictable and unforeseen *topoi* of homoeroticism (both in the encounter between Lucien and Herrera and in the tale that Herrera tells) and the *mise-en-abyme* of writing and its consumption occur in the locus vacated by suicide. Homosexuality and writing occur where suicide is no longer possible. Homosexuality, born into or given into this locus, is thus the turning away from the possibility of the noble (if technically indefensible from a religious point of view): goodbye to Werther, goodbye to any last vestige of romanticism, hello to a renewed, yet cynical realism, in which suicide will ultimately turn into the amusing, maudlin, or pathetic deaths of Emma Bovary and Anna Karenina. Suicide will be valid for women who have undoubtedly read about it in novels but not for men for whom it is now less than a brave act. Along with a new, complex relationship staked out for writing itself (writing thus tinged by homosexuality, by orality, and by a complete change in ontological status), homosexuality thus is a spot of rebirth, yet a solution whose very placement occurs at a supposed locus of death, even if that death is always already foreclosed by narrative logic.

The moment of suicide that cannot occur in the novel is thus the moment of rebirth, the moment away from the world in which Lucien had lived, and the moment in which he is reborn as other, as a suitable object of affection and attention for Herrera. Thus what has happened before that meeting is subject to reinterpretation, as his very clothes (reminiscent of those of Charles Grandet), donned as a shroud, become glad rags, for he is "dressed as if he were going to a party, for he had made a shroud of his Parisian clothes and his pretty dandy's togs [*harnais de dandy*]" (5:688). So the homosexual relation into which Lucien is heading is marked by death, marked by the impossibility of suicide, marked by the impossibility of choice for oneself: Lucien seeks to kill himself and winds up involved with Herrera. This is not to say that for Balzac homosexuality is predicated on death or even that it is a condemnation to death. It is a point of rebirth in which all previous relations cease to exist and in which all constructs and all semiotics of meaning once attached to the structuring of meaning around a semiotics of heterosexual transcendence now fade.

Lucien dies as the one who he has been; he loses relations to family, to others, to lovers, and to the poet that he had been, the poet whose verse remained unread, the poet who sang, Faust-like, the

praises of the feminine. Reborn as other, reborn as fundamentally ex-
iled from all that had preceded, Lucien will become a new singularity. But this will not occur before a rewrite of Balzac's earlier *La Peau
de chagrin*, in which the equally bereft hero threatens to "deliver an
undecipherable body to society." In the earlier novel, Raphaël de
Valentin does not meet the events that will change him from this suicide. Already, in this early novel, there are the limitations of free will,
which has to do with the enactment of power by the skin itself and
the way in which it shrinks, metaphorically, measuring the shrinking
of Raphaël's life with each of his wishes. In *Illusions perdues*, Balzac repeats the same coded possibility of the problematic nature of a suicide for a society that likes to control death: " . . . he heard ahead of
time the noise that his suicide would make; he saw the awful spectacle of his deformed body bobbing on the water's surface, object of a
coroner's inquest: like some suicides, he had posthumous narcissism
[*amour-propre*]" (5:688–89). This envisaged suicide is the public figure, the coded body of the self that, even through that imagined
death, remains susceptible to a recognition of the self as simultaneous subject and object, with a moment of self-absorption.

Difference occurs here and now because there is no code, there is
no position validated for the subject he will become, nor any for that
as the object of the gaze of the other. The avoidance of suicide turns
into a question at the level of semiosis: how is homosexuality signed,
how does one sign as a homosexual? Let us carefully examine the
moment of entry, which is the refiguration of Lucien's life and signs,
the moment of meeting, the moment at which Balzac has set out a
different set of codes that are detached from his habitual semiotics of
placement and in which he attempts to mark both this difference and
the impossibility of, as yet, describing what he wishes to describe.
The tale that Herrera eventually tells will thus have to serve a double function: a moral lesson to Lucien and a metarepresentational
ploy to talk about what language as yet has no code for.

The moment of encounter, overdetermined by a plethora of details, still focuses on these patterns of death and rebirth, of heterosexual order and homosexual novelty:

Lucien, who did not wish to be seen, hid on a hollow path and began to
gather flowers on a vine. When he was back on the main road, he had a big
bouquet of *sedum*, a yellow flower that grows in the gravel of the vineyards,

and he wound up exactly behind a traveller dressed entirely in black, with powdered hair, shod with calfskin [*veau d'Orléans*] shoes with silver buckles, a tan complexion, and scarred [*couturé*] as if he had fallen into the fire as a child. This traveller, in such an ecclesiastical mode, moved slowly while smoking a cigar. Hearing Lucien jump from the vineyard onto the road, the unknown man turned, appeared to be transfixed by the profoundly melancholy beauty of the poet, his symbolic bouquet, and his elegant dress. This traveller resembled a hunter who finds a prey that he has searched for in vain for a long time. As if in the navy, he let Lucien reach him and slowed his pace while seeming to look at the bottom of the hill. Lucien, who made the same movement, saw a small carriage with two horses and a postilion on foot. (5:689–90)

One rebirth is matched by another, as Lucien's coming up into the world anew, flowers in hand, as if for some unknown beloved, is matched by the phoenix-like rebirth of Herrera (Bauer 73). The latter, reborn from fire, is thus given a chthonic or infernal origin. Both come up from an underworld, from a netherworld, from below. Having escaped from the law anew, having escaped from his life sentence, Herrera finds new life in the garb of another, in the life of another, and in the spiritual cloth that hides his difference. Each is dressed, born into a set of clothes that marks difference for him from what had gone before. Beyond that, the first motif continues in the smoking, as if the hellish origins of Herrera continued to impose themselves as the two characters get to know each other. The smoke and the fire are constant reminders that the immediate salvation from suicide means a Faustian pact with the devil, and rather than being saved from committing an un-Christian act of suicide, Lucien is just sealing his own fate and his own condemnation to hell.

The effect is immediate, a *coup de foudre* that marks the instant attraction of the older man for the other, without there being any discrete vocabulary that can capture the precise meaning of the event. Herrera is instantly taken with the beauty of the other, a beauty that is now completely separated from every social context that had previous marked Lucien as effeminate. Balzac often uses the allures of feminine beauty in a man as a sign of weakness, indecision, or a feminine nature. Here, the beauty is just given without interpretation, as if it stood for nothing but itself: pure beauty and an aesthetic of desirability. Balzac moves us from the acceptable social world toward the cynegetic world of gay cruising. Herrera becomes a hunter who, having sought an elusive prey, finally finds it, or him. Both immediately change their pace and make the encounter occur. Significantly, Balzac chooses as an analogy a pointedly all-male society, the navy.

Thus, in one short paragraph intended to produce a meeting between these two characters, the author orients the work away from a Hugolian kind of coincidence and toward a semiotically charged field of male beauty, of hunting and hunted, and of male-only society. Lucien is thus thrust into a world that he has not known heretofore and that Balzac has only alluded to in the descriptions of Vautrin in *Goriot*. The task here is the construction of an all-male world in which the quick bonding between the two characters will come to be assured; this is a bonding not based precisely on a sexual contact but on an order of devotion, love, and homoerotic desire that does not have to be translated into a sexual discourse. This passage is the intertextual predecessor for the meeting of Charlus and Jupien at the beginning of *Sodome et Gomorrhe*, but whereas Proust needs his characters to engage in sex, Balzac can simply set up the model into which same-sex desire is ostensibly coded for the first time in the realist novel.

For it is that, too: even in the earlier *Le Père Goriot*, while Vautrin's homosexuality it mentioned, it is given by negation: "il n'aime pas les femmes." Here, Balzac is attempting to codify by positive attributes, by marking what is loved and beloved, what is hunted and captured. Whereas once Lucien's beauty set him against others as a mark of psychological tenderness, here his beauty is worshiped as an unavoidable thing in and of itself, the very positive attraction that one man produces or incarnates for another. Bride, bridegroom, and flower boy all in one, Lucien has instantaneously been transformed into the beloved: "'You seem to have concerns, at least you have the sign in hand, like the sad god of the hymen. Here . . . all your concerns will go up in smoke . . . '" (690). The displacements, safe solutions, and sleights-of-hand are used to ensure the safety of the narrative and the viability of what the author is describing, an act of seduction. Balzac uses the word "seduction" but displaces the object: "And the priest offered his straw box again, with a sort of seduction, casting upon Lucien looks filled with charity" (690). The seduction is real but is protected by a smokescreen.

At the same time that there is a concern with safety and propriety, the author has no choice: there is no vocabulary, no code of behavior or any sexual code, at least denotatively. The acceptable codes of homosocial bonding are those afforded by the military and clerical ways of life. The latter is invoked here, as Balzac uses Herrera's clothing, just marked a few lines earlier as the clothes of a man who, reborn as a (false) priest is also the devil or his emissary sent to steal the soul of Lucien. No one can refuse a priest, no one can fail to be accepted by the priest, no one can fail to be caught by the invocation of a deity: "Oh! Young man, is it divine providence that made me walk a bit to shake off the sleep all travellers are faced with in the morning, in order for me to obey my earthly calling by consoling you?" (690). The church, given the sacred nature of its mission, allows for place to translate unrepresented desire into a pseudoreligious, pseudofamilial discourse in which Herrera's lustful love, homoerotic in nature, becomes the very epitome of motherly devotion: "'*Santa Virgen del Pilar!* . . . you are an atheist,' exclaimed the priest while putting his arm under Lucien's with a maternal eagerness" (691).

The famous anecdote told by Herrera to Lucien has received much commentary, and Roland Chollet, one of the editors of the Pléiade volume, remarks the importance of the passage as the point that, despite its seeming gratuitous presence in the novel, is one of the richest for all the threads, narrative and thematic, that it ties together (104). Not the least of these is the substance of tale that deals with the eating of paper, a theme that is tightly related to the passages on paper production in the novel. Herrera seduces through language by suggesting a language that is not directly expressed but that winds up by marking Lucien as capable of being enraptured by a language of homosexual admiration. The tale itself is told in a way to suggest a similarity in situations between what is told and the situation in which Herrera and Lucien are now found: the Baron de Goërtz is traveling to Sweden, "as I am going to Paris." One needs a secretary, as does the other. Herrera immediately shifts the tale into an act of seduction: "The Baron met the son of a goldsmith, remarkable for his beauty though it could not equal your own" (5:692). So by placing Lucien in the tale told, by placing him in a position better than the character in the anecdote, Herrera flatters, cajoles, and seduces. Lucien accepts being the narratee, Lucien accepts "*de te fabula*" as his, and as his due. By not interrupting, Lucien marks his ear as already being taken over by Herrera, in a seduction that conquers him body part by body part. Right after the story, "The Spaniard put his hand under Lucien's arm, forced him literally to get into the carriage, and the postilion closed the door on them" (694). Or again, "You rascal [*Petit drôle*], the abbé said with a smile, while taking Lucien's ear to tickle it with almost a royal familiarity" (698). Lucien accepts giving his body, just as he accepts Herrera's flattering, familiar, and seductive language. But it is this double position of Lucien as narratee and subject that does him in. Lucien accepts the language and therefore accepts his own renewed position as the object of a familiar discourse that under normal conditions would never have occurred. Lucien accepts being picked up by Herrera and accepts being the object of a discourse that seemingly does nothing at first but delay his suicide. Impossible here and now, this suicide is metaphorized into a different kind of fate, the Faustian bargain of accepting Herrera's offers.

Lucien belongs to Herrera, but how? No one acceptable description fits, for there is no way to describe the nature of the younger man's servitude. Balzac offers Herrera a variety of comparisons that flow between standard emotional and acceptable relations and a rewriting of desire in which it is translated into full possession:

"That beyond all your beautiful qualities there is a force that is *semper virens*," said the priest, wishing to show he knew a bit of Latin, "and nothing will resist you in the world. I like you a lot already. . . . " (Lucien smiled incredulously.) "Yes," the unknown man continued, answering Lucien's smile, "you interest me as if you were my son, and I am powerful enough to speak to you heart to heart, as you have just spoken to me. Do you know what pleases me in you? . . . You have made a *tabula rasa* in yourself, and you can follow an ethics course offered nowhere. For men, gathered in a herd, are even more hypocritical than they are when their interest makes them play comedy. Thus one passes a good part of one's life hoeing what grew in one's heart during adolescence. This operation is called getting experience." (698)

Herrera's revelations are of everything and nothing: he has maternal or paternal feelings toward the young man he has just picked up; he alludes to a masculinity that is a power behind Lucien's physical beauty. This is a man attracted to another man, and to that very masculinity he says is incarnate in Lucien. It little matters whether we believe that Vautrin is attracted to that masculinity or not, or whether or not that masculinity is even there. In fact, it is arguable that Lucien has not been marked by a power *semper virens* and that he has let his charm guide him far more than an act of will.

In this reading of a few parts of *La Comédie humaine*, I have attempted to show how Balzac continuously enlarges the sphere of the "proper," the same, the narratable, and the understandable. At the same time as he increases the scope of his vision, other things come into play that had not necessarily been thinkable when the world was a nice, neat place. In these readings, the broadening of the scope brings about a kind of textual unconscious, not necessarily an *unheimlich* one but one that certainly makes the edges of narrative more *flou*, and one figured as an eruption within narrative: questions about civil status, bachelorhood, virginity, circumcision, and homosexuality abound. Matters relating to value, justice, and propriety are brought into question. Balzac does not answer the questions, but in bringing them to light, and again, often in spite of his own conservative ideology, he shows the reader that the complexities of narrating the human comedy are both endless and endlessly intriguing.

# Flaubert's Figures

Then the legion of Interpreters appeared, coiffed like
Sphinxes and with tattoos of a parrot on their chests.
—Flaubert, *Salammbô*

## I. Critical Prologue

Balzac recognizes the heterogeneity of the real as he is faced with the
problematics of depicting it. He encounters a myriad of contradictory,
discontinuous, and competing structures and systems; he constantly
has to present the history of a moment or a situation for the reader to
understand what is at stake. The retrospective glances are, in fact, one
of Balzac's most visible narrative techniques: he presents the current
situation and then immediately turns the clock back ten or twenty
years to give the necessary background that shaped the present moment. Some might attribute this to the fact that Balzac's expository
technique was less honed than that of "better" writers; others might
see the hand of a mercenary writing novels in installments for newspapers and reviews, and for which he was ultimately being paid by the
word. Both of these may be partial views of the truth. Balzac perceives
the basic impossibility of homogeneity, as did Stendhal, in somewhat
of a different way before him: Stendhal perceives diffusion (the mirror) and confusion (the Battle of Waterloo), and his efforts are focused on streamlining reality to its essence. Concerned far more with
the material than the core, Balzac *never* streamlines; even his shabby
gentility is abundant, his poverty, luxurious.

What Balzac recognizes, in particular, in this heterogeneity are the differences between the supposedly homogeneous, material world created by men, and the discontinuous, somewhat alienated and distanced world of women. Unequally formulated, this latter world is seen through the difference between the sexes and what they have (as well as, implicitly, what they are or might be). The differences are never clearer than in the massive dysfunctionality, fractionalization, fragmentation, heterogeneity, competition, rivalry, and discontinuity associated with the depiction of the family (which means the two sexes in all their disparate glory) in *La Comédie humaine*, as a glance at the articles in the recent collection by Claudie Bernard and Franc Schuerewegen amply shows. But families are only the most essential figures of this discontinuity, to which are added sexuality, communication, discursivity, and so forth.

Writing after the massive undertaking of Balzac's *La Comédie humaine*, Gustave Flaubert is faced with a problem of gargantuan proportions: how to write. Without a repetition of the arguments of Jean-Paul Sartre's *L'Idiot de la famille*, suffice it to say that Sartre's existential psychoanalysis of Flaubert has both a familial and material base and that Sartre concludes his 2500 pages having recognized the agony of the would-be author faced with writing the simplest line of prose. At the same time, Sartre never gives enough attention to Flaubert's aesthetic dilemma, which, in terms of a filiality, might read as follows. Having recognized the fundamental heterogeneity in a writing style that will congeal as realism in works such as *Le Père Goriot* and *Eugénie Grandet*, Balzac chooses to illustrate it through myriad examples, though, arguably, the "other" in Balzac is almost inevitably the feminine, which is itself always already present in the real. Thus the real and realism share the same other. For Flaubert, however, this coincidence is too good to be true. Refusing Balzac's facile oppositional model, Flaubert wants to show the artificiality of that automatic alterity, one that Balzac himself always conveniently explains through a kind of exculpatory genealogy of the other. Second, Flaubert wants to demystify that very process of incorporation and assimilation of the other, as if it were not a necessary historical moment but merely a kind of participation in what Bourdieu would call the habitus. Each individual incorporates the other; it is up to the novelist to display that process. Third, Flaubert wants to maintain the otherness of the other within the aesthetic of realism so that realism truly represents the real, and not just through the easy coincidence of the sexes that is so convenient for Balzac or, in another register, the coincidence of history and the individual on which Hugo bases his models of writing.

The beginning of this chapter focuses on what is at stake for Flaubert in his dissociation of realism from the real. Before examining his economy of assimilation, I present some of the problematics associated with the very concept of the novel *Salammbô*, a work so radical in its conception of that dissociation and in its rethinking of the relation to the exotic to the narrative. After that will come an examination of how Flaubert develops an intertwined model of desire and acquisition that not only is symptomatic of the "needs" and "wants" of his protagonist, Emma Bovary, but also resembles the realist enterprise as he implicitly conceives of it himself. The remainder of the chapter focuses on the idea of acquisition on a grander scale, which can be phrased as a problem of representation: how does the author account for the wholly, complete, radically other? Finally: how does an author make an adequation of the realist narrative with a transcendental?

Let us thus start somewhere between two novels, the watershed of *Madame Bovary* and the singularity of *Salammbô*. The goal in this part of the chapter is to examine the figures of alterity in the two: briefly in *Madame Bovary*, to show the anatomy of assimilation, then more at length in *Salammbô*, to show how that novel is a problematic figuration of the other. The aim here is not so much to provide global readings of either novel but to show the process of assimilation at work. In the second novel, as will become clear, the stakes are higher, as Flaubert has taken the courageous step of trying to write a "realist" novel without the benefit of an underlying reality. As the chapter develops, the consequences of that decision will become clear. For he seeks to so do in a way theretofore untried: present the other as other, subject it to the realist enterprise, yet resist Romanticism and its figuration of the "exotic."

So to the moment between the two novels, necessarily coming after both, for it is only then that the moment between makes sense, only then that one might chide Flaubert for having made an error in judgment. The eminent critic, Charles Sainte-Beuve, writing in his

*Nouveaux lundis*, reproaches Gustave Flaubert, who has written a second novel that is not at all what Sainte-Beuve would have expected after the celebrated and decried revolutionary novel of *Madame Bovary*. He writes as follows: "After the success of *Madame Bovary*, after all the noise made by this remarkable novel and the praise mixed with objections that it had provoked, it seemed that everyone unanimously agreed to ask Monsieur Flaubert to start another novel immediately, one that would be a counterweight and somewhat of a contrast to the first" (4:31–32). A second novel should repeat the success of the first, while correcting its errors or lapses in judgment and continuing to develop the positive aspects of that first success. To avoid repetition, the subject should be complementary or contrasting. Had Flaubert done what Sainte-Beuve subsequently recommended, *Salammbô* would have guaranteed the various solutions given in *Madame Bovary*. Specifically, one might have expected *Salammbô* to establish a refined impersonal narrative (which it does with some exceptions), a well-defined and well-developed plotting and pacing, interweaving background with close-up (which it does not do), and a use of the insights of psychological realism in a cogent analysis of the characters' thoughts (which does not even remotely enter the picture). One could imagine, therefore, Sainte-Beuve happy with a novel about city life, about men, or about something else proper. But Flaubert will have none of that.

If it is considered to be the repetition or refinement of *Madame Bovary*, *Salammbô* does not fulfill expectations. In fact, it is obvious that it is impossible for the work to conform to a set of previously defined parameters of textuality, either in form or in content. A psychological grounding that depends on an Occidental concept of identity, to wit, an Aristotelian division of the world, does not have a privileged place in a system heretofore ungrounded in a Greco-Roman theory of identity. Similarly, in terms of psychological realism grounded in causality, the novel is initially bankrupt. If *Salammbô* or Mathô eventually performs according to what might now be perceived as a psychologically valid and realistic behavioral pattern, that pattern should in fact come out of the novel's systems and not occur because these people have sudden glimpses of Occidental reason. As Forrest-Thomson (789) points out in her excellent study of the process of deconstruction that the reader performs through his or her construction of the meaning of this work, "The characters do not know why they act; the chaos of possible explanations, like the chaos of religious interpretations, makes any consistent motivation impossible."

Critics may not agree, but they are all faced with problems when analyzing the novel. When Lukács discusses the novel he points out a metaphor of Flaubert's in which Salammbô is compared to Saint Theresa. Ever the champion of realism, Lukács tries to provide an alternative explanation for Flaubert's psychologism. According to him (*Historical* 224), Flaubert chooses a "historical subject whose inner social-historical nature is of no concern to him and to which he can only lend the appearance of reality in an external, decorative, picturesque manner." Thus Flaubert, for Lukács, is really giving us only a version of the exotic that one might expect from a lesser writer. Given his Marxist perspective, it is natural that the critic value *Madame Bovary* over *Salammbô*; he sees the latter novel's flaws or its differences from the earlier novel as the very evidence of the weakness of the work and the lack of a solid structure and solid act of signification:

> The artistic superiority of his bourgeois novels lies precisely in the fact that in them the proportions between emotion and events, between desire and its translation into deeds correspond to the real, social-historical character of emotion and desire. In *Salammbô* the emotions, in themselves quite unmonumental, are falsely and distortedly monumentalized and hence inwardly unequal to such artistic heightening. (225)

Is it certain that Flaubert is even concerned about the "inner social-historical nature" in *Madame Bovary* any more or less than he is with his Carthaginian work? Is Lukács not somehow projecting Flaubert as a second Balzac concerned with the "inner social-historical nature" of his subject? And this in spite of the fact that Balzac's own personal biases might oppose him to an unsympathetic, dogmatic Marxist reading (which is certainly not the case for Lukács, whose readings of Balzac are among the most sympathetic ever penned) and that Flaubert's more sympathetic antibourgeois attitudes really relate to a total disdain of the social rather than to social activism.

What is Flaubert's concern? In a letter to Sainte-Beuve, dated 23–24 December 1862, he writes:

Mme Bovary is prey to multiple passions; Salammbô, on the contrary, remains stuck on an *idée fixe*. She is a maniac, a kind of Saint Theresa. It doesn't matter. I am not sure of her reality; for neither you nor I nor anyone, ancient or modern, can know the Oriental woman, for it is impossible to meet her [*la fréquenter*]." (*Corr.* 9:430)

Emma is multiple; Salammbô, maniacal. Both are women, prey to passion or passions, even if one cannot know Salammbô. Flaubert undercuts his own de-exoticizing of Salammbô by arguing that, just as with all Oriental women, we cannot know her.[1] At first glance, then, this would seem to categorize her under the typical, since she is veiled in an eternal, Oriental, feminine present. At the same time, no one can fail to notice that such a reveiling would put her under the sign of nought; so, even in Flaubert's blind spot, even in his fetishizing of the Oriental feminine, he does not illuminate his readers at all. In any case, Flaubert undercuts his comparison between Salammbô and Saint Theresa by calling it a moot point. Lukács (224) criticizes Flaubert, but, in so doing, he misses Flaubert's statement of alterity: " . . . for it is really quite immaterial whether one attributes to Hannibal's sister the psychology of a French petite bourgeoise of the nineteenth century or of a Spanish nun of the seventeenth." It really does not matter. For Flaubert, the reality with which he has to deal is absolutely (and not just relatively) unknowable. Moreover, it has never been knowable. If, along with Lukács, one posits a knowable sociohistorical reality, one cannot fail to agree with the type of criticism he levels against the novel. If, however, one chooses to follow Flaubert's project and the hypothesis that there is no ontologically or epistemologically determinable base that will ground the language of the work, then the work, as the novel of alterity, begins to take form as a coherent whole, radically different from the textual phenomenon Lukács creates as his object of investigation.

According to the late Charles Bernheimer, the problem in *Salammbô* can be resumed by its decadence and its failure, for Lukács and Sainte-Beuve, among others, to deal with this decadence adequately. Both Sainte-Beuve and Lukács want Flaubert to diagnose this symptom from a cause-and-effect perspective linking past and present and suggesting future development. But *Salammbô* shows that such a perspective can be nothing more than an imaginary projection that constructs history out of disparate, discrete events and things. Flaubert, here, according to Bernheimer (56), "follows no model of epistemological coherence . . . it almost seems that the opposite is the case: the document he is most enthusiastic about is likely to be the most difficult to assimilate, the most outrageous and incomprehensible, the most resistant to narrative recuperation." Flaubert's documents are like the body parts strewn across the barbaric battlefield: they are the cultural remains that constitute the novelist's inspirational resource in an age of decadence (56).

The decadence seems to lie in the language, in the subject matter, in the times in which Flaubert is writing. The language is what Marilyn Gaddis Rose calls the "decadent prose" of *Salammbô* (213): a multiple falling away of prose from the everyday world. Realism's move will be to recuperate that falling away, that exoticism, and that otherness in an endlessly revised definition of what might be a canonical work. Decadence then is the falling away of narrative and realist narrative, in particular, from the reality it purportedly is describing, precisely because that reality does not exist, cannot be constructed, and has no logic. Yet it is that very introduction of figures of otherness at the heart of the realist enterprise, and the construction of something heterogeneous and not homogeneous, that already lead to this seeming impasse. Flaubert will take narrative and show to what extent the development of the realist enterprise finally maintains its own consistency, regardless of the world it purports to describe.

The language of the novel relates neither to a determinable or determined reality nor to a mode of perception of a reality, whatever its nature. In a "bourgeois novel," verisimilitude comes about through a textual reversal. The writing that constructs a "realistic" world is returned upon itself, so it seems as if this language were merely posed a posteriori upon an already existing world that it then echoes or reflects. The language produces the world, and then the world takes precedence, putting the writing in a subservient position to the world created. Here however, the act of returning cannot take place, for there is no world to take precedence or any ground to anchor the writing. The writing will function as a metaphor for the world rather than as a metonymy of it. The construction of a reality behind the language will always remain in the realm of the "as if," the realm of resemblance: "According to all verisimilitude and my own impressions, I think I made something that resembles Carthage. But that is not the question" ("Lettre à Sainte-Beuve" 437). But even metaphor itself is excessive, for metaphor is a movement from one signifier to another or from one signifier to a constellation of signifiers. Such movement upsets the stability, or what Flaubert calls the "harmony," of the system. The point of the system is stasis: "As for the style, I sacrificed less in this book than in the other to the roundness of the phrase and the sentence. Metaphors are rare and epithets are positive" ("Lettre" 437).

A consideration of the psychology of the novel thus brings us to a conception of alterity for the work in which stasis replaces movement, and where the seamless whole will be of language and not of the verisimilar world created in the novel. Victor Brombert (80) is quite right, for example, to point to the immobilizing nature of Flaubert's style in the novel and especially to his use of the imperfect, even more immobilizing here than in the later *L'Éducation sentimentale*. If then the unity and seamlessness are of prime importance, given in the form of a stylized alterity, Flaubert's focus will be other than that of a bourgeois novel such as *Madame Bovary*, which derives some of its verisimilar strength from the insignificant realistic touches. The determination of a stylized alterity will come about only through an explanation of the other through language, which gives it form in terms of the (inevitable) grammar and syntax of French. It is not the world that language represents that will be made to cohere through the style, but the language of alterity itself.[2]

## II. Shopping with Emma

What is *Madame Bovary* really about? Has it not been set up as the normative work against which the radicality of *Salammbô* is juxtaposed? Perhaps the original damning critiques were right: *Madame Bovary* is radical, scandalous, outrageous, and censurable. During the conservative, hypocritical days of the Second Empire, *Madame Bovary* was considered to be a scandalous work: here was an author who dared impute immoral values to his female protagonist, who, far from the corruption of the big city, led a dissolute life, was not punished for her adultery, and who, in a most un-Christian way, committed suicide because she had done nothing more dastardly than the nineteenth-century equivalent of maxxing out her credit card.

For Emma Bovary, reading and writing are activities intimately associated with her belated romantic dreaming of a better world. When she was a child, studying in the convent school, she filled her head with images of historic heroines, tales of romance, and, most dangerously, excerpts from novels. As an adult, she continues with some of these unhealthy pursuits and reads novels, including works by Eugène Sue and Balzac. Showing signs of psychological illness, she is enjoined, on the advice of her physician, from reading novels, which, in a revival of Rousseauism, are deemed dangerous. Yet Emma must read, just as Gustave must write. To become Parisian, at least in her own mind, she subscribes to Parisian magazines and spends her time reading them, learning about the latest styles, fashions, and chic shops. The real Paris that she has never visited (and never will visit) is eclipsed by these writings, as she is given to taking these images as her own. For this Paris, which is "vaster than the Ocean [*plus vaste que l'Océan*]" (1:344) is the Paris described by Balzac in *Le Père Goriot*: "Paris is a veritable ocean" (3:59), but with interest, with addition, with speculation, and with symbolic capital hiding in the surplus value afforded by the comparison.

Emma's desire is her own apotheosis; far more banal and far less ironic than the deification of a parrot that Flaubert would later write, Emma desires merely to become the epitome of chic, *une Parisienne*. From the very beginning of Emma's Parisianism and of *Madame Bovary* as a novel, one thing is clear: Flaubert is consciously developing a realist aesthetic based not on the real, but on its phenomena and representations. From *Madame Bovary* through *Bouvard et Pécuchet* nothing changes: even in that last, unfinished volume, the hapless heroes are concerned with the representations of the real, as they sift through learned opinions of great men of science. Their only progress, if progress it be, is in having abandoned journals, newspapers, and reviews for weighty tomes. Implicitly, though not exclusively, one might add that in Emma's Parisian musings, greater weight is placed on the visible versus the legible than in Bouvard and Pécuchet's readings. In certain cases for the latter, one would expect scientific drawings complementary to the prose. One suspects that for Emma, the pictures and drawings of Paris fashion are more important than the prose—and this for two reasons. First, it is consonant with her personal reading style, in which, as a student, she was already given to "envisioning" part of the books she read. Second, if Roland Barthes is correct in *Système de la mode*, the written language of fashion is often, though not exclusively, a heavily coded (and stereotypically so) supplement to the visual representation of the thing itself, or, if there is no drawing or photograph, the stylized language would seek to describe what the photo or drawing would otherwise have represented.

Flaubert bases the economy of representation and construction of Emma, as well as other characters including Bouvard and Pécuchet, on the extent to which they read and write, internalize discourses to make them their own, develop their writing, and/or turn their writing or that of others into reality. From one end of the novel to the other, the endless leitmotif of writing appears. Emma's unhealthy activities extend to writing as well. She, too, can create, and at two points in the novel, she turns to the production of writing. When she wants to become the romantic woman she feels she is, she buys writing equipment, as she does when she decides to learn Italian, the language of love, romance, and adventure. Elsewhere, Flaubert describes in detail the writing that indicates Homais's pharmacy, and the ball invitation becomes a fetishized object. At the end of the novel, Charles is undone by his discovery of Emma's hidden cache of love letters. In that, he has finally fulfilled, through reading, the writing assignment he had at the very beginning of the novel, his pensum of *ridiculus sum* (1:295).

Lheureux profits because he has taken Emma's desires and turned them into material objects. But the desires were not originally hers. In a classic Hegelian or Girardian system of desire, Emma desires what the other desires. Yet in this case, the other is not some real rival but simply the images offered by her magazines, the packaged emotions offered by heroines of novels. Given as writing, these desires are translated into her requests from Lheureux, who, having delivered the material goods to her, also delivers bills—more writing, writing relating to the abstract of money and wealth as opposed to the tarnished materialist object that supposedly translates desire into reality.

Writing and reading serve as the general means by which Flaubert controls his characters. When presenting *discours indirect libre*, the characters are invariably marked as speaking other people's words: their subjectivity is always inherited from the general discourse that surrounds them; their original words are invariably clichés. With the description of Homais's pharmacy, the author focuses more on the writing on the wall, so to speak, the door, and the sign than on the contents. Flaubert's characters are imprisoned within a wall of a language that is never theirs, that is always imposed on them, and against which their only choice is silence. The culmination of this motif already obvious in *Madame Bovary* will be in the *Dictionnaire des idées reçues* and the abyss of received knowledge of *Bouvard et Pécuchet*.

For Emma, in particular, Flaubert adds a layer of figurality to that writing, and it is the unseen images of her envisioning the figures of history or literature that forms the basis of this figurality. And this figurality is not only the characters from books but also the images or figures of settings, backgrounds, and objects, half-remembered from her youth or learned through subscriptions to her Parisian journals. Emma conjures up—and this is the essence of her Bovaryism—a candlelit world of gossamer and romance. It is the world imagined in the famous waltz scene at the château de la Vaubyessard, a whirl of dance, music, and lust. The scene is one of eroticism and fecundation, a moment at which her figures reproduce to eventually produce yet another, the fantasmatic Berthe (Schehr, *Flaubert* 15–17). The character is so named because that name was heard from the lips of one of the guests at the château. It is also a name that hearkens back to les Bertaux, and one would not be wrong in seeing Emma's vision of Berthe as the feminized version of "Bertaux," the equivalent, the search for an origin or source. Long before Scarlett O'Hara and Tara, Flaubert gives a reinscription of origin through the naming and creation of a character.

In *Madame Bovary*, Flaubert fulfills the task of assimilation of the woman that Balzac outlines in *Eugénie Grandet*. Not that the younger writer makes his character an independent reader and consumer; far from it. Emma is the perfect subject for the ubiquitous dissolution of the singular. Everything becomes typical, mass-produced, and repeatable. Subjects are interchangeable with one another, endless fodder for Flaubert's mill, renewable prey in a system that digests figures and words with the same engulfing power. Halfway between Eugénie Grandet, who seeks a certain independence accorded to men, and

Gervaise in Zola's *L'Assommoir*, who has gained not that independence but the possibility of total dissolution formerly accorded only to men, Emma remains the conflated subject and object for whom sexual traits become one more set of figures and discourses to be bought, sold, or traded.

For all the abject status given Emma as a character because of her imprisonment in a Hegelian system of desire and even though she might be an example of a successful inclusion of the woman as other within the assimilating system of representation, this abjection and this inclusion are not enough. For the means by which Emma is included, the ironic reduction of the ekphrastic moment, and the desubjectification of all characters do not account for two things. On the one hand, the means by which this inclusion has occurred have deprived realism of the possibility of the figural, be it the figures of rhetoric or the emergent figures for which rhetoric cannot account. *Madame Bovary* is a monument to clichés, a summmum of the catachretic. Even the packets of romantic retrospective love, trivialized as they must be for the realist illusion to occur, are now nothing more than vain acquisitions, throwbacks to an earlier time that mark the narrative as being mottled, not by a real otherness but by stains that prevent realism from fulfilling itself. On the other hand, the novel does not (how can it?) account for the fully other, that which has no real support at the level of the material.

Some of the paths are clear after *Madame Bovary*; this novel is as much of a challenge to Flaubert himself as it is to others. *L'Éducation sentimentale* will be the final death knell to the romantic, as Flaubert reduces emotion, relation, and the basic units of desire themselves into these little packets of romanticism that are then excised by the styluslike pointed style of the author. Frédéric's truth, like Emma's, is caught in a system in which the expression of desire is always already coded by the generalized narrative to which, according to Flaubert, all are subjected. Also present is the possibility for the exotic: packets of codified orientalism that match the codification of the West. Long before the *japonisme* of the latter part of the century, long before Loti or others like him, Flaubert sets the stage for the possibility of the oriental as always already coded behavior, writing, meaning, desire, or the absence thereof.

## III.  The African Other

It is thus that Flaubert's next novel after *Madame Bovary*, *Salammbô*, takes on such importance, for the goal of creating a historical novel with no material support is even more radical than the contemporary representation of the earlier novel. *Salammbô* is Flaubert's attempt to create a narrative in a locus where there can be no comparison with either material reality or ideology; there is no mirroring from scientific (in the widest sense of the word) discourses to guarantee, justify, or even contradict impressions. This novel is an attempt to build a monument on the salted ruins of Carthage. Most importantly, this narrative monument must still be resolutely realist. Therein lies the problem.

All definitions of realism implicitly or explicitly rely on an avatar of the real of which they are perceived to be an adequation. This incarnation of the real may be, most simply, a surface reflection, or more complexly, a reflection of material reality, discursivity, psychological patterns, epistemes, or, more likely than not, as is the case with works as disparate as *Illusions perdues* and *Middlemarch*, some combination thereof. Here, no such adequation is possible, for there is nothing with which Flaubert can make the adequation. No matter how much he reads or reconstitutes and no matter how much seems to be known about Carthage, it is fundamentally other, as cut off from nineteenth-century France as is any other completely closed society. The oft-repeated cry of Cato in the Senate, "Carthago delenda est [Carthage must be destroyed]," is fulfilled, until the city exists no more, when nothing is left but ruins, the earth salted so that nothing will grow, not even the merest representation.

How then can an author represent that other removed in time to a period completely cut off from the present moment of writing and in space, because not only was Carthage destroyed, it was also always already other, an African other that is completely different? This is not the Alexandrian Africa of Cleopatra, the familiar Greek- or Latin-speaking Africa, the Africa of great pyramid-building civilizations. This is the Africa of teratology, the figure of deepest, darkest Africa. This is the Africa that eventually gives us the characters of *Salammbô*. This is the Africa that gives us monstrous figures that do not fit: the Africa whence comes Hannibal bringing his elephants over the Alps. How could one have a figure of realism when everything is heterogeneous?

Let us, for the moment, take a vaguely teleological perspective, starting from a *terminus ad quem*. What will Flaubert have produced by the end of his career? Flaubert's writing is an intensely lived, feverishly fought battle to the produce realist narrative, epitomized in the famous phrase of a "livre sur rien." The easiest thing to do would be to make believe that half his output did not exist: in a simpler world, a French author named Gustave Flaubert, who lived from 1821 to 1880, had a small output, a precious collection of masterpieces starting with *Madame Bovary*. Even a century after its publication, *Madame Bovary* continues to serve as measure for narrative praxis, for it is a work in which all the various problems and solutions of realist(ic) narrative appear, without the writing ever becoming formulaic or sterile. *Madame Bovary* is an exemplary work that defines and delimits the linguistic, social, aesthetic, and psychological transcriptions of reality into narrative. For students of literary history and those interested in literary reception in particular, it has the added cachet of having been a *succès de scandale*—above all, the masterpiece of realist narrative. Add to that one work a few others, including *L'Éducation sentimentale*, the work of irony; the small stylistic jewel of "Un Cœur simple"; the unfinished, brittle work of genius of *Bouvard et Pécuchet*. If one rounds out the presentation with selected correspondence, Flaubert is humanized, and he takes his place among the immortals.

Certainly such a simplistic presentation of Flaubert is somewhat ridiculous. It straightens out a career and life that are far more tortuous and contradictory; it eliminates a whole host of problematics of writing and production. This myth of production remains appealing because it streamlines literary influence, literary history, and *Rezeptionsgeschichte*. It is a way for us to understand how Flaubert had an influence, how a certain Flaubert had an influence: he of the lapidary style, he of the figure-less prose, he of the anti-Romantic fervor; this is the Flaubert that marks Zola, Maupassant, and Proust, just to name a few. Even in a work like *La Tentation de Saint Antoine*, excess can be brought to the realm of the understandable, for the work is not really a flight of fancy but a list of heresies, themselves discursive practices that are a set of differences from the writing of the absolute truth, the logos that determines sign and meaning. The novel is in part a tableau of those heresies; the *Tentation* becomes not a metanarrative of realism, like *Bouvard et Pécuchet*, but a realist meta-narrative of a series of differences from the absolute truth. Thus, in its representations of the hallucinatory and of heresy as other, *La Tentation de Saint Antoine* subsumes that other to the model of the ab-solute truth. If the *Tentation* has little relation to the real, it has a thorough relation to the discourses of realism, as it manages to de-velop a world, though nonexistent or fantastic, is governed by laws of discourse and laws of form that resemble those of the everyday world. For the *Tentation*, "Saint Julien l'Hospitalier," and "Hérodias," the religious motifs of monotheism, consonant with the West's view of itself, are a means of grounding the writing.

Through the process of acquiring the figural, Emma does not need metaphors as such but can introduce the figural by trying to ac-quire what she has seen or envisioned. So, while Proust is correct to criticize Flaubert for lacking beautiful metaphors ("A propos" 586), he does not see that each of Emma's purchases is a combined figure, metonymy and metaphor, introducing an other into her realm. Emma reverses realism's focal points of self and other as she tries to swallow the real whole—Paris and its figures—but she will succeed at swallowing only that most Romantic (and least romantic) of poi-sons, arsenic. The reversal she operates, ironic because it is so sim-ple, is already inscribed within realism. Just as the author includes the slightly less than foreign and slightly more than nonlegitimated provincial other within his realist absorption of what lies external to the real, Emma does the same, just doing so through the wrong end of the telescope. While illustrating the very practice of realism, Flaubert is doing something revolutionary with this novel, and a short parenthesis is in order here, because it is important not only to show how this revolutionary moment operates for itself (for *Madame Bovary*), then, but also to show what will really be at stake in *Salammbô*.

*Madame Bovary* completely reinterprets and redefines the Paris/province dichotomy. Traditional narrative interpretations of province come in two generic forms. The first is the generic *Bildungsroman*. The provincial protagonist, after having spent some time on his (or her) home turf, comes to the big city (generally Paris) and makes his or her way in the world. He or she learns a few lessons and either triumphs or fails. Paris may or may not be a better place; indeed, examples abound of Paris being the figuration of hell for the pure or not so pure protagonist. So do Julien Sorel, Eugène de Rastignac, Lucien de Rubempré, Frédéric Moreau, Gervaise, and Claudine come to Paris and have varied experiences, but each follows some sort of a learning curve. Some go back to the provinces, older and wiser; some stay in Paris to enjoy their success or wallow (or die) in their failure. The other generic form is that of the provincial (or even bucolic) novel where the provinces are, by and large, self-sufficient, where the local is more than enough. No better examples of such a vision of the world of the narrative exists than in the numerous brilliant novels in Balzac's series, *Scènes de la vie de province*.[3] Paris tends to be far away from the scene of the narrative; Paris figures as a vague amorphic group of echoes that enter with little lasting fanfare. Even when a pure Parisian enters (Charles Grandet), he is subject to local law. It is a model that Proust will use in his depictions of provincial *petite noblesse*.

*Madame Bovary* changes all that by resetting the relation of Paris and province. The novel is scandalous precisely because the provinces are not Edenic and pure, precisely because, at every turn, Paris infiltrates, seduces, sneaks in, or better yet, is welcomed in as Emma herself opens a Pandora's box to let its often diabolical figures out. With *Madame Bovary*, Flaubert changes the relation between the two: Flaubert has Emma open the door, but the narrative makes it clear: in a nineteenth-century version of globalization, realism will subsume the provinces. From there to the subsumption of the exotic is one small step. Yet Flaubert does not take the simple path of assimilation, and *Salammbô* stands out even more as a remarkable experiment in testing the figures of realism.[4]

*Salammbô* is a problem novel, much as certain of Shakespeare's late plays are considered to be problem plays. *Salammbô* is the one novel that stands outside the myth of Flaubert's realist production, not assimilable to the rest of the output, precisely because there is no way to ground it in any version of the real or reality: it is a realist narrative without the safety net of the real. So it is a problem work, both because of its singularity and because it seems hard to fathom after the defining role retrospectively given to *Madame Bovary* as the essential novel of high French realism. Significantly, the aberrant nature of the work has been frustrating to critics because it is so difficult to engage.[5]

Let us take a case in point: Andrew McKenna's remarks (307) about Flaubert's phrase, "impossible de rien distinguer," in Chapter 8 of *Salammbô*, point to the impossibility of distinction at that point in the novel in which Flaubert is describing the battle of Macar. Whereas Stendhal strategically controls the chaos in his depiction of Waterloo in *La Chartreuse de Parme*, and makes it indistinct only to Fabrice, both the narrator and the reader understand Fabrice's incomprehension and at least theoretically understand the battle: readers know it is "Waterloo" and what "Waterloo" means. Even if the readers are not military historians, faith abides in the narration that presents, without fear of contradiction, the competence of the generals, the linearity of the historical time line, and the truth of history: even before reading the passage, readers know that Napoleon will not win the battle. The chaos is that because the optic used at the local level is inadequate and because the hapless hero is inadequate to the task.

No such guardrails exist in *Salammbô*. When the narrator says "impossible de rien distinguer," he is bringing the chaos to a general level. There cannot be distinction; one thing, person, or event cannot be separated from another; the basics of a logic of identity do not obtain. Simultaneously, this ambiguity is not placed under the sign of irony as it might be in any other realist narrative. For, given the absence of solid ground on which to found distinction and decision, irony itself becomes an impossible figure. The frame that would allow for irony to obtain just is not there, even in narrative, where it is impossible to distinguish anything as well. If the reader cannot distinguish at the level of narrative, how is he or she to define the figures of the work?

Flaubert's phrase discussed by McKenna is the general watchword for the novel: *Salammbô* is the novel in which it is impossible to distinguish anything and in which it is impossible for anything to be distinguished. Critics sometimes seek foundation but have to impose structure on the novel to justify that foundational move. For example, in *Salammbô*, Catherine Lowe (87) sees the founding polarities (or bivalent oppositions) of inside/outside, city/country, male/female, and so forth as foundational but not dynamic. For Lowe, the polarities are caught in the narrative's mirror structure, a trap formed between "the story and the illusion that it produces of itself," a locus that creates the trap of the imaginary (in the Lacanian sense). In view of that proposed mirror stage, the reader is hard-pressed to create a valid relevant psychological position.[6] How can it be said then that there are characters in the classic sense? In her analysis of this novel, Jeanne Bem bluntly remarks the impermeability of Mathô and Salammbô to any psychological approach (18), and to find meaning in the novel, she sees it as a displaced historical allegory of modernity, with its violence, its capitalist system, and its colonialism (23).[7] In both these cases, the device—mirror stage or allegory—is a way to escape the impenetrability of the novel. What is compelled is a literal, realist, or readerly reading of the language, a language voided of allegorical content, real referentiality, psychology, and anything other than a system of signifiers that have replaced a system of material or referential reality. Everything is a figure that would interrupt the narrative, were there a realist narrative to interrupt that somehow seemed to relate to the real.

*Salammbô* is not a comfortable continuation or a dialectical reversal of the textual and technical problematics developed in *Madame Bovary*. The conjunction of points of view is a result of necessity, the absolute need to have a neutral if not to say a neuter position of enunciation, a zero-degree metonymical version of the French language itself. The French language (as *langue*) is taken as a clear or potentially clear and transparent medium, as both means and ground. Similarly, the point of view of the neutral third-person, or nonperson, narrator is assumed as a position from which to start the writing of alterity.

Consider the simple example of writing a job description for a druggist, by comparing Flaubert's two *pharmakoi* Homais and Schahabarim. Homais is described through a combination of metonymy and synecdoche, followed by a statement of tautology. It is primarily the pharmacy described in all its glory, from which the nature of the man behind the counter can be inferred, because metonymy, even ironized, works in this world; it is an acceptable law of form. Not even the whole pharmacy is given but only salient, remarkable, and representative objects that indicate the shop and the man behind it.

The whole is emblematically marked by the iterative inscription of nomination at the locus itself, joining sign to the object represented and identity to the authority of the Other, all under the nominative power of writing and language:

> From top to bottom, his house is covered with inscriptions written in Italian hand, round hand, block letters [*anglaise, en ronde, en moulée*]. The signpost, as wide as the store itself, has "Homais, pharmacist" written in golden letters. Then, at the back of the store, behind the large scale fastened on the counter, the word laboratory unfolds above a glass door which, halfway up, repeats "Homais" anew in golden letters on a black background. (1:356–57)

Marked by letters in gold, the names and signifiers metonymically signify a complete world, one identical to that synecdochally given by the "red bottles that garnish [*embellissent*] the front." When Homais himself is given, sign and reality agree: "his face expresses nothing other than self-satisfaction." That Flaubert's narrator is using irony with the word "embellissent" or in his characterization of Homais's smugness changes nothing in the realist paradigm, which allows for such irony and often depends on it, since the basic laws of representation, displacement, and condensation are all those of the real world.

Opposed to the preestablished self-consistency of Homais who can be signaled by metonymy and synecdoche and by the adequation of a language to the world is Schahabarim:

> Salammbô turned. She had recognized the sound of the golden bells [*clochettes d'or*] that Schahabarim wore at the bottom of his clothing.
> He climbed the stairs: then, at the threshold of the terrace, he stopped, crossing his arms.
> His deep-set eyes shone like the lamps of a sepulcher; his long, thin body floated in his linen gown, weighed down by the bells [*grelots*] that alternated with rounded emeralds on his heels. His limbs were feeble, his skull oblique, his chin, pointy; his skin seemed cold to the touch, and his yellow face, worked by deep wrinkles, as if contracted in a desire, in an eternal chagrin. (1:750–51)

At every point in the description, because there is no ground, there are more questions than there are answers. Here are just a few: How does Salammbô recognize the sound of the bells? What does stopping at a threshold mean? What does crossing one's arms signify?

What is the weight of a comparison between eyes and lamps? Should answers be formulated relative to the world of France in the nineteenth century or the unknowable world of Carthage during the Punic Wars? Why emeralds? Should Schahabarim be considered grotesque, repugnant, and repulsive, because in the West such an association would obtain based on his physical description? To whom did his skin seem cold? What is the value of his desire? What would an "eternal chagrin" mean in this context?

In the description of Homais, the various elements taken together underscore the banality and the commonness of this all-too-common figure. No real idea is given of his physical appearance beyond the minimal sketch; the narrator is content to indicate that Homais is "somewhat marked by smallpox and is wearing a velvet cap with gold tassels" (1:358). For Homais, the marks are identical to themselves and to what they signify through tautology and stereotype. A physical description of Homais would be superfluous, for the readers' mental image of this common character is easy to complete: singular in the book but plural in the real world. Thus, in addition to being *representational*, by figuring a verisimilar character through language, the description of Homais is also *representative*: the part stands as one of many. The operative figures of rhetoric that control standard narrative production, metonymy and synecdoche, are figures that allow for representative representation and verisimilitude.

These figures are excluded from *Salammbô*. Everything must point to the singularity of the phenomenon that Flaubert is seeking to represent. No metonymy can come to stand in the position of narrative description, for the effectiveness of metonymy depends on prior received knowledge by the reader. Similarly, synecdoche must be excluded as well, for one must have an idea of the whole in order to make sense of the part.[8] The description of the priest is exemplary of what Flaubert has to use to produce singularity out of neutrality. The description is as devoid of original figures as the author can make it, with the metaphors and similes pushing the limits of the banal. The movement toward a trope points to the writing itself as *ergon* and not to any other signifiers or to the real world. The singularity comes from the single details that here mark the identity of the character: "She had recognized the sound of the gold bells [*clochettes d'or*] . . . his linen robes, weighed down by bells [*grelots*] alternating on his heels with rounded emeralds [*pommes d'émeraude*]." The reality-effect derives from association made within the description: the *grelots* repeat and refer to the *clochettes*, already accepted by the reader, and the *pommes d'émeraude* are thereby made "real." The unknown or the different is brought around to the known by being placed on the same level of ontological and epistemological certainty.

Both in terms of the generic parameters for the novel that aims to be neither a *roman bourgeois* nor a *roman historique*, and in terms of the structuring of the subject of enunciation, *Salammbô* is seen to depend on the conception of language as being essentially a system of alterity. Neither at the general levels of genre or subject of enunciation nor at the more specific level of the description of the textual subjects and objects does Flaubert use language in a way that makes an adequation between sign and object. Apart from the necessary gesture made by the author that amounts to using French as a medium—but a French dissociated from all connotation and all figures—there is no linguistic or social contract between writer and reader. The novel is not posited as a mediate construct representing a set of subjects through a process of verisimilitude but is a given absolute with which the reader necessarily must struggle.

What could the novel represent, given the system of alterity on which it is founded? Like *Madame Bovary*, *Salammbô* is an attempt to rid realist praxis of any vestigial traces of romanticism, of sentiment, of imposed meaning, and of clichés. *Madame Bovary* is a careful analysis of the heart of Romanticism as received knowledge; it goes far in devalorizing a transcendental signifier of romantic love. The figures with which Flaubert constructs his first mature novel are images ironized in its construction: for Flaubert, the figure is not that which cannot yet be represented but that which has been represented too often. *Salammbô* continues that project of dismantling any a priori valorization of a transcendental signified of desire. We shall return below to the question or status of desire in this novel, but, for now, what is relevant is the status of desire as mimesis. This is received desire, desire as the desire of another, prepackaged desire that marks not only a Hegelian or Girardian world but also the development of Western narrative, crisscrossed by received concepts of desire in general and romantic love in particular.

Epistemologically, this gesture is always already accomplished for the narrative: the realm of identity, with the "philosophemes" or epistemes of Greco-Roman and Judeo-Christian tradition excluded. The ontological feature remains: an analysis with neutral tools of the problem of alterity. Within Romanticism, the problem of alterity is often reduced to a negativity of the self. Alterity—the dream world, the Orient—is considered to be the crypt into which is cast what differs from the self of identity, conceived either objectively or as the transcendental subject of knowledge. Thus, the realm of alterity is by and large the repository of desire; it is a world of the dark side, the impossible, and the eternal. The gesture and the movement of rationalization away from Romanticism, which consist in recasting or decrypting the desire, still are imprisoned in the romantic mold. The return of desire to the realm of identity is ultimately less the rationalization of this desire than the placement in question of the priority of the rational subject itself.[9]

Flaubert sets out to determine alterity for itself and not as it relates to the realm of identity. As I have already noted, he situates the narrative at a spatiotemporal point removed from the epistemes that define alterity in terms of difference from, negation of, and relation to identity. He thus gives himself the advantage of being able to dispense with the philosophy and textuality of the Occident. Relations are accidental and never causal. Building from a set of differential sources, Flaubert sets out to construct an alterity that has never been encrypted in a known world. He also attempts to enlarge the purview of realism by extending the narrative praxes and their presuppositions to something that is basically unverifiable. Individual facts, statements, and conjectures will find corroboration in recognized authorities on ancient times, though together they amount perhaps not to a real whole but to a zero-sum. Flaubert broadens the verisimilar into a more loosely defined and more artificial form of realism, the self-consistency of the narrative:

According to all verisimilitude and my own impressions, I think I made something that resembles Carthage. But that is not the question. I don't care about archeology. If the color is not uniform, if the details are off-key, if the mores do not derive from the religion and the facts from emotions, if the personalities are not developed, if the costumes are not right for the uses and the architecture for the climate, if there is not, in a word, harmony, I am wrong. If not, not. Everything holds together. ("Lettre" 437)

His archeological gesture is realism's own; he gestures toward Carthage just as realism as a whole gestures toward the real. In believing he has made something that looks like Carthage, Flaubert nevertheless knows that there is no mirror that can be held up to the light to see if there is such a resemblance. Language itself cannot essentially resemble something material unless the linguistic is itself denied, and language is viewed as transparent. The key is that he has made something that resembles the actual or real Carthage: something that no longer exists as a measurable, absorbable whole. Carthage is in ruins, and the linguistic artifact resembles that ruin. There is no order save that imposed by the system of representation, not the system of mimesis. Flaubert's assessment is correct: the resemblance to whatever Carthage may be conceived is not what is important, for the mimesis is always false: language does not resemble reality except in its artifice and its decomposition. What counts in the narrative are the thickness of the representational system, its internal coherence, or for that matter, its harmonies, disharmonies, slippages, and self-references. Flaubert's continuing description does not match any coherent position in the novel, but that is another matter: harmony is in the eye of the reader/beholder. The merest comparison, whose theoretical validity is based on the logic that Flaubert has deemed necessary for coherence in the quote just mentioned, is a threat to the system as a whole in its disruption of harmony.

Equated with a more easily classifiable type of realism (narrative as *Wiederspiegelung*), verisimilitude can be perceived as such because the reality that it is thought to reproduce is a continuum. What does this mean? First of all, there is no need to give laws of nature or laws of form in the verisimilar narrative, for the assumption of verisimilitude means that the created universe does not differ from the recognizable real one. Verisimilitude allows for a great deal of agreed-on received knowledge: in short, it allows for gaps. While *Salammbô* observes laws of nature and of form, the latter imposed in part by the assumption of narrative neutrality, tantamount to a normalization of the narrative and what it relates, in no other way does it or can it use the short cuts of verisimilitude. There can be no gaps in the discourse. For such gaps would correspond to gaps in the "real" world. What is not told cannot occur phenomenologically. What is not written cannot be known. But it is not simply that what is not written cannot be known, for there is one additional law: what is not written does not exist. In and for this world, writing is all.

A perspective on the novel as a whole, or a reflection on this purported harmony, shows the very impossibility of grounding that founds, yet cannot found, the novel. No anchor exists to found an interpretative system, except for the style of the piece: the syntax, the use and choice of words, the plotting of the novel, the detail. Each of these is immediately itself a problem. Beyond the basics of French syntax, the degree zero of grammaticality, how can any meaning or interpretation be imputed to linguistic form other than as an *écart* from language itself and not from the representational system?

Let us consider the famous opening lines of the novel, which have been viewed as monumental, stolid, and static by many and which can be perceived as such only against a more fluid or flowing style. Speaking of style means speaking of its effect, a phrase becomes an ekphrastic moment because of the implication of the represented object. Thus, with a simple phrase like "C'était à Mégara, faubourg de Carthage," followed by extensive description, there are only two ways to determine the effect of that staticity, each of which is already excluded by the challenge or problem of the novel. Flaubert lingers over an initial scene of description by giving details and sketching figures. But these details relate to no image, and any preconceived notion of what to linger over becomes an arbitrary choice. Why describe a city or a scene in detail, when, within the invented hermeneutic circle for this imaginary world, what is important is a veil that cannot be described? For the world that this is supposed to be (and again, this imaginary existence is hypothetical at best), the rest may just be dross, immaterial details that do not speak to the reality supposedly represented. It is only by imposing categories thought of as logical in the West that sense can be made of the world described, but that imposition, the anathema of anthropological investigation, is a destruction. Concomitantly, at the level of the narratological act of communication, the implied reader is an impossibility. It is a given that the implied reader of a work is, even at the most basic level, an informed reader: he or she has some understanding of what is given to him or her. This understanding does not simply mean the ability to parse the sentence, to know that in the sentence "arma virumque cano," *arma* is an accusative plural, *virum*, an accusative singular, *que* a conjunction, and *cano*, a first-person singular of the present tense. Some basic meaning must also be given. But in *Salammbô*, that meaning cannot be given, for no meaning preexists the narrative other than grammar and syntax. We can say then that *Salammbô* is already translated from some unknown and unknowable language. Nor does Flaubert know that language even if he seeks to "give people a language in which they have not thought" (*Corr.* 9:170).

What is this language? The language within the novel and the language of the novel, of its narrative, are both languages of the other, the "same" language of the other, if "same" has any meaning, a language of pure figurality bursting through the narrative to which it is identical or "identical." The language of alterity is triply other. It is ontologically other because there is no reality, either real or verisimilarly determined, that is the ground on which the written word can come to rest and which it can indicate. It is epistemologically other because there is no means of knowledge other than the signifiers that compose the narrative; there is no preexisting signified, other than those given by laws of syntax and by catachreses, appropriately known as "dead metaphors." Finally, it is other, as all writing is other, marking an absence. This last absence, inscribed into the language of metaphysics and the metaphysics of language, is not radically other in the way that the ontological and epistemological considerations are. For the writing itself, present (though as the sign of an absence) is the only means of marking the radical alterities alien to the novel's metaphysical constraints. Calling on the *langue* as a neutral whole, written language will be the means of determining the alterity of the work.

To pursue his radical inscription of alterity in the novel, Flaubert needs to arrive at an impersonal, voiceless voice of narration. It is a safe and basically unassailable position, one from which the falseness or bias of overt subjectivity is absent and thus one from which a discourse about alterity can be undertaken. In a totally alien world, it is an absolute necessity that the assumption of authority by the author, or by the rhetorical construct of the invisible narrator, have already taken place. This neutral discourse that pushes *parole* toward *langue* is not simply objective narration opposed to a subjective one. It is a totally other narrative that allows no spot for the encrypting of the authorial ego. The subject is not hidden behind the objective; it is instead completely dispersed in the search for language.

Let us now look at another example, taken from the beginning of the novel. Classical expositions are usually rich in information, as they provide setting, time, characters (if not necessarily protagonists), and even a sense of the plot. But here, all is figure, *écart*, difference, otherness. The novel begins with the parameters for readers' understanding of the novel having been determined by habitual reading praxes, preconceived notions, and collective understanding. There is nothing radical at the starting point, whose "zero degree" is that of the third-person, omniscient narrator. Throughout much of the first chapter, while building the description of Carthage, Flaubert begins to put a system of narration in place into which the third-person objective discourse can be dissolved. It is an economic strategy: despite all the problems with a type of verisimilitude determined in the normal manner for the work, Flaubert nonetheless starts the novel out by playing on the reader's desire for verisimilitude. As he is beginning to construct the mechanism whereby the third-person narrator will disappear, Flaubert grafts this new novel onto the verisimilar patterns of *Madame Bovary*, as he recalls for example, the description of the banquet at the Château de Vaubyessard (1:335) in a remarkably similar description of the *festin* (1:711–12).

As Flaubert begins to develop the false verisimilitude of the new novel through grafting, he distorts and upsets the very same paradigm for interpretation. As a general rule, Flaubert substitutes a multiplicity of objects for the unity of the earlier work. The object in *Madame Bovary* tends to be fragmented by the sequences of syntagmas used in the descriptions, as, for example, in that of the *casquette*. In *Salammbô*, the descriptions produce multiple fragments in a hall of mirrors: the fragmented images given by the mirrors replace the diffraction of light. Organization and classification give way to chaos. The singularity of Charles Bovary's cap is replaced by a plethora of hats, tongues, and signs that compete for readers' attention, each of which serves as a figure interrupting narrative flow.

The Greek could be recognized from his thin waist, the Egyptian, his high shoulders, the Cantabrian, his wide ankles. Carians balanced the plumes of their helmets with pride, Cappadocian bowmen had painted themselves with vegetable juices, drawing big flowers on their bodies, and some Lydians wearing women's dresses were dining and wore slippers and earrings. (1:710)

Instead of one series of determined signs that is the metaphor for the clear-cut edges of verisimilar representation from which the tangential has been trimmed, there is a multiplicity of sign-systems that do not dovetail. In this world, the production of verisimilitude begins to come apart as various fashions of semiosis compete and interfere. At the heart of verisimilitude lies an Aristotelian logic of distinction and distinguishability. But from the first, Flaubert breaks down the barriers that determine self and other and those that determine perception and apprehension of self and other. Distinctions between animate and inanimate and between human and nonhuman begin to disappear. Flaubert interweaves descriptions of the two, not simply from paragraph to paragraph or even sentence to sentence but from phrase to phrase: "One saw kitchen slaves running among the trees, scared and half-naked; gazelles on the lawns were fleeing while bleating; the sun was setting, and the odor of the lemon trees made the breath of the crowd even heavier" (1:710). While remaining internally self-consistent, even the description of Salammbô (1:718) compares animate parts with inanimate objects. In the process, the efficacy of metaphor to communicate meaning within an understandable sign-system is undercut.

Take, for example, a simple description of a musical moment, which involves three comparisons, reflecting an objectively determinable external reality, the second reflecting categories of classification, the third reflecting language and semiosis: "The slave raised a sort of harp in ebony wood higher than herself and triangular like a delta [*L'esclave souleva une sorte de harpe en bois d'ébène plus haute qu'elle, et triangulaire comme un delta*]" (1:748). One could posit that measures of extension in space, regardless of the culture or the semiotic system, are consistent or could be perceived to be consistent, and most readers would instantly agree with such a supposition. Thus whether the slave is Carthaginian or subject to general rules of form, members of both groups would probably agree that there is an objective way of determining that the harp is bigger than she is—though what "a sort of harp" actually means is far from determinable. The opposite consideration is possible but remote: that somehow the perception of measurable external reality might differ because, for example (hypothetically), different castes or classes might be seen as being of different heights relative to their social status, no matter what the objective measure tells us. For example, a slave might be perceived as always being shorter than a king even if Western subjects might place the height of the former at two meters and that of the latter at 1.7 meters.[10]

The key is measurability, which implies literacy. A literate society is one that physically, actively, consciously has acts of transcription, a written language (or several) that in its writing of the absent object (in the Derridean sense) can be understood by another, to a greater or lesser extent. With literacy goes the possibility of measurement and of objective criteria, even if such criteria are not always respected in all situations. The problem of classification is far more generalized. Consider the expression "une sorte de harpe," by which readers are meant to understand, one would commonly suppose, a musical instrument with strings that are plucked. The strings are attached at each end to a wooden frame shaped roughly like a triangle. This is what any reader would understand or should understand. But, to split hairs, whose harps are being considered? The modern harp seems to have been a medieval invention, associated in Western mythology with the chorus of angels, and a descendant of lyres that were known in Greece and Rome. To interpret the harp as a variant of that modern classification is thus to produce a willful misinterpretation through anachronism just as one is reaching the only understanding possible. For one could assume that for the Carthaginians, or for the Carthage of Flaubert, harps were a category for all string instruments, or all wooden instruments, or all instruments used in sacred situations. While readers may want to understand the phrase in the simplest of ways, doing so eliminates the potential of other interpretations that are equally valid, if not equally probable, but all of which coexist.

This point is most clear in the third comparison, the most abstract of the sentence, because within the simile is the abyssal point of a catachresis. The harp is said to be triangular like a delta. The simplest interpretation is that the harp is triangular and shaped like the Greek letter delta, i.e., like an equilateral triangle. But how could the balance of style withstand such an egregious comparison with something totally foreign? A Greek letter is doubly problematic: it is foreign and thus external to the sign system of Carthage that Flaubert is presenting to us, and secondly and more importantly, even within that sign system, Greek is tantamount to barbarian and certainly not the appropriate comparison for a sacred and religious motif. Nothing is more distantly opposed than the sacred of the Carthaginians as personified by Salammbô herself and the Greek, materialist and mercenary, tantamount to the incarnation of the infidel.

A better interpretation is at one remove: the harp is triangular like a delta, that point at which the river fans out in various estuaries until it reaches the sea; perhaps the two most well-known examples are the Nile and the Mississippi River deltas. But Flaubert could not possibly mean this. For the naming of the delta as a delta is a reductive, to be shaped like a delta means to be shaped something like a triangle, but not really; it means an expansion, a melding of sea, river, and land, of liquid and solid. It means anything but a materially reproducible template, by which to say that the harp and the delta are congruent triangles. Moreover, any interpretation of the delta as geographic feature whose shape roughly resembles that of a triangle means forgetting the catachresis: that the name "delta" was given to the mouth of the river, because from one point of view (bird's eye, above, Greek, trigonometric), it resembled the Greek letter delta. Language forgets the etymology and renders what was once a figure into a dead metaphor, a catachresis; it is a figure that is now a common name but that historically started as a trope: the arm of a chair, a river delta.

This excursus on one simple phrase shows how even the seemingly straightforward language of this novel is mined from the interior and is potentially explosive and destructive of meaning. To have meaning, both readers' disbelief and the closure of interpretations have to be deferred; in short, readers must work against what the novel is and does in order to render it readable. Rhetoric and the deconstruction of rhetoric make every reading an impossible one. It will suffice to quote four other comparisons from the same chapter to see to what extent there is a problem with any poetic use of language. That problem necessarily makes a more straightforward use of language, a prosaic work, itself complicated and unsolvable. Nature is invoked, as if somehow the natural kingdom remained objective, even if that of humankind does not: "fishing nets were spread from one house to another, like giant bats [*chauves-souris*] deploying their wings" (1:746). Not the least of the problems here is the catachresis in French, for the animal "bat" has no proper name other than that of a "bald mouse." Again nature seems to be explicable but is not: "the great salty laguna shimmered like a piece of silver" (1:746). What kind of shimmering this is can never be known. Again, in that example and in the following, the appeal to nature peters out in a vagueness that cannot be pinpointed: "the pyramidal cypresses murmured like the regular waves that beat slowly along the breakwater" (1:746).

As a final example from the same few pages, there is a description of Salammbô herself: "She raised her arms as high as possible, bending her waist; she was pale and light like the moon with her/its long robe [*pâle et légère comme la lune avec son long vêtement*]" (1:749). We have already wondered about the extension of a character or object into space, so Salammbô's raised arms do not necessarily tell us what we want to know. Most significant in this comparison is the final phrase: "pale and light like the moon with its/her long robe." It is impossible to determine what, for Carthage, the paleness and lightness of the moon might signify. And whose robe is it? Logically, it is Salammbô's; grammatically, it is the moon's. So the moon is perhaps a female goddess, clad in a flowing robe. Perhaps, but only perhaps. Ambiguity reaches far greater extension here than it did even in *Madame Bovary* (Culler).

In his descriptions, Flaubert is trying to destroy the anthropocentricity of the linguistic system itself, exchanging the object of third-person discourse for an undifferentiable amalgamation of animate and inanimate, of what is capable of language and what is not. As if to insist, he has dehumanized language as well along with the act of reception: "One could hear, next to the heavy Dorian dialect, resound Celtic syllables murmuring like battle chariots, and the Ionian endings collided with the consonants of the desert, as bitter as jackals' cries (1:710). Language is divided into its component but meaningless parts of syllables, endings, and consonants. As the object of third-person discourse begins to disintegrate, the third person begins to be transformed into a total alterity not bound to the hierarchic modes of first, second, and third persons. The nonperson has begun the process of turning into the other of totally dislocated discourse.

Emile Benveniste (1:255) reminds us that though the third person remains paradigmatically related to the two persons (first and second) of the linguistic system, it is essentially a nonperson.

From the very beginning of the novel, Flaubert insistently uses the word "on"; as the perceptive, semiotic, and representational systems dissolve, the eyes and ears of the omniscient narrator give themselves over to this position of indeterminacy, of undecidability, and of neutrality. To decide is to be human. To be human is to allow, even in the form of the nonperson, the language system itself to become skewed by a specific *parole*. Flaubert continues the process of altering the position of discourse in the second chapter through his repeated insistent use of the generalized indeterminate pronoun "on":

Some of the Elders were standing on the tower platform, and one did not know why a long-bearded person, in a dreamy attitude, was standing thus here and there. [ . . . ]
One assaulted them with oaths and embraces. Some even exhorted them not to leave the city, out of an exaggeration of politics and the audacity of hypocrisy. One threw perfumes, flowers, coins at them. One gave them amulets against sickness; but one had spit on them three times to attract death or put jackal's hair inside, which make the heart weak. One invoked the favor of Melkarth aloud, and his curse under one's breath. (1:726–27)

[Quelques-uns des Anciens s'étaient postés sur la plate-forme des tours, et l'on ne savait pas pourquoi se tenait ainsi, de place en place, un personnage à barbe longue, dans une attitude rêveuse. . . .
On les accablait de serments, d'étreintes. Quelques-uns même les engageaient à ne pas quitter la ville, par exagération de politique et audace d'hypocrisie. On leur jetait des parfums, des fleurs et des pièces d'argent. On leur donnait des amulettes contre les maladies; mais on avait craché dessus trois fois pour attirer la mort, ou enfermé dedans des poils de chacal qui rendent le cœur lâche. On invoquait tout haut la faveur de Melkarth et tout bas sa malédiction.]

The position of the "on" is a roving one, neither related to a specific person (or referential nonperson) nor fixed from phrase to phrase. Action occurs, if it can be said to occur, but the agent is vague, ambiguous, contradictory, and impossible. Even if the position of the "on" is a generalized one, spread out among the people of Carthage, it remains just as ambiguous, for at every turn, it negates the validity of its own position, thereby canceling the bond of symbol and discourse. The speech act of "on" is subject to a double interpretation: the offering of a symbol or sign of a communicational bond affirms and denies the validity of the bond. The two positions cancel each other out, and all traces of the personal, even as the impersonal third person, are removed from the discourse that will henceforth be a neutral one. Neutrality is defined in opposition to positive or negative, an impossible definition here, and thus even neutrality has lost its meaning.

As the nature of representing the subject is put into question and as the radical requestioning of the act of representation takes place through a dislocation of the process of representation, the object to be represented is made problematic as well. Flaubert conceives of the object as singular and unique. Figurality is abstracted or negated; if a word is used to describe an object is not justified through denotation, the word is (or becomes) a catachresis. The description of Carthage, for example, is as specific as possible to the point of over-precision. All words that might once have been figural in nature are reduced to the simple physicality of the represented object: "Behind, the city's tall houses shaped like cubes, spread out like the rows of an amphitheater. They were made of stones, planks, pebbles, reeds, shells, mud. The wood of the temples seemed to be like lakes of greenery in this mountain of blocks, diversely colored" (1:754). The "montagne" represents nothing more than the shape the pile takes from the usual denotative meaning given by the neutral French language. The simile does not function as a figure to further poesis. It concretely gives a material form to a physical representation that would otherwise be difficult to describe. There is no correspondence between nature and culture, no real comparison made between temples and lakes and mountains; nature itself is denatured through a use of language that allows no flight to metaphor as a poetic figure.

Because of the equivalency made at the beginning of the novel, and continued throughout, between inanimate and animate objects (of discourse), it does not matter to which category the object described belongs. All objects of discourse are treated with the same purpose:

Outside the walls there were people of another race of unknown origin. They were all hunters of porcupines, eaters of mollusks and serpents. They went to the caves to catch living hyenas, that they had fun racing in the evening on the sands of Megara, among the tombstones. Their huts of muck and seaweed hung on the cliff like swallows' nests. (1:756–57).

Again, the comparison is a shorthand way of communicating an imposing physicality to the reader without having to resort to an endless series of paraphrases, circumlocutions, or explanations of explanations. Moreover, the linguistic determination of an object is seen to be intrinsically related to an ontological imperative for the imposition of a singular reality. Even an epistemological barrier—"d'une origine inconnue"—that amounts to a limitation on either the language or more probably the parameters for communication does not interfere with the act of description of singularity.

Let us turn to another aspect of representation, which is the use of symbols. The act of symbolization is normally excluded from strict verisimilitude, not being in conformity with an act of representation of a reality that knows no symbols, that makes no a priori correspondences between systems, except those that are transcendental. But if a less strict attitude is taken toward the act of verisimilar representation whereby the semiotic field is locally expanded or distended so as to allow for the possibility of a symbol, a symbol is a local excrescence within the semiotic or representational system, a point that does not correspond to the field in which it was found. Such a point would transcend (though not necessarily with a transcendental signifier) both the immediate semiotic parameters and climate in which it was found and the rules for representation given by the novel. To be more specific, there is a local disturbance, epiphenomenal in nature, that transcends the continuity of the semiotic system or the theory of representation posited for a narrative. Thus "la mouche d'or" in Zola's *Nana* both deictically and semiotically transcends the "naturalist" system of representation in which it is found, in order to signify Nana and her destiny *en abyme*. Zola's poetic license often takes the form of a flight of fancy reified into a *mise-en-abyme* in which a global and transcendental semiotic system takes the place of a local, "naturalist" one.

In *Salammbô*, precisely because there is never any certainty as to whether or not there is continuity, the status of the symbol itself is jeopardized. In a novel in which every moment of the narrative has become a Lyotardian figure of disruption, the "symbols," so to speak, are just more intense versions of those disruptions. Flaubert's attempt at symbolization turns into a caprice of semiosis. Even more (or less) than the *casquette* of Charles Bovary, this attempt at symbolization in *Salammbô* is a symbol that is not a symbol. Charles's cap is overdetermined, and the description turns into a parody of symbolization. In *Salammbô*, the description of the serpent, pointing all too clearly toward the symbolic, is undercut by the absence of a figural significance in the work:

Salammbô's [serpent] had already refused several times the four live sparrows offered to it at the full moon and every new moon. Its beautiful skin, covered like the firmament with spots of gold on a completely black background, was now yellow, soft, wrinkled, and too big for its body, a fleecy mustiness extended around its head, and in the angle of the eyelids, one could see small red points that seemed to move. (1:869)

The serpent is a symbol, understood all too easily, for Flaubert can paint with a broad brush at times. But it is precisely because of this facile—and correct—symbolism that the reader must have cause to be suspicious. The symbol adds nothing aesthetically to the structure of the work; in fact, understood as a symbol, the description seems so heavy-handed as to weaken the novel. This is a symbol that is not a symbol; this is a world given through representation in which, or in whose transcription, a symbol—or any figure—has no transcendental or figural value.

The symbol—or the nonsymbol—has to have a function. Though Flaubert was certainly not above playing a game with his readers, it seems highly unlikely that Flaubert the perfectionist would risk the trivialization of his writing just to get the better of the reader. The symbol serves as a paradigmatic marker, as an index and reminder within the writing, of the one object always in excess of the system of representation, regardless of the system used. The symbol of the serpent indicates the object that is the very object of alterity: the zaimph, antimatter made into writing.

Although it is found at the beginning of a chapter, the description of the serpent immediately follows a reference to the zaimph (1:868). The multiple imbrications of the serpent with its purportedly chthonic origins correspond antithetically to those of the divine zaimph and recall the object itself. Thus the local disturbance in the system the attempt at symbolization is a reminder of what exceeds all systematization:

> But beyond, one would have said a cloud in which stars twinkled, figures appeared in the depths of its folds: Eschmoun with the Kabirs, some of the monsters already seen, the sacred animals of the Babylonians, then others they did not know. It was like a coat on the idol's face, and spread out against the walls, hanging at the angles, simultaneously bluish like the night, yellow like the dawn, purple like the sun, numerous, diaphanous, the holy *zaimph* that one could not see. (1:776)

The zaimph can be understood as a metonymy of the novel as a whole, as Sima Godfrey shows in her weaving of the zaimph with themes and textualities of tissues, textiles, fabrics, and textures.[11] If the zaimph is generalized as the figure of the novel, the reader finally has some epistemological certainty in knowing how to read. The description of the zaimph indicates an impossibility of epistemologically revealed truth, and Flaubert purposely undoes any reading that might be given in his very contrary attitude: "yellow like the dawn, purple like the sun." The "positive" metaphors no longer seem to have any value. As McKenna indicates, the veil "represents the absolute otherness of the sacred, the difference of divinity—its difference from all other objects being grounded in its more radical difference from itself" (314). The veil "does not represent anything in itself beyond a certain mute opacity to signification" (317). Precisely because the zaimph is the object of alterity, it does in fact indicate the novel. It is not only in the understandable, though ultimately unproductive, series of metaphors and constellations of signifiers that can be abstracted from the figure of the zaimph: text, texture, *tisser*, textuality. It is also and especially in the impossibility of description, in the multiplication of folds, and in the undecidability of the object itself that it signifies the work as a whole. The zaimph is the sign of the object and the writing of alterity. Not a hymen, not an inversion of the phallic—or nonphallic serpent—not a symbol in any way whatsoever, the zaimph indicates the entirety of the writing of alterity without ever indicating meaning, sense, signification, or significance. The symbol of alterity thus gives the theory of representation of alterity for the novel of alterity: each act of representation is identical to itself, and it bears no metonymic or metaphoric relation to a world, real or imagined. Ultimately, no theory of representation can be determined for the work because there is no perceivable continuity that can be posited a priori, ontologically, epistemologically, or even phenomenologically, and there is no act of figuration or any figurality that can be interpreted as anything but a positive determination of denotation.

Thus, in the novel of alterity, there is a strange chiasmus. Whereas in the writing that participates either as a representative or as an inversion of Occidental metaphysics, language and writing are understood as the other of the reality they represent; here, in the novel of alterity, language is identical to itself. Within language and within writing, there is no otherness. It is what it is. But what is language? The question is not as simple as it seems, because one of the fundamental aspects accorded to language in the West is its alterity, its difference from the structures and systems that it describes, its imposition of a system of partial relations—syntagmas, morphology, figures, and so forth—on a world that it is seen "naturally" (i.e., artificially) to reproduce. In fact, it does not reproduce the order of the world; it imposes an order, making the world both "natural" and ordered through the imposition of that alterity. In that imposition comes the denaturing of the world (its humanization) and the naturing of language (its harmony).

In *Salammbô*, understood as a theoretical experiment, Flaubert seeks to create a seamless world of the other. What he accomplishes is a far more radical result: a world so completely other that the presence or absence of such seams and harmonies is completely beside the point. Language, the French language, is used to create a disparate other whose identity is so completely different that the merest phrase hides not a coherent world but the endless possibilities of dissolution. No ordering of the world is possible in a response by the reader that itself does not somehow fetishize one or another aspect of the writing. Thus even fetishizing the fetish leads to a result that seeks to recuperate the novel into some normal system.

The identity of the language to itself necessarily brings us to a consideration of generalities. For even if there is a radical and abyssal difference between language and what it purports to describe, even if that gulf can be bridged only at the expense of a perversion of the writing, there still seems to be a kind of linguistic identity, in which language, wholly other, maintains a kind of self-reflecting and self-fulfilling sense of unity: impenetrable, except in its own dissolution or deconstruction, bereft of meaning, except if one chooses willfully to misread. Stylized and penetrating, it is like so many wounds from a stiletto that eventually leaves nothing but the phantom idea of representation where once there might have been a body. If the sense of identity comes at the expense of meaning, so be it. As Flaubert himself says, "Là n'est pas la question." The harmony is in the language itself, in the writing that gives an illusion of those salted ruins where now there is nothing.

Still, that sense of identity produced by a more or less seamless whole of textuality begs the reader to reconsider what abstraction and generalities may be in this world. For the individual object may not exist in having a textuality wed to a materiality through an ideological process of "representation," but the abstract has not yet been considered; and, in that light, three generalities come to the fore. First, language itself, the very material of which the novel is made. Second, the structuring of narrative, as the architecture and archeology of the work. And finally, desire, that which, aside from the objective, stands for subjectivity.

Barbarians babble. The clever speaker, parasiting the system, speaks to each in his own tongue, controls the discourse as Spendius does, or manipulates it, inspiring or inciting to action or revolt through mistranslation. Within the false world of specious verisimilitude, all this makes sense. But from a perspective in which a simple description is a *non-sens*, how can one be so sure? What does Flaubert mean, what does he want to say (*veut dire*), when he makes language something determinable by difference, as will the structural linguists of the twentieth century?

Language becomes a point of difference and distinction, where there is no other, and yet, because it is only other, only different, it is like a set of imaginary numbers (numbers based on the square root of $-1$). Language has its differences, languages have their differences, but there is a breakdown between them or among them signaled from the very first: "They called for wine, meat, gold. They yelled for women. They raved [*déliraient*] in a hundred languages" (1:717).

Language means material objects (wine, meat), symbolic objects (gold), and desire (women). But finally, language means the delirium of babble or Babel. Their delirium in a hundred languages—cacophony and madness—is reproduced on every page and in every line. Flaubert questions sanity and doubts the validity of an organization of systems ordered through opposition and difference. Flaubert makes distinctions, because he must write, but those distinctions are as futile as any attempt at organization. Whether it is many ululating in a babble of supposedly separate idioms, or one, many-voicedly, speaking all, it is the same. Only that which cannot be understood remains unique; for Salammbô "sang all that in an old Canaanite tongue that the Barbarians did not understand. They wondered what she would be telling them with the scary gestures with which she accompanied her speech" (1:720). Nonmeaning, the impossibility of communication, and hermetic uninterpretability are the unique values and certain meanings attributed to language and to languages in this work.

For the rest, there is a falsification, the lie of language: "She used simultaneously all the tongues of the Barbarians, a woman's wiles to calm their anger. She spoke Greek to the Greeks, then turned to the Ligurians, toward the Campanians, toward the Negroes; and each, listening to her, rediscovered the sweetness of his country in this voice" (1:721). There is the false belief and forlorn hope that language can tell the truth, communicate, render desire, mark the proper, and be immediate. By hearing a voice that remarks their own origins, the Barbarian soldiers falsely believe that language will give them a truth that had been taken away, as well as a return to an origin and to meaning. Anonymous soldiers and protagonists alike are treated to and by language exactly as the reader is: everyone is lulled into a false belief in meaning. That meaning is there only when textuality is perverted to make believe that the voice of the writing gives a sense of the proper, a call back to an origin, and a writing that reproduces and represents home, source, and origin.

Any structuring of the narrative or within it is itself subject to the same interpretative questions, the same rigging of the material through grammar and syntax. In *Salammbô*, however, the distortion in ekphrasis is more radical than in a work such as *Madame Bovary*, because there is no interpellated vision on which a narrative description is based. So the description of the Acropolis at Byrsa (1:754), which is similar to that of the Bovarys' wedding cake or that of Charles's cap, takes on new dimensions in its anarchy, as the ekphrasis is no longer even a commonly shared approach to the limitations of language. In a realist narrative, convention dictates that a description is diachronically given of a synchronic object that cannot be captured by the author except over time; language is used to construct what is given, but the possibility of construction is buttressed by the universals of space and time and their equivalence. Here however, the spatial and temporal orderings buckle and give way, for there is no order of things.

McKenna's observation about the disorder of the battle can now be fully generalized: the adverbs that normally reflect order and universals, even when nouns fail to signify, are also put into question. Finite states cede to transitional and undecidable ones. Between life and death; the description of the dead, caught to such an extent *in medias res* (*in medias belli*) that they do not have the time to fully die: "Cadavers, too crushed in the crowd did not fall; upheld by their companions' shoulders, they stayed upright a few minutes, with unmoving eyes. Some, the two temples having been pierced by a javelin, held their heads like that of a bean. Mouths opened to yell remained agape; cut-off hands flew away" (1:932).

Desire represented here is artificially produced by the effects of language. Even if the desire of the characters, given life through the critic's act of nomination, analogically resembled the system of desire at work in the real world or its representations, the resemblance would be parodic at best. The analogy cannot hold water precisely because all acts of figurality have been excluded. But there is a doubled desire that needs to be taken into consideration: the desire of the author, itself metonymized in the will-to-write, and the desire of the reader, the will to *jouissance*. Flaubert undercuts the standard reader-writer relation by interposing a world *qui n'en est pas un*. Thus, at the same time, he undercuts the insistence of desire that usually accompanies the act of representation in more traditional nineteenth-century narratives—works that seek to move metaphorically toward the white light of wholeness that signs Occidental mythology. This is a mythology formally excluded from the novel. The desire of the author has to be placed elsewhere, but there is nowhere for it to go, nor is there a locus into which the desire of the reader can fit.

One example, because it is a telling one, is the question of homosexual relations. It should be understood that the example is chosen precisely because of the egregious nature often ascribed to the activity, its categorization within the realm of the different or odd, or its placement in a set of things that must be explained or accepted. So here my interest is not in the representation of homosexuality but in the representation of something usually considered to be either assimilated or distanced: something, in short, always and already different. Let us look at the most serious mention of the activity:

Then in this perpetual wandering across all sorts of countries, murders, and adventures, strange loves had formed—obscene unions as serious as marriages, where the stronger defended the younger in the midst of battles, helped him to cross precipices, wiped the sweat of fevers off his brow, stole food for him; and the other, a child found along the side of the road and who had become a Mercenary, paid for this devotion with a thousand delicate cares and wifely duties. (1:967–68)

Flaubert puts desire into question by characterizing this specific desire as strange and obscene. Even if Flaubert is being ironic in characterizing homosexual love as obscene, in order to mock the repressive mores of his time, by what measure would one be absolutely sure that he is being ironic? By what standards or measures could these norms be validated? Desire itself is strange in all its manifestations, but in this world of Carthage where everything is strange, this love is now just one among many, something to be described as if it were perceived as distinguishable, when it in fact is not.

The textual thickness of the novel does not allow for a repository for the desire of the writer or of the reader. It is true that Flaubert writes the novel of alterity, but in so doing he excludes the most important extratextual relation possible, the sympathy between writer and reader, the intermingling of states of desire, and the creation of the novel itself as a repository, through linguistic transformation, of desire—both *plaisir* and *jouissance*. Ultimately, alterity does not work, and not simply because Flaubert needs to make the necessary forfeit of writing in a language in which people have never thought. The creation of a novel of alterity cannot take care of the frame of reading and writing. The novel of alterity is ergon without parergon, writing without frame. As such it remains one of the most noble failures in all of nineteenth-century literature.

## IV. Flaubert against Kant

After all that, perhaps there is still the last possible bastion of certainty: transcendental measures of space and time. Already in the Carthaginian novel, space itself is fractured by the multiplicity of descriptions with which Flaubert fills the work. Time remains reasonably constant, though the novelistic reflection of time that compresses or dilates events is present. In *Bouvard et Pécuchet*, Flaubert takes on this last certainty. The novel is generally understood as a massive undoing of Western systems of thought, epistemology, and ontology. Each chapter engages a field of knowledge and proceeds to show its contradictions, its incompatibilities, its opinions taken for fact, and its inconsistencies. By challenging these most basic categories, Flaubert succeeds in putting the very possibility of identity into question. Or, more radically, by challenging time, Flaubert makes the self into an other; he finally dissociates, once and for all, realism from the real.

By Chapter 8, time is out of joint. Certainly Flaubert has made time questionable in this novel, a nameable or unnameable figure that cannot be put in perspective. It is partly a matter of the language itself: French has no clear word for the abstract concept of time, the equivalent of the English "time" or the German "die Zeit." In everyday language, time itself is marked by its division into a system of notation: "Quelle heure est-il?" Though one can say, "il est temps de faire quelque chose," "le temps" itself is touched both by verb tenses and by meteorological considerations.[12] Time itself is untimely for Flaubert, too little too late. The first time the title characters turn their attention to philosophy, Pécuchet says: "it is time to no longer wallow [*croupir*] in egotism" (2:867). But what does time mean here? Time for Bouvard and Pécuchet is always something of which there is too little or too much; the moment is always belated or premature; the time to do something is never now but always earlier or later. This "now" looms in the near future, a future that will, by the end of the novel, become an eternal present.

During their meditations on philosophy, Bouvard and Pécuchet seek to define human thought. The work of the mind, pure cerebration, leads to a revolt against a material basis for thought, investigation, and analysis. As their interest and their belief in philosophy *per se* develop, they remember their previous investigations into agriculture and even politics as being pitiful, and even their masterpiece, the museum, "disgusts them" (2:904). In the "faculté de connaître," they find that "memory makes one correspond with the past as clairvoyance [*prévoyance*] does with the future" (2:905). There is no way of proving that analogy, for both points are defined against an unknowable moment, and the order of the comparison is itself illogical. As is known from its introduction in the mnemotechnic system of the shadowy Dumouchel, memory is always already an act of inscription. So the timeliness of the present moment, even as Bouvard and Pécuchet attack the matter, is questionable, unknown, and unknowable, for it is caught between writing and the sixth sense of prediction and premonition.

Still they forge ahead through the universals, through immortal works, as they hope to find the moment, the right moment, the moment that is *juste, correct, propre*, or *droit*. But they are unimpressed by the discussions of epistemology, which are filled for them with a lot of wordiness that just proves platitudes, and so displeased are they that they skip over the "faculté de vouloir" in order to concentrate on Logic (2:905). Having learned what analysis, synthesis, induction, and deduction are, they also discover the "main causes of our errors." To no great surprise to the reader, "almost all [of these errors] come from the misuse of words" (905). The examples are telling: " 'The sun is setting,—the weather is clouding over [*le temps se rembrunit*],—winter is approaching. . . . ' " (905). Could the question of time always be a lexicographic or linguistic one?

The examples that Flaubert chooses are telling since they involve a second meaning of *le temps*: time as weather. The first and third examples confuse the two, for the first, with the advent of night, is a mark of time but is usually a mark of changing temperatures and humidities. The third example as well ties up weather and time since a change of season signals a change in meteorological conditions. The second example is perhaps the most interesting, for out of context, its meaning can never be certain. As much as context indicates that it

is a reference to a change in weather, it can also be understood apoc-
alyptically as a comment on the darkening of time itself. In this
novel, it is time, not weather, that is clouding over, darkening, and
becoming unreadable, unmeasurable, and confused. This does not
bode well for determining what is right, as once again, figurality and
narrative become scrambled.

Time will always have been a problem in this novel and a singular
one at that. In previous works, I have noted two types of problems
that mark the limits of Flaubert's realist narrative. The first is a problem in representation itself, as the author, through various mechanisms and models, shows the limits of the possibilities of realist representation: the classic example in this novel is the *bahut de la
Renaissance*, in which, through illustration, discourse, and figure,
Flaubert deconstructs the processes of representation, the means by
which meaning is given and taken away. Second is the apparition of
black holes in the novel, problems in knowledge, in epistemology, in
the breakdown, dissolution, or liquification of the model itself, as
everything becomes awash in a sea of mud. The third problem is the
transcendent one in which the other two are implicitly or explicitly
predicated: the impossibility of time itself.

In *Bouvard et Pécuchet*, time and space are distinct. Space remains
continuous, though Flaubert certainly acts on it: the change over
time of the farm and its lands, the compression and expansion of human space wherein a cadaver always seems smaller than the sum of
its parts, and the shifting sands that turn solids into liquids. In its extension, space remains complete, and ultimately as solid as the pages
on which Flaubert is writing. Not so with time, for aside from the
impossible word of time, time is figured as both continuous and discontinuous, as both expandable and contractible, as both figurative
and literal. The problem with time is that it is both transcendental
figure and representation, always already translated into a chronological representation of itself, a means by which its very originality
is brought into play as being suspect.

If time and space are distinct in the way they maintain their transcendental status or not, this has not always been the case. It is an effect of the human to confuse transcendentals and the representation
thereof, a confusion that gives rise to one projected backward to the
very origins of the planet. The hapless protagonists have problems

with the nomenclature of the various eras of evolutionary history: "Why Devonian, Cambrian, Jurassic, as if the lands designated by these words were not elsewhere than in Devonshire, near Cambridge, and in the Jura?" (2:787). If space is exchangeable, time is fleeting, distorted, and distorting; it is ultimately incomprehensible as a measure always too big or too little, incapable of marking time: "The six days of Genesis mean six great epochs" (936). Moving from a literal version of the Bible to an allegorical one takes into consideration the possibility of evolution, and, yet, such a move challenges the possibility of providing a firm temporal base on which to build. Representation and epistemology can have a solid base only if the transcendental figures on which they depend are solid. It is no wonder then that Pécuchet, studying philosophy, winds up espousing a position that depends entirely on perception: "Having read an analysis by Berkeley, Pécuchet says that he [Pécuchet] denies extension, time, space, and indeed substance" (910).

For all that, time remains different. Flaubert safeguards space, extension, and substance by the constant stream of place and space, by the constant reference to the material. The Berkeleyan defense is just one among many that neither fully engages nor fully explains the problem of time. Berkeley's phenomenological position depending on the perception of the observer, though decidedly modern, cannot take into consideration the two key factors of the disruption of time in this novel. The first is the confusion between cosmological or natural time, depending on a past that remains identical to itself, and human time, which includes the added factor of the perception of time in what would soon be known as the Bergsonian sense of duration. The other problem, linked to the first despite all preliminary suppositions, is the confusion of time and tense, the confusion of the transcendental with the language and signifiers humans have invented to measure it.

The question of tense and duration is itself a relevant one. From his earliest writing, Flaubert uses the imperfect more frequently than do many other novelists. His insistence on the imperfect ultimately winds up in a confusion of the descriptive, the iterative, and the habitual, so that the tense of description and the tense of finite action become confused with each other, and nothing is necessarily or essentially foregrounded against other elements in the writing.

The insistence on the imperfect confuses the past as well, in an end-less series of repetitions whose relation to one another is ambigu-ously muted: "Ils bâillaient l'un devant l'autre, consultaient le calen-drier, regardaient la pendule, attendaient les repas [They yawned in front of each other, consulted the calendar, looked at the clock, waited for meals]" (870). The measure of time becomes confused in this iteration of boredom, as if the moments marking time and marked by time themselves dissolved into a sea of endless non-events. So, too, does duration of narration become confused as Flaubert varies the time covered by each chapter as an uneven and wildly changing matter.

Both these matters pale when faced with the bigger problems of the novel with its destruction of representation, its collapsing of re-alist paradigms, and finally, its dissolution of the time that enables everything else, as the transcendence of time is both posited and de-stroyed in the same work. The destruction of time amplifies the ef-fects of destruction of the rest of the novel: the dissolution of lines of logic and order, the questioning of any sort of genealogy, be it fa-milial or epistemological. When the time is out of joint in this novel, all dissolves into a sea of melted watches of which Dalí himself would have been proud.

Relatively comprehensible, at least at the outset, is natural time, until it is complicated by a cosmological order that approaches the universality of time. Natural time is represented in the experiments in agriculture. Initially, as in all the characters' future endeavors, a regular order seems to reign, and it is only with their investigations and knowledge that entropy begins to take over. So too, the three senses of *temps* start out in this chapter as being consonant with one another: "Then the bad days arrived, snow, cold spells. They lodged [*ils s'installèrent*] in the kitchen and did lattice-work, or went through the rooms, chatted by the fire, watched the rain fall" (733). Perhaps the meteorological order is already beginning to fail as rain follows snow; perhaps the order of tenses is beginning slightly to fray as well. In the natural world, time tends to be comprehensive, even to them, even when they get it wrong. In the natural world, it is space that is problematic, with a production of entropy that is a level of disorder relating to things: "But the bed swarmed with larva; despite compost of the dead leaves, under the painted frames and the bespattered bell-glasses, only rickety vegetation grew. The cuttings did not take root, the grafts unstuck, the sap of the runners stopped flowing; the trees had white in their roots; the sowings were a disaster" (738–39). Time here remains a constant and a transcendental force giving support and credence to what happens. Things proceed regularly as space crumbles, with the "delirium of fertilizer [*délire de l'engrais*]" (741), the spontaneous combustion of the haystacks (744), and the destruction of the fruit harvest by the storm (748).

When the speculation on time goes beyond the historical concept of the natural, matters go awry, as Bouvard and Pécuchet look to discover the origin of the universe: "The majesty of creation caused them an awe as infinite as its object" (780). Time as related to nature divides and circumscribes a nature decided to be such by human beings. The nature in which time works is one created by culture, by agriculture in specific, valid for seven millennia, but not before then. Nature exists naturally only in retrospect, after agriculture, an inscription on the earth, comes into being.

The moment at which time works correctly is thus the agricultural moment and is thus an invention of humankind. Before it, time does not work at all, because time is, for Flaubert, an act of writing that can work only when there is culture. The initial retrospective glance at creation and evolution is informed by such a concept of nature. Seemingly wild and untamed, it is subject to a *Sturm und Drang* type of overreading and overwriting that marks evolution and the beginning of the world as romantic fantasies projected back from a concept of nature informed both by excess and by the act of inscription: "the paleotherium, half horse and half tapir, overturned the anthills of Montmartre with its snout" (782). And finally: "All these eras had been separated from one another by cataclysms, of which the last was our flood. It was like a fairy-play [*féerie*] in several acts, having man as its apotheosis" (782). Evolution is like a play, whose time and timing are sequenced according to the rules of art. The final act of the play is preceded by "our flood." On the one hand, this flood, the biblical flood, is the figure inscribed as such in a book, a written production of humanity to take creation into account. On the other, this flood is ours, a complicity of belonging, sharing, and agreeing, that Flaubert uses as early as the first line of *Madame Bovary*—"nous étions à l'étude"—to establish complicity and communication by grammatical design, even if there is none. So the flood, a moment in nature and time before the human conception of time and writing, becomes "our" flood retrospectively inscribed within human time, and the latter is, in this mystical version of the march of time, consecrated as Christian time, the locus of the gospel, and the figure of transcendence. And yet, it is precisely a *féerie*, a magical fairy tale with no more relation to the truth than any of the other doctrinal elements the narrative has skewered heretofore.

Flaubert often alternates conceptions of time within a passage, through which he underlines the artificial nature of the concept of time that sees it as unified. Right after the description of this romanticized evolutionary moment, Flaubert alternates moments in human time, like "an afternoon," with moments in a supernal time marked by the truth of creation: "The church bell rang the angelus" (783). The curate approves of the science of evolution because it "confirms the authority of the Bible in proving the Flood" (783). Science itself then, is marked by time but marked by an inscription of time as writing, albeit religious writing. Elsewhere, they read the Bible on Sundays at the hour that the bells are ringing for vespers (921), and when they make a pilgrimage to the Virgin, Flaubert assures us that they enter the chapel at six o'clock. If the religious or eternal is in one way a guarantee, albeit ironic, of human time, human time cheapens (for lack of a better word) any appreciation of superhuman time that is a mark of the eternal. Even the existence of God is brought into question and proven by the intertwining of the inscription of human time and eternal writing. The argument for the existence of God contains the following exchange in which the logical reversal is matched by a metaphor that displaces divine matters onto the horological: "'When I see a clock . . . ' 'Yes, yes, of course. But where is the father of the clock-maker?'" (901).

If time is intrinsically related to writing, then the death of writing would provoke the death of time as well. By the end of the novel, or more exactly the last chapters Flaubert completed before his death, the iterative nature of writing, the eventual "copying as before [*copier comme autrefois*]" is tantamount to the death of time as well. For at this point, writing has lost its incisive ability, and time is depleted. By the end of the novel, with reading having been accomplished as the stocking of memories and the internalization of antinomies without resolution, with reading having finally been reduced to the complete wash of inscription, the same can be said for writing. Writing as repetition—writing as eternal repetition—means that writing is now there without a trace, without difference, either with an "e" or an "a."

Just as the past is voided of meaning by a limiting of the past to that which can be perceived—this is the *reductio ad absurdum* of Berkeley—the future is limited by the impossibility of writing. When Flaubert indicates that "for children, the future does not exist" (968), the statement is valid for all characters, including Bouvard and Pécuchet themselves, who have been reduced to the state of *infans* in an eternal achronic present. When Flaubert finally writes, "copier comme autrefois," that unending past of the imperfect, the oft-used imperfect of all of his novels, finally meets its complement in a future that is nothing more than the Sartrean hell of an eternal present in a Second Empire drawing room. But this time there is no bust or letter opener, just the detritus of a museum, a stuffed parrot, and a pair of humming computers endlessly caught in the idiot loop of a year that is "oo," a Y2K explosion over a century before it fizzled out.

# Naturalist Ultraviolence

Their scenes of terror are composed of gloomy woods,
deep vallies inaccessible to the sun, impending barren
rocks, dark caverns, and impetuous cataracts rushing
down the mountains from all parts. . . . Gibbets,
crosses, wheels, and the whole apparatus of torture, are
seen from the roads and in the most dismal recesses of
the woods, where the ways are rugged and overgrown
with weeds, and where every object bears the marks of
depopulation, are temples dedicated to the king of
vengeance. . . . And to add both to the horror and
sublimity of these scenes, they sometimes conceal in
cavities, on the summits of the highest mountains,
foundries, lime-kilns, and glass-works; which send
forth large volumes of flame, and continued columns
of thick smoke, that give to these mountains the
appearance of volcanoes.

—Chambers, *A Dissertation on Oriental Gardening*
(36–37)

## I. *In flagrante delicto*

As modest as a bed may be, as soon as one enters a bedroom, it is
what occupies the eyes. It is, as Balzac might have said, "one of those
things" whose multiple functions relating to sleep, sex, and death
have such a high symbolic value that they cannot be ignored.
Whether it is a question of a simple mattress, a hammock, a futon, or
of a big four-poster bed swathed in gauze and covered with a canopy,
the bed is presented monumentally, more than any other object dec-
orating the house. The bed is the spot in which desire is fully and
most completely invested. It is thus an object that, whatever its position, organizes space around it, controlling the surroundings and re-
centering the room. The force lines emanating from a bed create
something like a magnetic field or, as the Chinese would say, help to

direct the *ch'i* in the room, and consequently the *feng shui* of the room and the house as a whole.

Before focusing directly on Zola, I have evoked these force lines on the phenomenological level, without seeking any theoretical consistency, for it is necessary to revisit and review the ways in which we consider energy and force in narrative, the way in which an object, a description, or a figure interrupts those flows. So the references to *ch'i* or even to the magnetic field should be taken at that level: a bed organizes the space that we perceive, in which we sleep, in which we make love, and in which we lie dying. How can we feel these force lines in a novel? For, no matter how verisimilar, a novel does not offer us a bed as such but the word "bed," the written signifier for bed, which invokes, for the reader, the meanings of "bed" and the signified that appeals to an idealized or generalized referent.

In Zola's work, an object that seems to have a symbolic value functions as an intensification, an interruption, and a translation of the semiotic lines of the text. It is a literary version of what Lacan would call a *point de capiton*, a bundling, a gathering spot, or a locus in which the text is reflected, reorganized, and renewed. It is also a locus in which the figure emerges from the warp and woof of textuality. A bed is one of those bundled objects. Somewhere between the interwoven space and neutral space (textual spaces both), the object becomes special, as it is invested with power and desire. When, in Zola's novel, *La Bête humaine*, we read the following, we immediately realize that something is about to happen: "Both had fallen to sit on the edge of the bed." It is not a narrative statement like another; it predicts action; it is pregnant with possibility. In this liminal locus, both beings and things are transformed. Caught in a power game, Séverine and Roubaud are near the love bed. The closer they get, like sailors hearing a siren, the more they are irrevocably caught by the energy of the bed, the actual energy that the object radiates in textuality, and their own potential energy as well.

The bed calls for an excess and for a move toward overstepping the lines of propriety and property. A bed is certain only if it is at home, for other people's beds, even when one is totally and legally married, do not work: they squeak, reminding us of something illicit or out of place. Either for sleeping or for engaging in sex, the only true place is one's own home. Failing that, one has crossed a line into the realm of the taboo:

Bit by bit, without a word, [Roubaud] had wrapped her in a tighter caress, aroused by the warmth of this young body he held in his arms. He was getting intoxicated from her smell, she drove him mad with desire bending at the loins to get free. With one move, he moved her from the window, which he closed with his elbow. Their mouths met, he crushed her lips, then carried her to the bed.

"No, no, we are not at home," she repeated. I beg you, not in this room [*Non, non, nous ne sommes pas chez nous, répéta-t-elle. Je t'en prie, pas dans cette chambre!*]. (1010–11)

Already the presence of a bed other than their own manipulates them and lowers them to a baser level. Far from home, one becomes more an animal, less a human. The bed of another changes both partners, though it is the man more than the woman who undergoes this change, and both become less proper and less human in the process. And with that shift, evil begins to lurk.

Why speak of evil? The world of the *Rougon-Macquart* is not a benevolent universe but one in which the baser impulses of humans are most frequently represented. Still, in what Franchi and Ripoll call the "world of violence" (80) of *La Bête humaine*, Zola makes evil the central figure of the novel. In specific, in this drama of the bed that implies Séverine's refusal to do her wifely "duty," Zola willfully confuses violence and evil, dehumanization and becoming animal. And all this takes place around a bed. This bed has nothing less than a memory, a memory of all that had taken place in it. In specific, the bed remembers the repeated rape and sexual abuse of Séverine by her guardian Grandmorin, who took care of her in a less than chaste, avuncular manner. Whatever the moral value of the acts that occurred in that bed, the bed remembers them indiscriminately, and Séverine remembers them along with the bed. If, for some reason, Séverine refuses to do her wifely duty, she cannot tell him why. To say the least, that would have provoked anger. One should take Zola literally, indeed etymologically, here when he says that Séverine is "in an inexplicable anguish" (1011). She can say nothing, she cannot explain—indeed, how could one explain the horrible?—nor can she remove the folds and creases—*plis*—from the bed. Yet it is the bed itself, the locus at which the inscription of this illicit love had been recorded, that tells him. Source of negative energy, be it malevolent or antihuman in origin, the bed is a locus of writing read both silently and immediately. Roubaud knows it, as a man and as a reader, for, as Zola had already indicated: "That was the unique novel of his existence" (1001). To be associated with the novel means to be knowledgeable, even in a primitive state, of the ways of reading and misreading. Thus the relation to violence is already in place, for a novel can offer violence to the reader even before reality does: Roubaud "once again became the unconscious brute of his force; he would have crushed her, in an outburst of blind anger" (1001). Thus, we can understand what Zola offers Roubaud to understand in the reading of the bed that has been permanently written on:

"Goddamn bitch! You slept with him! . . . slept with him! . . . slept with him."

He got madder in repeating these words, slammed down his fists each time he said them, as if to make them enter her flesh. (1013)

The very spot invokes violence and makes him a beast, even before he recognizes that there has been a violation of the law. For violence knows no temporality, and evil does not respect human laws of diachronic logic. Evil circulates in a novel, bumping up against objects or coming out of them, overpowering human beings without recognizing their needs for logic and order. Thus, he says indirectly and unconsciously what he has yet to say directly, even before he realizes what has happened there. He is trying to coerce Séverine into bed: "He was trembling; he would have broken her. 'Fool [Bête], no one will know. We'll remake the bed'" (1011).

What Roubaud does not understand is that once undone, the bed can never be remade. In this universe, it will always keep all the marks and all the traces, creases, folds, and crumples that mark the actions and events that have taken place in it.[1] Each little mound and valley remains, even if the sheets are boiled, bleached, starched, and ironed. Regardless of what one does, the writing remains. As Zola says, it is inexplicable, that is to say, it can never be unfolded. Everything is there in an eternal present and in a dehumanization, for to be human is to mark the passage of time. This present is confounding, and all evil and all excess that had been seen melt into it, mixing with each other and becoming indistinguishable. In becoming a "human beast," as the very title of the novel suggests, one loses one's memory of the past, while the bed strangely keeps it as a permanent database, and differences are no longer understandable. Becoming a beast annuls the past, a past remembered by the bed, as well as the knife: "It was a knife that she had just bought for him, to replace one he had lost and that he had missed [*qu'il pleurait*] for two weeks. He shouted, found it wonderful, this beautiful new knife, with its ivory handle and shiny blade. He was going to use it immediately. She was thrilled with his joy; jokingly, she made him give her a sou so their friendship would not be cut" (1002). Still, he marks the knife as another object with a memory: "He would have killed her; she read it clearly in his look. In falling, she had seen the knife open on the table; and she saw the glint of the blade again; she thought he would reach out. A cowardice took over her, an abandonment of herself and everything else, a need to finish" (1014).[2]

Zola evokes such memories but for the moment merely underlines what happens to Roubaud in his transformation to something other in which evil and words become mixed together:

> Roubaud's fury was not calmed. As soon as it seemed to dissipate a bit, it returned immediately, like drunkenness, in great reinforced waves that overtook him in their dizziness. He no longer had control of himself, he flailed wildly [*Il ne se possédait plus, battait le vide*], thrown to each change of wind the violence whipping him, falling back to the singular need to appease the human animal screaming inside him [*bête hurlante au fond de lui*]. (1017)

Everything is clear, and Zola ends in this way: "He shuddered. The idea of possessing her, that image of their two bodies falling on the bed, had shot through him. And in the murky night of his flesh, at the heart of his bleeding, sullied desire, the necessity of death brusquely arose" (1019). Thus everything is there: the bed, source and memory of everything, is the locus of death, impurity [*souillure*], and bleeding desire. The bed produces an energy that prevents solids from remaining solid, that insists that desire becomes flows of desire that are necessarily mutable. As Michel Serres has shown, in Zola's work, it is a question of a thermodynamic flow or flux akin to that of fire. But it is necessary to say that this fire is always changing, that it never maintains a form. And that, moreover, these flows are novelistic more than they are pseudoscientific. The result is clear: even solid objects participate in this flow of negativities. For it is a question only of negative flows: good cannot be sullied without writing. However, the bed, the locus *par excellence* of this sullying and this transformation, which is the very locus of writing, never remains what it is at any given moment. For all the other beds are in it, all the beings who were in it, all the infractions of the law of man, nature, and civilization. *In flagrante delicto*—a fiery dereliction, literally on fire: "flagrante" comes, as we know, from the Latin *flagrare*, to catch fire.

Like communicating vessels, one bed calls to another, recalls another, and communicates with another. Each bed remembers the first locus of sullying, in the inscriptions woven into the cloth; each bed recalls the initial inscription of the woman's body, repeated in her flesh: "He got madder in repeating these words, slammed down his fists each time he said them, as if to make them enter her flesh." (1013). There is not even a need for a physical bed, for it is sufficient that the action (love, sleep) that would have happened in a bed occur in order to evoke the bed. Wherever one sleeps becomes the bed that haunts and returns and with it, violence, a mixture of ills and negatives: "Then Jacques, legs broken, fell on the edge of the line, and burst into convulsive sobs, lying on his belly with his face [*face*] in the grass. My God! Had that abominable evil come back of which he'd believed himself cured?" (1042). The word "face" that Zola uses to describe Roubaud's face, instead of *visage*, the usual word for a human face, appears again in the description of Jacques. It is merely necessary for Jacques to lie down on the ground for the flow of negation and evil to return. The violence associated with Roubaud is obvious in Jacques as well and is described in the same terms. As Roubaud has killed, kills, and will have killed, Jacques recalls that he (too) is a violent killer: "It returned in him, sharp, awful, as if the scissors had penetrated his own flesh. No reason calmed him/it; he had wanted to kill her, he would kill her if she were still there, unbuttoned, bare-chested. . . . The next year, he remembered having sharpened a knife to stick in someone else's neck, a little blonde he saw walk by his door each morning" (1043).

Evil runs rampant; evils spill from all sides. Unlike the flows of energy of *ch'i* that I evoked earlier, whose energy is positive and different from thermodynamic energy that bears no ethic or moral value, the energy that flows in *La Bête humaine* is negative; it is a vehicle in which evil can circulate. Zola shows not the circulation of good, even if goods circulate but rather the haunting of the text through negation. Good is what rests essentially equal to itself, while negativity, never clearly defined, can circulate, haunt, and invade the loci of the novel: "Immediately they had decided to sell it, that house [Croix-de Maufras] of debauchery and blood that haunted them like a nightmare, where they did not dare to sleep, given the horror of the ghosts of the past; and to sell it as is, with the furnishings, without repairing it or even dusting it" (1134). This locus of debauchery and blood, as Zola says, can function in no other way than as a machine to generate evil, to create flows of evil that can circulate without obeying either the laws of physics or those of humanity.

From *Thérèse Raquin* on, Zola develops this line; the reader will recall that the characters in that novel are literally haunted by the specter of death and by spots of blood that endlessly appear wherever they turn their eyes. It is a technique of which the most well-known example is Poe's story, "The Tell-Tale Heart." Poe's title should be understood literally, haunting, which is the same thing as the circulation of negativity or the circulation of the antiheart is the equivalent of telling the tale. It is a technique, image, or process that Zola rediscovers in *La Bête humaine* after long years in which the flow for him, as in a novel such as *Au Bonheur des dames*, has to obey material laws as well as those of energetics. In *La Bête humaine*, however, having reduced materialism to the inevitability of the railroad and the unavoidability of the physics of the machine, he is ready to abandon material laws to rediscover a novelistic *esprit* detached from the physical.

It is thus that evil, blood, desire, and murder circulate in the novel:

But, holding Jacques in that way, Séverine burned again. And with desire, the need to confess was awakened in her. For so many long weeks, he had tormented her! The round spot [*tache*] on the ceiling grew, seemed to extend like a pool of blood [*tache de sang*]. Her eyes hallucinated when she looked at it; the things around the bed spoke, telling the story aloud. She felt the words rise to her lips, with the nervous wave that raised her flesh.[3] (1194)

It matters little if Séverine is in bed with Jacques, for Zola uses the same burning vocabulary to indicate how he sees this guilty love.

Desire becomes the equivalent of murder, for the locus and its energy reinforce the system of circulation and exchanges. In other words, Grandmorin raped her in bed and that was a crime. Period. Every bed in which Séverine sleeps after that will be marked by that multiple violation: the rape of the young girl, the deflowering of that girl, and thus the violation of the marriage to come—evil knows no temporal restrictions. As Grandmorin's sister, Mme Bonnehon says: "He kissed her, perhaps tickled her. There's no crime in that" (1092). My point exactly: where there is no crime, there is no displacement. Grandmorin is killed in an act of vengeance—and I remind the reader that the vengeance is for actions that took place before Séverine's marriage—his blood spills everywhere but especially in two directions. One is a material direction: blood and violence spread according to the lines of the railroad. The other, more specific, would be a metonymic or congruent displacement: where there is a bed, there is blood; where there is desire, there is blood; where there are a bed and desire, there is murder.

This negative energy of which Séverine is now the witness is translated into the novel, in the story told, once again, the story of the telltale heart. Everything surrounding her speaks, as if blood itself has begun to speak, to tell the story and thus to become a novel. When negativity begins to speak, it is the novel that is being written. This possibility of the novelistic is redoubled by the need to tell: Séverine feels the movement of language in her like a regurgitation, a negation of solids, a negation of good, or a return of what has been digested into words spewed forth. What does Séverine say? She tells of the rapes, but at the same time, foremost is telling Jacques how Roubaud forced her to admit them to him. Negative acts are repeated anew, haunting the characters by the force of repetition, by the translation of negativity into language and by recalling negation through novelistic language. Telling one's novel, a novel marked from one end to the other by negative energy, is reduced to the repetition of this eternal haunting. And living desire lets loose the same mechanism at every turn: "The shudder of desire was lost in that other shudder of death that had returned in her. As at the heart of all sex [*volupté*], it was an agony beginning again. For a moment she seemed to be suffocated by a slowed feeling of dizziness" (1197). Thus, while Séverine recalls and repeats Grandmorin's murder, so often evoked in the novel, it is normal for the return of repetitious identity—negativity—to occur as well. As this murder is evoked, they all are: "He could not close his eyes, which an invisible hand had obstinately seemed to open in the dark. Now he distinguished nothing in the room, drowned in the night . . . Every time, through an act of will, he seemed to fall asleep, the same haunting returned, the same images paraded by, waking the same feelings" (1205–06). The evil that is lived by Séverine is lived exactly in the same way by Jacques as well.

The examples could be multiplied, for such inscriptions of evil are the substance of the narrative, but there is a final example that is the last link in this cycle of negativity and in this transfer of haunting. At a given moment, a breach is opened. Or rather, to use the word from the novel, there is a crack [*fêlure*] (1092). In *La Bête humaine*, the crack in Jacques, or even in the Macquart family in general, opens at the moment that the Lison has its/her accident. A psychological reading is easy to do: Jacques loses his sanity at this very moment because he is in love with that machine that has become cracked in the crack-up. Still, there is a novelistic dimension that is not accounted for by a psychological character analysis. This is the vehicle of that negation through the language of the text, which puts everything up for grabs.

As long as it circulates, evil remains in the bed, inscribed in each crease and recorded in each object that emits something like infrared waves without stopping. When the accident occurs, Jacques is—naturally, novelistically—taken into the famous bedroom at what used to be the house of Grandmorin: "It was in the big bedroom in Croix-de-Maufras, the room covered in red damask, in which the two high windows looked out over the rail line a few meters away. From the old four-poster bed facing them, you could see the trains go by. And for years, not one object had been removed nor any furniture moved" (1275). It was inevitable that he be brought there: it is perhaps a parlor trick, the stuff of melodrama. But Zola is not Hugo, for whom coincidences make the plot move forward. In Zola's work, it is important that the novelistic work through this negative poetics; the predictable drama of the machine of gears and pulleys constructed by Zola is not even in question. Jacques must be the witness to the scenes in which evil is transmitted. To place Jacques in this same bed is a way of bringing things home and of making the system of representations coincide, a system that normally distances the signifiers of objects from the objectal system as such. Putting Jacques in this bed means that evil has returned to its origin and can totally overtake him. All that he did to avoid that his own crack reopen becomes useless henceforth. In the light, at the very moment that evil returns to its origin, everything is played out: "He was completely lucid, he recognized that room that she had described, the night of her confession: the red room where, at sixteen and a half, she had yielded to Grandmorin's violence. It was that very bed he was in now . . . " (1275).

The end of the novel could be deferred, and it is, at least twice. The first is a false hope or a means of delaying the inevitable. As Jacques is going to strangle Séverine, they make love instead: "It was one of their most ardent nights of love, the best, the only one in which they felt intermingled, dissolved into each other" (1286). Repeating the initial actions—the origin of evil and negativity—and recalling the interweaving that exists among all sorts of negative acts make the reader remember how the origins of negation are confused and how these multiple negations can erupt as a figure to interrupt the text. But that does not last long. The second deferral is a decision made by Jacques to place the evil elsewhere: "A brusque decision that he had often made, took him over: kill Roubaud so as not to kill her. This time, like the others, he believed he had complete, unshakeable will" (1288).

But of course, the end comes as it must. Jacques winds up strangling Séverine, as he had always foreseen he would, for nothing can interrupt the flow of negation that is, at the same time, the fulfillment of the novelistic. Evil triumphs as the other assumes a role beyond the human.

## II. The Garden of Evil

Whereas Zola provides a compelling figure for the circulation of evil in *La Bête humaine*, it is up to a later (and lesser) writer, Octave Mirbeau, to provide the most sustained nineteenth-century narrative of evil, pain, and negativity all intertwined. The narrative is so laden with a demonstration and description of this evil that it becomes fixed in a scene of static description. But we are not there yet, and we have a lot to learn from this strange, singular novel that provides a more generalized analysis of the figure of negativity than does Zola's work. Mirbeau's 1899 novel *Le Jardin des supplices* is a narrative exploration of a prison in China in which the principal activity seems to be the torture of criminals. Scenes of bloody torture are set in counterpoint against a story of a decadent love affair between the narrator and the female protagonist, Clara. The novel is divided into three sections, of which the first is a frontispiece, which consists in the main of material reworked from earlier texts, "Divagations sur le meurtre" (1896) and "La loi du meurtre" (1892). The frontispiece is a somewhat sardonic and ironic defense of murder reminiscent of the pre- and postcoital philosophical treatises in Sade's novels. The second section, "En Mission," the first part of Mirbeau's novel *per se*, is a flashback told by a man with a "ravaged face" (60). We are told how he was "brought to undertake" a trip to the Far East, and, specifically, to the Garden of Supplices, "one of the most frightening episodes" of his trip to the Orient (63). If there are other comparable episodes, we never learn of them. In any case, this flashback treats Mirbeau's readers to a disquisition on the petty and tawdry politics of Europe. In the middle of this section, the narrator sees Clara for the first time, after which they wind up in the Indies and then head toward the China of hallucinatory scenarios, fantastic justice, torture, eroticism, and death. The third and longest part, properly entitled "Le Jardin des Supplices," is a tour of the Chinese torture garden that gives its name to the book as a whole and is a series of tableaux serving as fantasized image of Chinese justice and punishment.

At the end of the section of the novel set in France, as the narrator boards ship in Marseilles, he has a first vision of Clara, in a decadent reinscription of Frédéric's sighting of Madame Arnoux: "One especially violently attracted my notice. She was a marvelous creature with heavy red hair, green eyes spangled with gold, like those of wild beasts" (103). The very first vision of Clara is the stereotype of the decadent female figure of the "*belle dame sans merci*" (Praz 182). She is the incarnation of the violence and animal lust of the entire world. It is through these eyes, inured to violence and destruction, that he and we will be asked to see this world. These eyes become ours as we associate our voyeuristic vision to hers, as we accept to read the supplices of the Chinese prison system, each more cruel and exquisite than the previous.

More singular, however, is the disquisition on politics. Through its construction that opposes a satire about European politics and institutions to the depiction of the scenes of torture, *Le Jardin des supplices* has often been seen as an indication of the author's disgust with the Western world's hypocritical smugness about its democracy and freedom. For Mirbeau, modern Western societies parade their violence as virtuous justice, their abuses as economic and moral strengths, and their chicanery as a fair political system (Ziegler 162–65). Mirbeau rails against the inhuman, depersonalized world of the West for which Kafka will provide the most poignant literary version in works like *The Castle* and that Hannah Arendt describes in her book *On Violence* more than half a century later: "Today we ought to add the latest and perhaps most formidable form of such domination [of man over man]: bureaucracy or the rule of an intricate system of bureaus in which no men, neither one nor the best, neither the few nor the many, can be held responsible, and which could be properly called rule by Nobody" (38).

It is not difficult to pinpoint a precise moment in the political affairs of France that focalizes Mirbeau's disgust with the systems of justice and politics that are supposedly the apotheosis of democracy and freedom but that are, in fact, a parody of all the West says it holds sacred: the Dreyfus Affair. As Reg Carr (100) remarks, "It was only the full implication of the Dreyfus Affair, which horrified Mirbeau by its injustice and its cruelty, and the consuming passion which it awoke in him, which provided him with the stimulus he needed to complete his novel, to tie his free-ranging mind down to one central topic, and to give motivation and meaning to *Le Jardin des supplices*, the long-awaited follow-up to *Sébastien Roch*" (Carr 105–107; Schwarz 113). For Mirbeau, railing against Western justice, the story of the Dreyfus Affair is about the torture of an innocent, indeed, of innocence itself.

The Garden of Supplices becomes the metaphor for a Western society that insists on torturing all its innocent members and in which each individual is a scapegoat for the system (Girard). The difference is that the "real" Western world insists on pathos as it personalizes each victim and finds reasons, that is to say, a rationalization, for victimizing them. Mirbeau removes what he perceives as hypocrisy by taking out the pathos and poignancy of the individual subject; reduced to anonymity, the victim is the suitable mirror for Arendt's "Nobody." In a political reading of the nature of the Garden of Supplices, the totally inconsequential nature of any individual victim is merely testimony to the honesty of the system: it little matters who is tortured, as long as there are torture victims (Gouyette 86–87). The crux of the political reading is clear: European society is as bad as this prison system, if not more so. Indeed, according to Schwarz (117), Mirbeau stresses the idea of the Chinese prison as mirror of the West in the closure of the book: "Mirbeau ends the book by returning to his starting point. The Garden of Supplices is the symbol of European society, the torturers representing the institutions working together to suppress man's *élan vital*."

Mirbeau reverses the stereotypical Eurocentric opposition between the presumed despotic nature of the East and the liberty of the West. In so doing, he echoes what some might perceive as the apologetic ethnology of late nineteenth-century France, in which the presumed despotism is actually seen to be liberty and in which, by implication, the presumed freedom of the West hides an ever greater threat to freedom because it builds corruption and terror silently into its institutions. In this, Mirbeau echoes Simon's classic study of the Chinese city:

Many Europeans believe that China is, *par excellence*, the country of despotism. But I ask what kind of despotism could, for more than 500 million people, have only 25 to 30,000 government workers, that, to protect itself, has a permanent army of only one hundred thousand Tartars, more or lest lost amidst such an anthill? In reality, the Chinese govern themselves and do their own administration: in the family, by all the family members; in the city, by the delegates they have elected and whose official government employees are only those who preside [*les présidents*]. (15)

Government and power are local; there is no need for any overarching structure. In the minds of many late nineteenth-century writers including Mirbeau, big, central government rewrites the aftermath of the Revolution a century before such government equals the institutionalization of terror. China represents freedom because the voices of the many are not silenced by the terrors of the few.

This is not yet supplice; it is just one of the several preludes that build up to an act of violence. The whole first part of the novel

contains varied descriptions of hypocritical European politics, chicanery, backstabbing (in a symbolic sense), spin-doctoring, damage
control, and general phoniness. It replaces a vast tissue of "civilized"
lies, against which the horrors of the second part of the novel will be
set (Schwarz 112–18). China becomes the unfettered world of absolute liberty in which nothing interferes with the expression of one's
desire (Schwarz 115). Mirbeau's China is a construction where there
is no need for figures, translations, or modifications of violence.
Though violence is not necessarily subject to measure in that it can
be given free reign, there will still be a reason and science of violence
that will be the science of torture, the precise measure that will determine the form that this torture will take.

In one sense, however, the Garden of Supplices becomes the symbolic or allegorical figure of the Europe that has been rejected as a
lie, for Europe has sweeter ways of torturing people to death with its
velvet-gloved institutions (Schwarz 117). And so one has all the ne-
cessities for a moral reading of the novel. In sum, as Carr says, "The
basic thesis of this nightmarish novel is that society is organised in a
way which encourages and fosters the animal instincts of humanity,
giving free rein to the cruel and homicidal tendencies of man, and
producing a world full of suffering, of exploitation and of death"
(104). In a moral reading of the novel, the garden that becomes an
allegory for the West is the reversal of the tropic figures of the West
that seek to mask the violence that they incarnate with their languages, metonymies, and laws.[4]

The political reading is necessary because it is an available structure on which the author and the reader can peg the text, a safe, certain paradigm and a hermeneutic that permit an interpretation to occur within acceptable norms. One could, clearly and cleanly,
construct a set of political ideologems and a concomitant rhetoric by
means of a political hermeneutic. At the same time, however, such a
political reading is necessarily aporetic because there is no solution.
The Chinese system both is and is not a reflection of the smoother,
but ultimately more dangerous, system of the West. It is a fair representation of the contradictory truths behind the system: the Chinese
are just and the Chinese are not just. Thus, the prison as mirror reflects the same thing in the West: the West is just and the West is not

just. Such an impossible position may be corrected by conceiving of the universe as fundamentally evil and cruel, a Sadean universe in which all is evil and in which the freedom of the individual can be expressed only in an act of cruelty that reflects that universe.

Such is, I think, the role given by decadent writers to the universe as a whole. It is only in a universe considered to be run benevolently that we can accurately decide what is just and what is unjust in the Kantian sense. In an evil universe, a universe in which the evil is inevitably incarnate in the decadent woman such as Clara, the true society reflects the endless repetition of the universe that visits pain on each and every individual in a repetition of the subjection to the social.[5] Thus the individual subject becomes a tool of the universe and the law as a whole. The individual consents to the evil of the universe, and the expressions of crime and punishment become the exemplary method of illustrating the truth of that universe. As Jacques Lacan asserts in a 1950 essay on criminology: "Every society shows the relation of crime to the law through punishments whose realization, through whatever method, demands subjective assent" (126). If this universe that Mirbeau creates seems to us far from the ideas of Kantian justice, perhaps it is not so far from Kant's *Critique of Practical Reason*, of which Lacan writes in his later essay from 1962, "Kant avec Sade," that Sade not only completes the critique but gives its truth (765–66).

The political reading begged for by *Le Jardin des supplices* presents us with at least two contradictions that cannot be resolved on a political level. First, it remains unclear to what extent the rhetorical China of Mirbeau's prison is deemed to be the truth of the West. As far as that is concerned, would this truth be a transcendental one, beyond any geotemporal restrictions, or would it merely be a truth of the moment, a paradigm by which to operate? Second, is the universe in which this truth or nontruth is said to occur a benevolent one, or is it more likely than not an evil one? In the first case, the punishments meted out would be some reflection of the punishments to come, a Dantean *Inferno* before the eternal fires of hell. In the second case, the expression of supplices would be an expression of the truth of the universe, its diabolical power, and its damning judgment; it would be a set of decisions in which the vehicle is the eternal feminine that does not come from Goethe's heaven but from Baudelaire's hell. The impossibility of deciding here relates to the fundamental undecidability of any cosmological situation. Mirbeau's universe is both good and evil, both just and unjust. The contradiction neither is resolved nor can it be through some dialectical process. The contradiction is not a means of affirming an ideology but of denying the possibility of any cogent ideological or political position.

So let us move from the directly political to the poetics of the novel, for even more important in the understanding of it is that the entire rhetoric of representation on which this novel depends is in fact founded on the imaginary construct of the *supplice*. Coming between Poe and Kafka, and in many ways, serving as the acme of such writing, Mirbeau's book is one of a handful of modern works to describe the specific kind of torture known as *supplice*, a word for which English has no specific equivalent. Supplice is the torture that happens between the act of judgment or condemnation and the death of the condemned prisoner; death is often viewed as a release for him or her, as it is a means of ending the pain. And whereas the love affair and the political critique are inscribed within the parameters of standard decadent writing, the torture belongs to a more restricted set of narratives, whose rhetoric is unfamiliar and uncertain because of the extraordinary subject of which they speak and the paucity of narrative norms into which they may or may not be placed. Clara's eyes and her vision invite us to look at, force us to see, and seduce us to get off on a narrative of supplice that fascinates and excites as we view the unspeakable supplices described in the second half of the work.

In the West, the supplices of the Christian martyrs, and *primum inter pares*, the Crucifixion of Jesus, are the forerunners of Mirbeau's work, along with the myriad iconographic depictions of Christian martyrdom in art (Villeneuve). Add to that a mythic component that would include the tortures of Marsyas, flayed alive by Apollo for having been a better musician (Ovid 6:385–400). And if the tortures are Sadean, they are not those relating to the participatory masters and victims but to the listeners and voyeurs, indeed, to the readers of Sade's works, as is the case in *Les 120 Jours*. Through Clara's eyes, Mirbeau inscribes the reader at the locus of sadistic voyeur, a position Praz associates with the decadence already implicit in "frenetic French Romanticism" and specifically, in Pétrus Borel's *Contes immoraux* (293).[6]

This specular position of voyeurism finds numerous echoes in the phantasmagoria relating to the figure of supplice: the members of the Inquisition looking down on the narrator/victim in Poe's "The Pit and the Pendulum," the modern, "supplice-less" panopticon proposed in nineteenth-century penology, the tales of Pétrus Borel, and indeed a specific kind of supplice called the torture of Venetian mirrors, which seems actually to have been used or proposed more as a torture to extract information than as a supplice unto death. This torture "imagined by an Italian Franciscan friar, took place in a room whose surfaces were entirely covered with mirrors. The subject was brought there naked, suspended by his hands above the pointed seat; he was progressively and slowly lowered onto it so that his anus always bore down on this point." Villeneuve quotes a Dr. Cabanés, who allows that "the subject thrashed about and attended his own supplice multiplied by the mirrors." The element of specularity is an integral part of the process of supplice, a quality it shares with torture and simple penal punishment. In supplice, there must be a visual witnessing to the act having taken place, which amounts to a catharsis of the system for itself and a specular reinscription of the law as law, both on the victim on whom it will be seen or read (Kafka) and in a generalized, all-pervasive sense of specularly reinscribing the world in this penal prose. The specularity and voyeurism are always constructed on a model of sadistic homosexuality, and even when a heterosexual model exists—as is the case here with Clara and the narrator—it is cathected on that homosexual model. Thus the introduction of this specularity renders all the models of (re)production sterile.

Supplice is particular and singular, and it defies representation. Supplice has silent screams and howls of pain. It little matters. Supplice is to be read, to be watched as a silent movie or a snuff film, to be imprinted on the mind of subject and observer alike. Kafka's sufferer will eventually understand his sentence after it is inscribed in arabesques and curlicues on his body. Not exchanged, but counted. And at the same time, Kafka's version necessarily involves the breakdown of the machine, precisely because there is a *décalage* between the suffering and its readability. Far away from the immediacy of the Venetian mirrors, the lapse introduced into Kafka's machine is a breach that turns into an abyss. Not so with Mirbeau:

even if the victim cannot see himself being tortured, even if he cannot be a specular subject unto himself, we can read immediately, with no visible *décalage*. At the same time, Mirbeau will hint at the beginning of a physical *décalage* (203) in the torture involving skinning a victim alive; this introduction of absence is that on which Kafka will capitalize.

We have set the gaze, but what exactly are we looking at? What really is supplice? Let us stop, much as Mirbeau's novel stops over and over again, to consider it in detail. What makes it, at least within this framework, the factor of undecidability? Supplice is the act of punishment for one who is condemned. Its forms are varied: the auto-da-fé, crucifixion, drawing and quartering, keelhauling, flaying, flensing, burning at the stake, stoning, flagellation, impalement, defenestration, decollation, gouging, electrical shocks. Add the elements of a martyrology: St. Sebastian's arrows, St. Lawrence's grilling. Sometimes, mere actions are supplemented by the tools of the trade, to paraphrase Sartre who needed no such tools in his hell: the boot, the iron maiden, the rack, the stake, the cang, ropes, whips, garrotes, strappado, the pillory, the knout, the Russian scourge, the wheel of torture, pincers. There is a difference between torture, before the speech act, and supplice, after the speech act but before death, before all is said and done, even if they look alike. Torture should not fully succeed. As Elaine Scarry says: "Torture consists of a primary physical act, the infliction of pain, and a primary verbal act, the interrogation. The first rarely occurs without the second" (28). Torture is pain and action exchanged for words. With supplice there is no exchange.

As Michel Foucault notes, there is an economy of presence in the public performance of supplice *Surveiller* (47–49). The guilty individual is considered the herald of his or her own condemnation. His or her voice and screams reinforce the meaning always already given to the scene: there is neither opening nor difference. The subject's discourse is identified with the double act of judgment and the retelling of the crime. The voices form a chorus of condemnation, and the supplice is an antistrophe to that chorus of woe. Supplice makes an adequation between the criminal action and its confession, between the law on a universal scale and its translation into a specific case, between the counting of acts of supplice and that law, and between the screams of the condemned criminal and the law that is once again reestablished in its universality. This mathematics is one of fractions that add up: the events add up and, through a combination of numbers, one can return to the universal whole.

Supplice is a mathematics of pain, of knowing just how much to induce, how much can be inscribed, how it can be meted out. As Foucault says: "Supplice depends most of all on a quantifying art of suffering" (38). The marks are counted one by one, as are the turns of the wheel, the distances moved, the number of lashes, stones, flagellations, the marks of the knife. How much air can be removed in what amount of time during a slow asphyxiation? How tightly can a garrote be pulled? All this is a science, specifically, a science of numbers, mathesis and mathematics for your viewing pleasure. It is power with a difference, power over a difference, a capacity for storage and distribution of countable "acts of violence." The universal in this world is an impersonal mathematical discourse that assures the link between the world of supplice and the economy of capital punishment, which counts its dead bodies. They are not the same mathematics though: capital punishment, even on the wholesale level of genocide, is involved in the counting of integers. Supplice involves partial counts, fractions, irrational numbers, and even differentials.

Supplice disappears in the West. The Inquisition is over; the Salem witch trials lead to no purification of the virgin lands of New England; the Terror leads to no new birth of liberty, equality, and fraternity. Penology is reborn as the very concept of the law and punishment changes, for between 1769 and 1810 many of the penal codes of the West are radically revised as they undergo a "modernization." And among all the reforms and modifications, as Michel Foucault says, one stands out: "the disappearance of supplices" (13). In a few short years, "the supplied, cut up, amputated body" disappears, the body that had been the "major target of penal repression" (Foucault 14). No longer is the criminal a victim. The law remains universal, but each case is individual; the law never could have predicted it. While the victim of a crime is ever more innocent, the criminal is ever more guilty by definition. We no longer need to represent the crime on his body. The sentence, his punishment, become ever more abstract, ever further from the scarification of the guilty person's body. Punishment meets the crime and is mete to the crime in a count of years or fines or both. Numbers are abstract in this world.

The disappearance of supplice in the real world of the West, somewhere in the early years of the nineteenth century, with the concomitant ending of the public spectacle, means rethinking the act of representation of supplice. In the world of the literary supplice there is no real object, just a fantasmatic recollection of a past, an elsewhere, an otherness. Without an object, the world becomes a construct made of words, in which language must repeat both the differences of the world of the art of supplice: the mathematical precision, the representation of the crime, the reinscription of the pain both as theater and as punishment. Can the literary language of the nineteenth century represent such extreme ultraviolence? Is there the possibility of an alphabet or a rhetoric of violence that maintains the precision of the art or the science of the supplice? And indeed, without an object, the writing may take off. As the officer says in Kafka's tale: "It is no calligraphy [*Schönschrift*] for schoolchildren. One must read it for a long time" (121).

Can there be an aesthetic of the writing of supplice and a rhetoric as well? Can we even mark an act as an act of violence that properly fits into a category? Certainly classical aesthetics would resist a figuration of supplice in mimetic representation. In the most well-known argument about classical aesthetics, Lessing's *Laocoön*, the author provides a sharp contrast between the representation of pain and the reality to which it refers. For Lessing, there must be a difference between the two; pain must be muted and softened for there to be an aesthetic moment: "Pain, in its disfiguring extreme, was not compatible with beauty, and must therefore be softened. Screams must be reduced to sighs, not because screams would betray weakness, but because they would deform the countenance to a repulsive degree" (13). The Marquis de Sade, of course, would not have agreed with Lessing, but his works cannot be said to be typical even if they didactically represent the ideological world in which he writes.

At the end of the nineteenth century, art may imitate such horrible reality to a perfect degree, insofar as the pain can be represented. Consider Mirbeau's aestheticized version of supplice in which pain and torture are presumed to be represented in every figure in the multiple hollows serving as a museum of prison art:

I then noticed that opposite each cell, deep alcoves had been hollowed out in the wall on the left. These alcoves contained painted and sculpted woods that represented, with that frightening realism of Far Eastern art, all the kinds of torture practiced in China: scenes of decapitation, strangulation, flaying, hacking of flesh . . . , demoniacal and mathematical imaginations that push the science of supplice to a refinement unknown in our Western cruelties, as inventive as they are. (174)

Art differs from life. Art can maintain a mathematical precision, a degree of the law, where life is excess, truth and poetry: "'Don't look at that! . . . said Clara with a look of disdain. That is only painted wood my love. . . . Look here, where it is true." (174). In imitating life, art corrects life's little errors, and this even extends to the art of supplice. Mirbeau follows Poe's descriptions of the images of the locus in which the supplice is carried out; staying mostly in the realm of the image prevents the emergence of a breach in representation, the very breach that Kafka will explore as his machine goes awry. Mirbeau introduces inscriptions (223), but logic dictates that they be Chinese, thus remaining unreadable for the reader. Mirbeau stays with the image, perhaps in recognition of the fact that the textualization of the scene will lead to a destruction of the mechanism, because machines always break down sooner or later.

In this image-oriented anatomization of the subject in pain, the act of supplice both fragments and isolates the parts of the body, as if they no longer belonged to a human being, as if they were being shoved under an enlarging lens to the detriment of the rest of the body. This fragmentation of the human body is present in the description of the prison, where the prisoners' necks are in iron collars that are so wide that "it was impossible to see the bodies; one would have said they were scary, living heads of decapitated men" (171). In the first scene of direct physical supplice, Mirbeau, reinscribing Balzac's branding of Vautrin, marks the victim's back as the locus on which the punishment will be inflicted and, in a prophecy of Kafka, written. With an iron switch heated in a forge, a soldier whips a man who has stolen a fish:

When the switch was red-hot, the soldier whipped the man [à tour de bras] on his loins . . . The switch went "shhh" through the air . . . and it deeply penetrated the muscles, which sizzled and which emitted a little reddish steam . . . Then the soldier let the switch cool down in the flesh which swelled and closed up . . . then when it was cold, he yanked it violently in one pull . . . with small bloody fragments. (165)

The part of the body that undergoes the supplice becomes isolated from the rest of the body and from the being that may inhabit that body. The body part becomes the unique object on which attention is focused. And indeed, it quite literally becomes the partial object that belongs at the same time to the subject of consciousness and the subject of pain: "with each blow, it seemed to me that the switch was entering my loins. . . . It was horrible and oh so sweet" (165).

In the text of supplice, the body is always potentially in its fragmentary state, the future is inscribed in the present, and the victims of supplice always mirror the flensing that will be theirs. As they grab for the unspeakably horrible victuals put before them, the victims become the equivalent of the pieces themselves: "There were only naked torsos, mixed or fused with the others, girdled with long thin arms, torn by jaws and claws . . . and twisted faces grabbing the meat" (178). Compared to animals in a cage, psychotic animals to boot, or sharks in a feeding frenzy, these humans have been reduced to nothing more than the mechanics of bodies in motion, a frenzy that produces, in the mind of the observer, an orgasmic frenzy of lust, as Clara becomes sexually excited by the acts of destruction: "'Kiss me. Caress me'" (179).

In Mirbeau's novel, supplice happens in a way that is out-of-measure. There is no correspondence between the criminal act and the supplice inflicted on the victim, and it is here that the economy of presence that Foucault uses as a model can be seen to be based on Western systems of justice and, essentially, on a somewhat benevolent universe in which the auto-da-fé or its equivalent is seen not as an act of torture but as an act of faith. In the universe created by Mirbeau, the Foucauldian model is entirely suspended in favor of an untimely, extravagant, decentered one. One man is condemned for having stolen a fish (165) and another for having stolen a bag of rice from some Englishmen (203). At the same time, certain supplices do seem to fit the crime but not necessarily in a metonymic fashion. Special punishments are reserved for "quality criminals . . . mutinous princes . . . high dignitaries who no longer please the emperor" (236). In another case, the punishment may seem to our eyes to fit the crime as a reinscription and a reperformance of the crime. It is the supplice chosen for a man who is condemned for having raped and disemboweled his mother, a man who is thought to be mad. For his crime, he is condemned to the supplice of the caress as he is masturbated to death:

The madman—he didn't seem so mad—was laid out on a very low table, with his limbs and body tied down with solid cords . . . his mouth gagged so he could neither move nor yell . . . A woman who was neither beautiful nor young, with a serious mask, dressed entirely in black, her naked arm ringed with a large gold ring, came and knelt next to the madman . . . She took hold of his rod . . . and she officiated . . . Oh! my dear! . . . my dear! . . . If you had seen this . . . It took four hours . . . four hours, think of it! . . . four hours of dreadful, artful caresses, during which time the woman's hand never stopped for a minute, during which time, her face remained cold and gloomy! . . . The patient expired in a spew of blood that spattered the whole face of the tormentor. . . . (166–67)

To our politically correct minds, the punishment fits the crime in that it seems to be a sexual act that quotes the original rape. Pushed to the extreme, violating all propriety, the sexual act equals death in both the crime and its appropriate punishment. But even beyond that, what is important is that the punishment may or may not fit the crime. Poe, in his rewriting of the auto-da-fé, and Kafka, in his reinscription of the sense of order, both create a supplice that, though excessive to our eyes, follows the economic model and is consonant with a logic and poetics of supplice as defined by Western standards. Mirbeau, however, avoids the decision that is necessary for such a poetics.[7] The punishment may or may not fit the crime; in this world and in this textuality, it cannot be decided, nor does it matter one whit. In Mirbeau's hands, literary supplice becomes an excuse for a description that penetrates the imaginary without any appeal to justice. Justice is served by not being served. Justice is served when there is punishment, regardless of who is punished, for whatever reason, and whether rightly or wrongly.

The West is not totally free of this violence of power, but it occurs at the margins of the West, at a confrontation between systems, and within an economy that, Mirbeau would undoubtedly argue, is the institutionalization of a system of torture far more brutal than this Chinese system. For the Chinese system has the decency of putting people to death, and in so doing, thereby ending the crime. The

West may choose its victims and kill them, but, in general, the system goes on perpetrating the crimes of imperialism, colonialism, and abuse through a generalized system of parasitism that prefers to weaken rather than to kill. When the West kills, it generally remains true to its mathematics, its genius of precise murder. And when the West does kill, it is not so much by abrasion, flensing, or wearing away but by the very tools it uses to bring life. Clara tells of a supplice administered by some French in Algeria to some Maghrebins:

There were thirty of them . . . thirty holes were dug in the sand, and they were buried up to their necks, naked, their heads shaved, in the midday sun. In order that they not die too quickly, from time to time, they were watered like cabbages. After half an hour, their pupils were swollen . . . their eyes were coming out of their head . . . their tumefied tongues filled their mouths which were horribly open . . . their skin cracked, roasting on their skulls. (189–90)

In Mirbeau's China, as in Poe's paranoid world, simple integers give way to fractions and unending divisions (Schehr, *Parts* 33–77). Heads are not simply lopped off one by one; bodies are slowly reduced from their integrality to annihilation, with the line between life and death, in an expansion of Poe's "Valdemar," a vague border constantly in flux. And beyond that impossibility of counting the dead is the fact that the line between just and unjust, between justice and injustice, is equally impossible to define. There may or may not be a relation between the crime and the punishment, between the act and its re-representation. What Mirbeau describes goes beyond a logic of representation, justice, and logic itself. It little matters whether there is a fitting judgment and execution, because guilt and innocence are themselves brought into question. In this sense, Mirbeau does occupy the middle ground between Poe and Kafka. In the former, the system, as abusive as it may be, is the absolute law, the Lacanian law of the father and the Inquisition. People are punished according to a strict code, and punished for their own good: an act of purification is an act of faith (auto-da-fé). The supplice purifies the victim and makes him one again with the law. For Kafka, everyone is always already guilty, always already about to be punished; in that sense, the punishment continues to fit the crime, which is the crime of existence itself. Poe's mathematical precision goes awry in Kafka, as the machine, already too old to be trusted, goes haywire in fulfilling its task, and, as I have suggested, the rupture occurs as well in the breach of representation. In Kafka, the victim is almost ancillary to the inscription of the guilt of the entire system. Mirbeau is there in the middle voice of undecidability and ambiguity. There is clearly still a system of justice and therefore a possibility of deciding on guilt or innocence. At the same time, that decision does not matter one bit.

The West has undergone a decadence that moves from a glorious past to a dismal present. Whereas Western justice and punishment still do clear head counts, supplice no longer exists in its carnal and physical form; it has been transformed into the stuff of politics, an endless abrasion of the soul and mind of man: Gambetta is described as a "dilettante of the voluptuous, who adored the odor of human rotting" (80). And cheating has replaced pain as the standard of abuse: political scandals, corruption, dishonest merchants, false science, and the like. Supplice itself has become banal, a mild discomfort from which one seeks distraction: "Nothing distracted us from the supplice of feeling ourselves cook with the slowness and steadiness of a *pot-au-feu*" (109). The West has turned supplice on itself in direct, self-inflicted pain; one is, as Baudelaire says in the poem, "Héautotimorouménos," one's own executioner: "I am the wound and the knife [*Je suis la plaie et le couteau*]." Or the West, in its own perversion of the system, has gone outside the system to provide grist for its mill, blood for its blood lust. The scopic madness of the West—the need to look—is tantamount to the need to control and vice versa:

They had provided for the upkeep of two secretaries and two servants, the very expensive purchase of instruments of anatomy, of microscope, of cameras, of collapsible boats, of hunting rifles, and of cages to bring back the captured animals alive. [ . . . ] It goes without saying that I bought none of these *impedimenta* and that I decided to bring no one along, counting on my own ingenuity to make my way through these unknown forests of science and India. (100–101)

Physical and visual control are there for a reason, for reason itself: the law, justice, need, the categorical imperative, or even pleasure, as in Sade and Lacan's version of Sade. As Pascal endlessly and sarcastically shows in his *Lettres provinciales*, in which he rails against the apologetics for murder of Jesuit casuistry, from the speakable to the unspeakable is just one short step. In an 1892 story, quite appropriately entitled "Colonisons," with its complicitous first-person plural imperative, Mirbeau is very specific about Western reason and hypocrisy: "Wherever there is a need to justify [*légitimer*] spilled blood, to consecrate piracies, to bless violations, to protect hideous businesses, one is sure to see this obsessed British Tartuffe pursue his work of abominable conquest under the pretext of religious proselytism or scientific study" (270).[8]

In Mirbeau's China, there need be no reason (i.e., cause or guilt) for punishment, even if the punishment is administered according to its own reason (*ratio*) and logic. Where the West has logic, knowledge, and cause, in China there is merely silence at the heart of the torture, a silence that Mirbeau endlessly reinscribes with his ellipses. Mirbeau's somewhat discontinuous style, in which he often resorts to ellipses (here and elsewhere) instead of continuous prose, finally gives meaning to figures of lazy writing: the story of the reason for torture cannot be told, because there is no real reason. And, as in the West, we are prisoners of our forms; there can be no narrative continuity. If form follows function, the ellipses on every page reflect the absence of logic, the absence of reason, and the silence at the heart of every supplice as it exists in the East and as it is represented in the West. At the heart of Western representation, there is an imaginary figure, a signifier hiding an empty signified, and an imaginary content that does not exist. No wonder that there can be no solution to aporias.

In a decadent novel, all must slide, and for all the oppositions, there is also slippage in the East as well. Few people know how to practice the noble art of supplice, and some of the more subtle forms of torture are reserved for special cases where rank has its privileges. As one of the torturers/executioners nostalgically remarks, things are not as good as they were: "You see, madam," the talkative fellow continued, "our trade, like our beautiful porcelain vases [*potiches*], our beautiful embroidered silks, our beautiful lacquer-ware, is becoming an ever more lost art . . . Today we no longer know what supplice really is . . . Although I try to keep the real traditions . . . I'm overworked . . . and I cannot stop its decadence all alone . . . " (204). Kafka will echo this nostalgia about the decadent state of supplice, as the worn and frayed machine breaks down. His machine cannot continue; it must come apart rent by forces from within, not by the parasites Poe introduces into the system (the rats) or the *manus ex machina* that saves the narrator from being squeezed to death and that is, ironically, the hand that will allow his hand to narrate his harrowing tale.

Supplice is not human alone. From Poe to Kafka, machines are involved as equally important participants in the execution of supplice. A machine of supplice or of execution is the figure of the ever-reinforced act of inscription on the subject, as if the subject, in his or her last moments, must be forced to reread both the aesthetic iconization of crime and its statement of the law in baroque curlicues and arabesques. Poe's victim initially believes that the machine is just a two-dimensional piece of art: "It was the painted figure of Time as he is commonly represented, save that, in lieu of a scythe, he held what, at a casual glance, I supposed to be the pictured image of a huge pendulum, such as we see on antique clocks" (498). But the figure is real: it is not art but the pendulum that slowly descends and whose edge is the finely honed blade that is supposed to cut the victim to shreds. Later, Kafka's machine, even in its dilapidated state, still has an aesthetic component, for the machine contains potentially the template for the inscriptions of the sentences on prisoners, a pattern to be remarked and written in order to produce an inscription that is simultaneously writing and art.

Between the two, Mirbeau offers the reader a guillotine "in black wood, whose stiles were decorated with gilt inscriptions and terrifying masks" (223). Mirbeau aestheticizes the entire space by turning it into the equivalent of a formal French garden, in which "beauty and horror cohabitate" (Solda 69) or where "the art of gardening and the art of inflicting pain and moral anguish find a 'harmonious' coexistence" (Gruzinska 72). And, as Allen Weiss admirably shows, such a garden is "a scenario of absolute power and desire" (33). The French garden marks space geometrically and submits disorder and chaos to the rules of orthogonal planting and distribution. Everything must be right. The garden is the locus of a distribution of power according to a perfect geometry of placement. Whereas Baudelaire chooses to have flowers of evil emerge here and there in no global pattern but only a local one in each poem, Mirbeau chooses to make a garden of evil: "And, from this floral enchantment, arose scaffolds, apparatuses for crucifixion, gibbets with violent illuminations, completely black gallows at the top of which snickered horrible masks of demons; high gallows for simple strangulation, gibbets that were lower and with moving parts for the flensing of flesh" (201). There must be no infraction of the law, though one may reconstruct a bit of wild nature within the formal pattern if one chooses: the wild bower in *La Nouvelle Héloïse*, the grandmother's roses in "Combray." The simulation of the natural through artificial means is one more way of introducing the aesthetic dimension into the framework of the space of supplice. By artfully marking the space, there can be a confusion between the aesthetic and the cruel. Aesthesis becomes a figure of supplice:

Here and there, simulating rooms of green and floors of flowers, wooden benches, armed with chains and collars of bronze, iron tables in the form of a gross, executioner's blocks, grills, gibbets, machines for automatic quartering, beds trussed with cutting blades, bristling with iron points, fixed iron collars, racks and wheels, boilers and tubs above extinguished hearths, a whole set of tools for sacrifice and torture. (226)

At various levels, aesthetic inscription repeats. The larger level of the garden that produces the general aesthetic is echoed or mirrored in a *mise-en-abyme* of the aesthetic and the cruel in the very decoration of the individual machines of supplice. Through the imposition of the aesthetic, supplice goes on to the infinitely small. The idea of refinement is just that: produce the entirety of the experience in the merest moment, in the smallest detail, and in the most exquisite of tortures. Supplice is cumulative as it builds toward a complete aesthetic of death. At the same time, it is ever more divisible into a set of tiny movements that reproduce the whole: "When I had taken off his skin and it was attached to his shoulders only by two little buttonholes, I made him walk, madam [ . . . ] You would have said that he had on his body, what do you call it? . . . Ah!, yes, of course! . . . an Inverness cape [*macfarlane*]?" (203). One imagines the infinitely painful moments of the performance, the slow flaying alive, followed by the evidence, the skin of the tortured victim hanging as if it were clothing: through the imposition of an aesthetic of supplice, the natural, that is to say, the skin of the victim, becomes the equivalent of the artificial, nothing more than an article of clothing to be donned and doffed at the will of the torturer.[9]

Supplice, then, is the creation of artifice from the natural. The individual subject's value is his or her potential to be a victim to be sculpted, flayed, or flensed; it is his or her potential capacity to be turned into an art object through the imposition of the law and the aesthetic of cruelty. While this is certainly the decadent aesthetic, there is a negative movement as well, a resistance, the impossibility of aestheticizing everything. The same victim who is being skinned alive and then forced to parade his new suit of clothing has something that resists an aesthetic of cruelty: "'His bones were so hard that I nicked my saw, the beautiful saw you see here.' Something small, whitish, and fatty had remained between the teeth of the saw . . ." (203).

This book is written in blood about subjects, objects whose very utility depends on their being solid: bodies are no good for supplice if they are not solid flesh. For it is only a solid that can be marked by an act of supplice: "bonds of rope and strips of leather had little by little entered the flesh where they now made pads of blood" (233). Hamlet's wish that this "too, too solid flesh would melt" is echoed in Mirbeau's prose, which needs the resistance of the solid to describe the acts of violence. But still and always, there is flow of blood, tears, and ink. Having been subjected to supplice, the solid bodies are eventually translated into these various liquids. Liquids can spread, diffuse, and fertilize a garden or a novel that is that garden, the dried liquids of the world turned to the flowers of rhetoric that describe the supplice. In this garden of unearthly delights, the liquid of choice is blood:

Pools of blackish blood, there, sticky and red. Pools of blood filled the empty parts; long tears of dried blood hung on the uncoupled apparatus . . . Around these mechanisms, the earth finished pumping the blood . . . Yet more blood spangled the whiteness of the jasmine with red, marbled the coral red of the honeysuckle, the mauve of the passion flowers, and little bits of human flesh, that had flown off because of the lashes of the whip and the leather strips, hung here and there on the tips of petals and leaves. (226)

Flows are the mark of the victim; the tears shed by the narrator (220) are characterized as women's tears, tears of someone who is prey to the will of the other. Just as the narrator's desires remain unfulfilled and just as he still remains somewhat European, his tears mark him as a victim as well. Clara maintains power over him (220), and she identifies with the executioners and their songs, with the flowers of the garden that speak volumes. These flowers are fertilized with the blood of the victims, as their voices and their silences are marked as one and the same: "She became still and, continuing to walk, she listened to the voice of the flowers in which she recognized her own voice" (222). We shall shortly return to the question of sound but not before looking at one of the singular acts of supplice of the novel, the supplice of the rat.

The supplice of the rat is perhaps the most well-known scene in the book, partly because of two of its reincarnations at the two ends of the twentieth century. Early on, the image of the rat biting and burrowing into the nether regions of a body was the central fantasm in Freud's 1909 study "Notes Upon a Case of Obsessional Neurosis." More recently, the same fantasm has taken on the status of an urban myth known as gerbilling, where some well-known actor is discovered in the emergency room of a hospital in either New York or Los Angeles with a gerbil in his rectum. These two versions, however, themselves speak volumes: the image of the gnawing rat preys on the unconscious, not only in the form of anal homoeroticism that Freud gives it or that is implicit in the story of gerbilling, an anal homoeroticism central to the specularity of this book. But there is also in an appeal to a classic demonology of torture and evil that includes the swarming images of rats in Poe's "The Pit and the Pendulum," the Dracula stories, the Pied Piper of Hamelin, and so forth. Here however, Mirbeau strips the collective image of its multiplicity and concentrates on the singular destruction of one rat, as if he were trying to determine the basic element of the act of supplice.[10]

Mirbeau's version is a detailed graphic description of an act of supplice second to none. A hungry rat is placed in a pot that is then placed hermetically over the buttocks of a condemned man. As befits the construction of the supplice, there is a primitive machine of belts and straps holding the pot in place. Through a tiny hole in the end of the pot that is not attached to the prisoner's buttocks, the torturer introduces a red-hot iron wire. As the rat fears both the heat and the light, it seeks an escape, and in so doing starts tearing up the flesh of the victim. Blood-drunk, the rat finally discovers the one natural exit available and penetrates the body of the victim to die asphyxiated, just as the victim himself dies from a hemorrhage, an excess of suffering, and/or madness (208–11).

As the novel develops, Mirbeau's approaches to supplice get both more sophisticated and more minimalist. There is a gradual dismantling of the machinery of the work by which some of the earlier tortures were constructed. Here, we have nothing more than a Luddite machine, a simple harness by which the natural animal energy of the rat does the work of the torture. The rats that had been the ultimate instrument of freedom in Poe's story become agents of supplice in Mirbeau's novel, which reverses the act of liberation by reharnessing the energy of the parasite itself. Where Poe has a gradual unwinding of the bindings as they are shredded into ribbons, Mirbeau substitutes a simple unchanging and unbreakable set of belts. Thus, in the supplice of the rat, Mirbeau uses the animal as a demonic copy of the human worker; it will be a short step to the dehumanization of humans themselves in Kafka's tale or in the images of dehumanized workers from the early part of Fritz Lang's *Metropolis*, contemporaneous with Kafka's work. The rat's natural instincts are neither good nor bad, for these are words that relate both the human world, and specifically to the ideologies and moralizing of the West, and to its projections of a cosmology. Mirbeau uses the neutrality of the rat's energy to perform the supplice, a mechanism that will find its way into the supplice of the bell, which will be the consummate image of torture in the book.

In the supplice of the rat, Mirbeau also introduces an element of invisibility heretofore unremarked: one can no longer see the act of supplice, one can only read its results. Supplice turns into its own representation, as the mechanism by which it is constructed becomes ever more removed from the light of day. Foucault points out that the reformation of the penal code devolves on the abstraction of punishment into a length of time. For Mirbeau, however, believing little in the Kantian universe on which Foucault bases his judgments, it is sufficient to abstract supplice itself into its invisible equivalent. For Mirbeau, it is not time that is the abstract or the universal but suffering; more than half a century before Camus's *Le Mythe de Sisyphe* and *a fortiori*, Beckett's entire oeuvre, Mirbeau posits suffering as a universal by which we measure all things human.

Similarly, in the next supplice, the act of violence becomes even more abstract as its violent nature has seemingly disappeared. Whereas in the earlier supplice of death by masturbation there was an abrasive action, here it is simply the sound of a bell that turns the everyday into the supplice of the damned: "One would say that the vibrations of the bell, ringing at full peal, penetrated this body like a hard, driving material . . . that they raised up its muscles, made its veins crack, twisted and broke its bones . . . A simple sound, so sweet to the ear, so deliciously musical, so moving for the soul, becoming something a thousand times more terrible and painful than all the complicated instruments" (235).[11]

In the supplice of the bells, Mirbeau provides a microcosmic version of the social machine of torture in which humans play all the parts, and in which the mechanical is reduced to nothing more complicated than a bell. This is the purest act of supplice described in the book, in part because it is the most economical; both the victim under the bell and the ringers of the bell are condemned and suffer alike. In this most refined version of torture, the mechanics are reduced to a minimum, though everything depends on a mechanical movement, but this time it is men who have been reduced to machines. Equally important, however, is that the supplice of the bell is the site at which the most basic unit of supplice is discovered. Moving from the mechanical to ever simpler machines, from the human to the animal, the progression of supplices has finally landed on the noncorporeal. No longer is there a need to distinguish between solid and liquid, between executioner and victim, between power and powerless. Mirbeau has categorized supplice's basic building block as the ethereal, but as an element of beauty itself:

Neither the knife that cuts up a body, nor the red-hot iron that burns, nor the tongs that yank, nor the wedges that spread the joints and split bones like pieces of wood could wreak more havoc on the organs of a living being or fill a brain with more horror than this invisible and immaterial sound of a bell that alone becomes all the known instruments of supplice, working simultaneously on all the feeling and thinking parts of an individual, doing the work of more than a hundred executioners. (241)

It is a building block already hinted at fifty pages before, as the sound of a bell is likened to the voice itself: "The words of 'death, charm, torture, love' that incessantly fell from her lips seemed nothing more than a far-off echo, a tiny little voice of a bell, that was hardly perceptible" (197). This voice is everywhere, whether it is in the clicking of nocturnal geckos (250) or in the flowers of evil and supplice that are so many corporeal translations of the innocent sound. Supplice happens in a decentered voice that is everywhere, in the most innocent sounds or in the wildest shrieks. The voice and the sounds are deterritorialized, the only sound or all sounds in one: "She became quiet, and while walking, she listened to the voice of the flowers in which she recognized her own voice, her voice of terrible days and homicidal nights" (222). So this larger-than-life cruel woman who stereotypically marks the novel as a decadent one, finally resumes the aesthetic at the heart of a poetics of supplice as she both incarnates and disincarnates the voice that is a sound. This is a sound of ubiquitous presence that is the sound of supplice, scream and silence alike. Just as there is no clear separation of the narrative ideologems of good and evil and just as there is an arbitrary infliction of supplice on the just and the unjust, on the guilty and the innocent, there is no distinction between sound and silence at the heart of the articulation of the supplice.

Among the final tableaux is one whose total confusion helps bring the novel to a close. Set in a "house of joy," the disembodied, decorporealized, and deterritorialized voices and bodies, the permanent dislocations of sounds and sights, the monstrous combination of the human and the bestial, and the intermingling of perversion, of writing, and of supplice are the fitting image for this novel:

In front of every door, there were screams, panting voices, gestures of the damned, twisted bodies, pulverized bodies, a whole grimacing pain that sometimes screamed under the whip of atrocious voluptuous acts and barbaric onanisms. In front of the entrance to one room, I saw a bronze group whose arabesque of lines was enough to give me a shudder of horror . . . An octopus wrapped its tentacles around the body of a virgin and with its ardent, strong sucker, pumped the love, all the love from her mouth, her breasts, her belly. (263)

What is there in the end but silence and screams, eroticism transformed into supplice and vice versa? Clara sinks into the hysteria of the dissipate, the decadent, the decayed. The narrator endlessly repeats her name, in a tattoo, a self-inflicted torture of the damned, in which the sound of his voice is his own permanent ringing of the bells, for which he plays all the parts. He has finally found its middle voice of sacrifice and unending supplice in which are finally reunited in a permanent gape of torture and supplication all the fragments of bodies, the depersonalized tableaux, the agencies of power and abuse, the flowers of evil, and the voices of seduction. And so he continues, ever torturing himself, ever dying, but never fully, wholly dead.

At the end of the nineteenth century, Mirbeau challenges the idea of Kantian universals that prop up Foucault's economy of punishments, the means by which Foucault can envision the transformation of the supplice model of punishment into an abstraction of time served, which is the basis for modern Western penology. Refusing the West and its universals from the very start, Mirbeau provides us with a representational system in which the abstraction is not a falling back on a universal of time but is only—and perhaps even more economically—an abstraction of supplice. In this garden, it is not time and work that make the flowers grow but supplice, the universal constant that will become the lowest common denominator of the twentieth century that is about to be born of a mother, who is, as Samuel Beckett says, "astride a tomb." The end of the universal is a fitting end to master narrative. Proust and Gide will continue it but in a highly personal vein. At the same time that they invent modern narrative, they will again expand alterity.

# Proust and Gide

At first glance, it may seem that to add Gide and Proust to the praxes or realism is to stretch the definition. Those who object have a point, for no better examples of high modernists exist in French. Yet several reasons come to mind that justify this addition. First of all, Gide and Proust continue to use the processes of realism in their works by situating the individual squarely within the social, by providing an accurate portrait of society, by emphasizing the real psychology of the individual, and by maintaining a highly classical discourse and style. Second, as with Mann, but not with Anglo-American writers, there is no radical bending of narrative form in modernist experimentation: no unguaranteed multiple points of view as in Woolf, no linguistic experimentation as in Joyce, no stylistic/linguistic events as in Dos Passos or Faulkner. Gide and Proust are the last of the realists and the first of the modernists. What defines their modernism is that, in their works, there is the expression of a particular point of view allied to the universal but not totally assimilable to it. It is a universal that has effectively disappeared in the non-French writers just mentioned. The reintroduction of the first-person narrative, which had been abandoned to a great extent throughout realism, is a world-shaking event in literature. Suddenly, with *L'Immoraliste*, there is a singular, and far-from-main-line narrative, addressing matters that had not been engaged before, alluding to discourses previously thought unmentionable, or if mentioned, always neatly cordoned off. Proust goes further in his development of singular voices and psychologies; Gide himself will take a different tack in a work like *Les Faux-Monnayeurs*, in which he creates a polyphonic work, with multiple points of view, yet they all are more or less subsumed under the framework of the universal voice. Still, the narrator in *Les Faux-Monnayeurs* will try to move away from the universalized bourgeois position as he tackles the dissolved, the dissolute, the fake, and the eccentric.

With Proust and Gide then, my goal is to look at the final step in the assimilation of the other in realist narrative. From the generalized other that marks nineteenth-century narratives, a turn is made toward the single voice and the position of one individual. Can he or she have a voice, separate from or in addition to the universals accorded everyone by the end of the nineteenth century? Can the individual maintain his or her singularity without being fully integrated into the French version of the melting pot? Can the French Jew or the French homosexual, to take the two examples at hand, resist total assimilation into the realist universal? Or, to put it another way: with the move from third- to first-person narrative, is there a parallel move to have a discourse by which the other continues to speak as other? In both the cases at hand, the Jew in Proust and the gay man in Gide, the problem is a fairly thorny one, and the figures that have previously surged up continue to do so in these cases. Where Proust will eventually become a modernist is in his treatment of the homosexual (as opposed to his treatment of the Jew). Arguably, for Proust, the Jewish question was intimately related to the question of Dreyfus and thus marked by and embedded in a precise historical moment, whereas the matter of the gay man (or woman) may have always seemed a question of freedom. As for Gide and the homosexual question, his solution is to turn fictional narrative into autobiography: the truth of the individual is confessional.

## I. Rachel, quand du Seigneur

"Rachel, quand du Seigneur la grâce tutélaire
A mes tremblantes mains confia ton berceau,

J'avais à ton bonheur voué ma vie entière
Et c'est moi qui te livre au bourreau!"

[Rachel, when the Lord's saving grace
Committed your cradle into my hands,
I devoted my entire life to your happiness
And it is I who hands you to the executioner.]

Scribe and Halévy, *La Juive*

For a long time in Proust scholarship, it has been standard to emphasize the functions of poetic tropes in the *Recherche* by considering them as one of the major buttresses of the work's structure and
architecture. A few examples, chosen almost at random, will suffice.
David Ellison (1–29) starts his poststructuralist reading of the *Recherche* with a discussion of Proustian metaphor; through an analysis
that depends to a great extent on a knot of metaphoric references,
Serge Doubrovsky analyzes fantasmatic structures in the novel. Both
Gerard Macé and Philippe Boyer choose a specific image (a Fortuny
dress and a yellow section of wall in a painting by Vermeer) and
weave their studies around the figures spawned by the images. Paul
de Man (57–78) devotes a whole chapter of *Allegories of Reading* to
the subject of reading taken as a trope in the novel. In a more traditional mode, Albert Mingelgrün devotes his monograph to a study of
what he calls "interferences" of Biblical images in the novel. While
Gérard Genette is often thought of as a Proustian scholar in reference to his narratological analysis of the work, "Discours du récit,"
which forms the bulk of *Figures III* (65–282), he also has produced
two major essays, "Proust et le langage indirect," included in *Figures
II*, in which he discusses "the poetic state of language" (233), and
"Métonymie chez Proust," in *Figures III* (41–63).

Equally well known in Proust criticism is that an interest in tropes
is one of Proust's own interests, whether it be in an article devoted to
the "style" of Flaubert, or more extensively, throughout the *Recherche* itself. Whether it is Swann's penchant for comparisons between
individuals he meets and the works of art they call to mind or the
grandmother's insistence on aestheticizing gifts to her grandson by
seeking an image with several thicknesses—a picture of a famous
bridge is good but a copy of a Hubert Robert painting depicting that
bridge is better—the thickening of the thematic of the writing

through an insistence on the tangibility of images is no surprise to any reader.

Though disparate, all the above have one thing in common. No matter if the approach is thematic, deconstructive, narratological, or psychoanalytic, all of them are concerned with the ways in which figures of language or of images are woven into and erupt from the Proustian narrative. If Genette shows how the figurations of temporal dislocation form and interrupt the narrative, de Man demonstrates how reading within the novel both explains it and deconstructs it. Doubrovsky, Boyer, and Macé all focus on the ramifications of a singular image. While some readings remain steadfastly thematic and closed, various studies of the construction of homosexuality in Proust's narrative (Lavagetto, Ladenson, Schehr *Shock*) look at how the figure weaves and interrupts the narrative at the same time.

This part of the chapter focuses on one such image with its own attendant ramifications, because it is yet another key to the Proustian concept of identity and to the way in which Proust takes the realist paradigm and makes it his own. The image in question is that of the Jewish woman as depicted in the *Recherche*, one that implies everything from maternity to prostitution to the Dreyfus Affair. Most interesting and rewarding for a reading of the novel is to follow the metaphorics of the construction of that image, for it is such metaphorics that determine the ways in which identity is constructed in narrative. As is the case with all the figures of alterity examined heretofore, there is a dynamic involved that moves between the stable construction of the figure, and thus its assimilation into the discourse of identity, and its permanent destabilization.

The figure of the Jewish woman in Proust's novel is based on two primary comparisons, emphasized and underlined by Proust in his discussion of them, in his repetition of the images, and in his reminder to the reader that the penchant for creating such images is a fondness shared by the characters making these images. The first of these images is the introduction of Saint-Loup's future mistress, Rachel, with the reference to Eugène Scribe and Jacques Fromental Halévy's 1835 opera, *La Juive*.[1] The second image is the well-known comparison of Odette de Crécy to the biblical figure Zipporah, depicted in a fresco by Botticelli in the Sistine Chapel.

If Scribe and Halévy's opera was well known at the time at which
the novel is set, it is far less well known today, though there have
been sporadic revivals in the last half-century, usually as vehicles for
the tenor role of Eléazar, the father of the title character. Some familiarity then will help the reader understand what Proust has
brought to the fore in his references to that opera. At the end of the
last act, Rachel, the Jewess of the title, is about to be burnt at the
stake. The only possible way for her to be saved from this fiery death
involves renouncing her Jewish faith and accepting baptism while
converting to Christianity. This solution, which she will not accept
because of the strength of her faith, is ironized by a revelation made
in the previous act. In a *coup de théâtre* at the end of Act IV, Rachel's
father, Eléazar, reveals that long ago, an anonymous Jew saved a Cardinal's daughter from certain death when she was a child. Eléazar
knows who her savior was and, ostensibly, her fate, too. Alone on
stage, Eléazar now sings "Rachel, quand du Seigneur," an aria well
known to the French opera-going public in Proust's time. Eléazar in-
timates that it was he who found the child; consequently, Rachel is
not actually his biological daughter but the daughter of the Cardinal
and, therefore, Catholic by birth. Born a Catholic, raised a Jew, she
is unaware of her own ambiguous status. The aria reflects an ambiguity about blood and birth, about love and family piety, about the
opposition between a father's love for his daughter, who has become
Jewish through that love, and a father's hatred of all that is not Jewish, again, his daughter by her birth. Throughout the aria, Eléazar
wavers in his emotions of vengeance on the Christian enemy (of
whom the Cardinal, ironically, is by far the most clement) and the
love he feels for his adopted daughter.

Needless to say, at the conclusion of this grand opera, Rachel does
not renounce her Jewish faith as she has been asked to do by the
Catholic hierarchy and, specifically, the Cardinal himself. He does
not know that she is his daughter, just as she does not know that she
is not Jewish. As she is thrown into the purifying flames, Eléazar follows her, but not before announcing that Rachel was in fact the Cardinal's daughter. The Jewess who refused to convert to Christianity
because of her faith was in fact a Christian by birth all along. Warned
by Eléazar's aforementioned aria in which he weighs love versus vengeance, the audience naturally expects this final blow.[2]

This melodramatic grand opera plays a pivotal role in several points in the *Recherche*. The grandfather is wont to whistle the music to "Rachel, quand du seigneur" when Bloch comes around, and later, and more importantly, the narrator describes a Jewish prostitute who eventually becomes the mistress of Robert de Saint-Loup and who is later recognized by the narrator as that former prostitute (2:456). Following his grandfather's own quotation of the opera, the narrator baptizes her with the nickname "Rachel quand du Seigneur." The first time this character is encountered is in one of the many scenes in the *Recherche* that engages a sexuality marginal to (though an integral part of) the proper and presentable bourgeois vision of quiet propagation through heterosexual marriage. Rachel is introduced when Marcel's friend Bloch, who is Jewish, takes Marcel to a brothel for the latter's maiden voyage into the world of prostitution (1:565). Far more advanced in his knowledge of this world than Marcel is, Bloch himself has long ceased going to this particular brothel, yet he still considers it the right place for the narrator's initiation. Time has wrought its usual effects, and the girls Bloch requests are not there. The madam is not fazed in the slightest, as she proposes an exotic solution to the problem of finding the right girl for Marcel:

> The madam of the house knew none of the women asked for and always proposed ones that one would not have wanted. With a smile full of promises (as if it were a rarity and a treat), she especially praised one of whom she said: "She's Jewish! Doesn't that appeal to you?" (It is undoubtedly because of that that she called her Rachel). (1:566)

The exoticism of the Jewish woman is a commonplace in the era, as her dark sultry looks are associated with a generalized orientalism and thus a generalized libidinal sexuality. In *La Maison Philibert*, Jean Lorrain (63) says much the same thing: "The type of the Oriental Jew prevailed in Rebecca. She had the pretentious and classical profile of the Fatimas of lithographs and Rachels at the fountain from Biblical prints." Whereas Lorrain, for one, is always eager to point out the physical and concrete nature of a situation (as well as its decomposition), Proust is content with naming Rachel as a Jew. Her Oriental air is conjured by the very fact that she is called a Jew by the madam. For her, just the fact that Rachel is Jewish is enough of a recommendation that her potential client will have a good time with this sultry beauty.

This is not to say that Marcel agrees with the madam's assessment of her girl.[3] Far from it, because of what he hears and not what he sees. Just as he will hear the grunts of Jupien and Charlus at the beginning of *Sodome et Gomorrhe* and know, without any visual confirmation, that what he is hearing is, in fact, "homosexuality," he hears Rachel's vulgarity and knows that she is not for him. Overhearing Rachel's conversation with the madam, Marcel finds the former common, despite an intelligent air, and he is not at all attracted to her. Even so, endlessly polite, Marcel allows that one day perhaps he will come to the brothel for Rachel alone:

Each time I promised the madam, who proposed her to me with a particular insistence praising her great intelligence and her knowledge [*sa grande intelligence et son instruction*], that I would come with the express purpose of meeting Rachel, whom I had nicknamed "Rachel quand du Seigneur." (1:567)

This promised version of the meeting never takes place, and Marcel never has carnal relations with Rachel. Much later, Marcel will meet and get to know Rachel after she has become Saint-Loup's mistress. Given what happens in the novel, it would probably have been a violation of a taboo for Marcel and Saint-Loup to have had carnal relations with the same woman because that would have been too close to an enunciation of the homoerotic bond between them. It is enough for Marcel to have had the possibility of having sex with Rachel or for him to have had a crush on Gilberte, the future wife of Saint-Loup, for this possibility to be evoked, in a safe way, but not actualized. There is no sexual rivalry between the two men, and to say that Saint-Loup bests Marcel with women is far from the narrative truth of the writing, which is the taboo that is of the homoerotic bond between the two.

As is often the case in the *Recherche*, a poetic detail in the novel is overdetermined by a plethora of connotative references. Since many narrative lines crisscross at any moment, a detail may seem to take on importance by being at that node. At this point in *A l'ombre*, it may be of little import that Rachel is Jewish, or is said to be Jewish; it may simply be a way of singling her out from the crowd, so that when she becomes Robert's mistress, the readers will remember that and have a singularity on which to focus. That is not sufficient, for the references to Judaism are not innocent in a novel that makes much of the Dreyfus Affair. There will be echoes of her Jewishness throughout the rest of the novel, as being Jewish becomes, through the explosion of the Dreyfus Affair, a stigmatized social quality. Being Jewish becomes part of a barometric system for social rise and fall. At the very least, being a Jewish woman means participating in an exchange system in which religion is whitewashed by money, power, or influence: "At the time I frequented Mme Swann, the Dreyfus Affair had not yet exploded, and certain great Jews were quite powerful. None was more powerful than Sir Rufus Israels, whose wife, Lady Israels, was Swann's aunt" (1:508).

This power fits into a grid or pattern far more complicated than social structure or social class. It is what the narrator will refer to in his discussion of the societal kaleidoscope, which turns to bring new patterns into play, as various qualities or details cause a character to move higher or lower in the social pattern:

But like kaleidoscopes that turn from time to time, society successfully rearranges elements that one had thought immutable to form another figure from them. When I had not yet made my first communion, upright women were stupefied to meet an elegant Jewess as they paid their calls. These new patterns of the kaleidoscope are produced by what a philosopher would call a change in criteria. The Dreyfus affair brought about a new one sometime after I began to frequent Mme Swann, and the kaleidoscope spun its little glass bits around once more. Everything that was Jewish fell, even the elegant woman, and obscure nationalists arose to take her/its place.[4] (1:507–508)

Rachel will be in part a barometer of the state or position of the Jew in the novel, as she is, by her very station in life, the purest Jewish "commodity" who, like the eponymous operatic heroine before her, can be exchanged from hand to hand. Like a commodity, a Jewish woman can be given and received; representative of the mercantile system itself, Rachel epitomizes the exchange. At the same time, because of the reference to the operatic heroine, this giving of the Jewish woman as object also means a giving of Jewishness itself. Further on, readers will discover how this gift of Jewishness operates. At this point in the novel, it is too early to tell her fortunes or even her nature, though the vulgarity is certainly as much of a clue as anything

else. Here, there is little more than the chance encounter that pre-
pares the longer meeting, much as the encounter between the young
Marcel and "the lady in pink" (a.k.a. Odette) in his Uncle Octave's
bachelor apartment is the figure of the relation between Odette and
Swann in "Un Amour de Swann." The madam is also playing the
card of the stereotypical exoticism associated with a Jewish woman
subjugated to the will of a non-Jewish man.

Rachel is Jewish by hearsay: the madam says Rachel is Jewish, but
there is no confirmation of the Jewishness of the character. The narrator underlines the problem of Rachel's Jewishness by a reference
to the opera: "But the madam, who did not know Halévy's opera, ignored why I had made a habit of saying: 'Rachel, quand du
Seigneur'" (1:567). Marcel's motivation for using that nickname
echoes his grandfather's own musical commentary on Marcel's Jewish friends. This is consonant with one of the rules of thumb for the
novel, which is that Marcel often does things because others before
him have done the same or similar things: the dynamics of his love
affair with Albertine, for example, are patterned to a great extent on
the patterns of jealousy, longing, and desire of Swann for Odette in
"Un Amour de Swann." So with this operatic reference, Marcel is
doing what his grandfather used to do. In Combray, precisely at the
point at which the very same Bloch has made a terrible impression
on the family of Marcel, the latter lets us in on his grandfather's idio-
syncratic behavior:

It is true that my grandfather believed that every time I got closer to one of
my friends than to another, it was always a Jew, something that would not
have displeased him in principle—even his friend Swann was of Jewish origin—if he did not find that I did not usually choose the friend from among
the best. Thus, when I brought home a new friend, it was a rare occasion on
which he did not hum: "Oh God of our fathers [*O Dieu de nos pères*]" from *La
Juive*, or "Israel, break thy chain [*Israël, romps ta chaîne*]." Naturally, he sang
only the music [*ne chantant que l'air naturellement*]. (1:90)

If the pattern of remarking a Jew through a reference to opera,
even to that specific opera, is part of the origin of this reference to
the opera, it is not the only explanation. For Marcel is certainly not
imitating his grandfather's ambiguous, ironic commentary on Jews.
Instead, he takes the gesture of reference to the opera and translates

it into an ironic commentary on who is and who is not Jewish. There
is the crux of the problem. For though the opera is entitled *La Juive*,
it is precisely at this point in the opera that it becomes clear that she
is not a Jewess, at least by birth.[5] But what of "Rachel quand du
Seigneur"? The narrator says that it was because she was Jewish that
the madam called her Rachel; by nicknaming her "Rachel quand du
Seigneur," by *baptizing* her "Rachel quand du Seigneur," Marcel is
making her out as not being a Jewess, a fact that he underlines by indicating that the madam did not know the opera in question. Implicitly, then, we are all supposed to be familiar enough with the
opera to realize the depth of the commentary. In referring to her
through a figure from the opera, in naming her, he is putting her religious background in doubt.

The word "naturellement" in the quotation about the grandfather's behavior is also problematic and ambiguous. It means, quite
naturally, that it was normal for the grandfather to sing only the
melody and not the words. Here, "naturally" means "artificially," i.e.,
out of culture, out of the laws of etiquette. The words remain silent,
for spoken or sung they would be an affront to all who might hear
them; a joke already in dubious taste becomes a prejudicial remark
when voiced. The words are there, haunting those who hear the
melody, those who naturally would have recourse to those words
when they hear the melody, those for whom, therefore, there is a
natural agreement with the somewhat prejudicial remark. Thus does
music play a new revelatory role in the novel in which it naturally
hides yet reveals the prejudices of high culture. It will be with the explosion of the Dreyfus Affair that high culture will not be able to
maintain its natural silence that tells all. Naturally, too, means that it
was a natural thing to have such a position, that by his very nature,
the grandfather, who is not "naturally" anti-Semitic, given his friendship with Swann's father, still naturally assumes that position of difference from and commentary on the Semitic position, for it is natural for a non-Jew to maintain that position. It is as if, within the
fulfillment of the natural law that is Christianity and its secular incarnation in the state, even in the Third Republic, the nature of law,
of meaning, of logic, and of culture naturally leads to a comment, albeit a nonvoiced one, rendered only melodically, on the other who
has not accepted that natural law.

What does it mean to say that in her baptism as "Rachel quand du Seigneur," this character is and/or is not Jewish? That is, ultimately, the most banal explanation, though in any case, it makes the reader focus on the act of nomination: someone is Jewish because she is said (by the madam) to be Jewish, and a similar act of nomination (by Marcel) makes her not Jewish. The magic of naming in Proust, as illustrated by the section of *Du côté de chez Swann* entitled "Noms du pays: le nom," is thus buttressed by a fundamental ambiguity in the problematics of naming, not the least of whose manifestations is the anonymity of two key characters, "l'amie de Mlle Vinteuil" and Marcel himself. Generally, the ambiguity of such nomination is generalized into an ambiguity of reference that echoes at various points in the novel, in which saying or indicating, rather than confirming a state, makes matters undecidedly ambiguous: Dreyfus's guilt or innocence, various characters' insistence on Charlus's heterosexuality, Swann's questioning of Odette, and the narrator's questioning of Albertine about her lesbian adventures. In each case, the statement of one of two alternatives always implies not a solution to the question but a *remise-en-question*, a remarking of the ambiguity.

So it is not a question of whether, on the most banal plane, Rachel is or is not Jewish. The reference shows that there are different theories about being a Jew, and more specifically, about who may be qualified as being a Jewess. Proust, who is going to build a poetics on such ambiguities, is focusing on the difficult and often contradictory nature of that categorization. There is no way of knowing if Rachel is really Jewish. Here, she does not speak, except to let the madam know that she is available; and it is the madam who calls her Rachel. It is not even certain if that is her name, or simply just another nickname, like "Red," given to a redhead. Or even if she is merely supposed to incarnate a fantasy and a sellable quality for clients as she plays the role of the exotic Jewish prostitute, while actually being a French Catholic or something else. As she is without a family—significantly, she is the only important Jewish character in the book without a family—one can never know for certain whether she is Jewish or not.

Who in fact is Jewish, and who is not? It is a point important in the extreme in wars of religion, in shibboleths, in grand opera, and in novels where a certain number of characters have features or traits

that separate them from the normative world of the contemporaneous population of France.[6] Is being Jewish genetic, or is it a social
construct? Is it religious or ethnic? Is one Jewish in the same way
that one is a man or a woman, in the same way that one is gay or
straight? Is being a Jewish woman indicated by the same signs as
those conventionally used for indicating a Jewish man?

Excluded from the covenant and unmarked by any circumcision,
the Jewish woman has to be said to be Jewish by some other: she
must be interpellated, called, or named as a Jew. The Jewish woman
is pointed to, indicated by word or by deed as the object of a discourse that defines and classifies, as the receiver of a discourse that
takes her to be Jewish. In turn, she has the power to determine who
else is Jewish. Or, at least, that is Jewish teaching. Judaism is a birthright passed through the mother. Judaism is a thing of the blood,
then, and it is the blood of the mother that is, according to Jewish
law, the only certain blood line there is, something to which we shall
return shortly.

Still, the question is not so easily answered, for there are competing theories of who is Jewish and who is not Jewish. The Jewish
woman is the one spoken to, spoken about, or written to. She is interpellated: the mother of the author, a Jewish woman assimilated
into non-Jewish, bourgeois, French society. Or there is the example
of Sarah, Abraham's wife, that can be seen in one of the many biblical images of the *Recherche*. In this case, it is a description of Marcel's
father looking like the figure of Abraham speaking to Sarah (1:36), as
the scene is figured in an engraving given to Marcel by Swann, a kind
of gift that is an example of the aesthetic "thickness" already noted.
The Jewish woman is quite literally before the law: before the writing
of the book, before the giving of the law to Moses, and before the
Jews become the people of the book. Like the mother of the author,
Sarah is there before the book and before any law of writing interferes with the production according to the rules of a society that has
no room for this interpellation.

Sarah and the mother of the author are before the act of writing.
Perfect inversion of that law, the position of Rachel is the reversal of
the Jewish paradigm: she is called Rachel by the madam because she
is Jewish. Her naming, her legitimacy, come after the act of nomination that says who she is, what she does, and who she must be. As

soon as the act of writing takes place, the appeal to the Jewish woman becomes not an act of invocation or an apostrophe to some pure perfection but an ambiguous naming: not a calling to but a categorization. For there are two different versions of deciding who is Jewish and who is not. According to the Jewish religion, as described in the tract of Kedoshim (in the *Gemara* [39.B]), the decision depends on the identity of the mother. If the mother of a child is Jewish, the child is considered to be Jewish. In a contrary fashion, if the mother of a child is not Jewish, regardless of the identity of the father, the child is not considered, at least in Orthodox circles, to be Jewish.

That matrilineal, all-or-nothing scenario does not appear as such in the novel: one might speculate that this pure maternity is what Proust cannot or will not represent in his writing. In its stead come two opposing theories of who is Jewish, two mechanisms of assimilation, though one leans toward an amalgamation of bloodlines and the other toward a view of racial purity. In one scenario, a character is Jewish because one of her parents is Jewish. Interestingly enough, the first character referred to outside the family circle of Marcel's family is a character who can be seen in this light: Mme de Saint-Loup (1:7), once Gilberte Swann, and thus Jewish through her biological father. Throughout the novel, there is an attempt to play down this bloodline by means of Odette's remarriage: Gilberte becomes Mlle de Forcheville, purified, as it were, of her paternal Jewishness, even unto her inheritance, which, though actually coming to her from Swann, everyone wrongly believes to be from Forcheville.

This is what one could call the degree zero of mixed blood. Unremarked and unremarkable, the character is three-eighths Jewish the same way the author of the book is half-Jewish.[7] In and of itself, there is nothing to that statement about a mathematics of blood and marriage. Opposed to this standard view of Jewishness that corresponds to a simple arithmetic problem, as remarriages determine the status of "half" and "step" siblings through the same mathematics, there is a conception of Jewishness that is more like the arguments of racial purity being expounded at the end of the nineteenth century by such writers as Drumont and Gobineau. In this scenario, the character is Jewish by infection, by intimation, by hints, or by allusions. Like any viral infection, like vampirism, one drop of Jewish blood is enough to adulterate a whole race: "as if it were a question of determining the infinitesimal quantity of 'Jewish blood' with a microscope" (2:106). Since Jewishness may be borne by a name, it is not necessary to have blood for there to be a Jewish infection. As the name is always a magical evocation of matter in the *Recherche*, it can sometimes be enough to convert or pervert the character:

"It really is what one says: Marsantes, *Mater Semita*, it smells of the race [*ça sent la race*]," answered Rachel repeating an etymology that depended on a great misinterpretation. For *semita* means "pathway [*sente*]" and not "Semite." But nationalists applied it to Saint-Loup because of the pro-Dreyfus opinions that he in fact owed to the actress. (And she was less qualified than anyone to treat Mme de Marsantes as a Jewess, for the ethnographers of society could not muster anything more Jewish in her than her relation to the Lévy-Mirepoix.) (2:476–77)

Thus, for Rachel, Madame de Marsantes becomes Jewish, not because of some distant relation to a Jewish family, whose name in fact suggests a mixture—*mirepoix* being a dice of aromatic vegetables—but with whom she has no direct filiation and therefore of whose blood she shares not a drop. As for Rachel herself, the naming of a woman as Jewish makes her suspect of being Jewish. Within the bloodlines and the naming process, just one drop of Semitic blood—or even one Semitic-sounding etymology—taints the whole individual. In her role as object of the dominant discourses, Rachel herself repeats those same discourses, albeit falsely in this case, naming someone as Jewish who is not Jewish at all.

This fear of Jewish blood, or, more precisely, this fear of the infection of the whole race by a Jewish woman, or even by a woman who has had intercourse with a Jewish man, is repeated in the *Recherche*. The two theories become conflated: whereas according to Judaism, the woman is the guarantee of the Jewishness of the child and whereas, according to the fear of the virulent spread of Jewish influence, one drop of Jewish blood can taint a whole Christian population, there is a quick remedy, but it has to be an antidote to both theories:

If the Prince de Guermantes received Swann, whose friend he had been forever, it is because, knowing that Swann's Protestant grandmother, married to a Jew, had been the mistress of the Duc de Berri; he thus tried from time to time to believe in the legend that made Swann's father the illegitimate child of the prince. According to this hypothesis, which was moreover false, Swann, son of a Catholic, who was himself the son of a Bourbon father and a Catholic mother, was pure Christian. (3:68)

Like his daughter purified of her Jewish money by the false beliefs of society at large, Swann himself becomes a changeling, a pure Christian in this fantasized world created by the Prince de Guermantes. It is a world quite similar to the fantasized world of pure heterosexuality that is the projected world of many of the characters in the novel, until the narrator's acts and eyes discover the truth behind the tailor's door, the characters' lies, or the facade of a heterosexual marriage covering up a character's genuine taste for inversion. While being Jewish and being homosexual are not absolutely parallel in the novel, with a divergence that is *a fortiori* true for the laws governing the representation of homosexuality and those for Judaism, there is a homology between the way in which each of those is exposed or hidden at any given point.

This virulent Judaism attacks blood, name, and reputation; it produces fantasies and determines roles and behaviors. Specifically, although in the mind of the Prince de Guermantes, Swann from time to time becomes a true Christian, it is precisely with the women of the novel that the ambiguity is a problem constantly renewed yet never resolved. Swann is and always will be Jewish: despite the Prince's episodic beliefs, he knows that it is only a passing fancy or an act of transparent self-delusion; most of the time the Prince de Guermantes does not believe that Swann is anything but Jewish. At any given moment, the man can be either Jewish or not Jewish; he cannot be both at the same time. Similarly, Dreyfus is either innocent or guilty. Regardless of how unheroic a character he may be, the innocence of the individual cannot be tainted by a measure of guilt: "'In any case,' the Duchess interrupted, 'if this Dreyfus is innocent, he hardly proves it. What idiotic, overblown letters he writes from his island. . . . What a shame for [Dreyfus's supporters] that they cannot change innocents'" (2:356). There is a precedent for the all-or-nothing Judaism of a character, which is the circumcision, the mark of the covenant, performed on the male and given to him as a mark of that covenant. No such mark is given the woman; in this world in which everyone may be suspected at one point or another of being Jewish, homosexual, or pro-Dreyfus, the woman can always be harboring a bit of Jewishness, for no cutting remark belongs to her. Whereas Swann is or is not Jewish, Madame de Marsantes may be a bit Jewish, by her name, by her distant relation, or by her son's pro-Dreyfus stance. Any of those is enough to make her *mater semita*.

By extension, it is not only those women suspected of having Jewish blood or a Jewish name who are possibly Jewish but also those who are said to be Jewish. By extension then, if a woman is compared to a Jew, she too may be considered to be Jewish. Such is the case for Odette, for whom Swann finds Old Testament comparisons. Odette will become somewhat Jewish because her husband is Jewish, but, even before that, she becomes Jewish because Swann compares her to a biblical figure. In making these comparisons, he becomes, in the oddest sense, her mother—for being Jewish comes through the mother—and the source of Odette's aestheticized Judaism: "She struck Swann by her resemblance to the figure of Zipporah, Jethro's daughter, who can be seen in a fresco in the Sistine Chapel" (1:219). But it is no different than for the Guermantes women, and specifically, the epitome of the Guermantes woman, the Duchesse de Guermantes, for she and her line have lent their traits to a figuration of a Jewish woman in a stained-glass window in the church in Combray: "According to tradition, Ahasuerus was given the features of a king of France and Esther, those of a Guermantes lady with whom he was in love" (1:60).

The two stories are exactly the same: in each case, an artistic representation of a Jewish woman is likened to a non-Jewish woman. In the case of the church in Combray, the Christian woman has provided the model for the features of Esther; later incarnations of that same woman resemble not the absent, unfigured ancestors but the stained-glass window. In the case of the Sistine Chapel, undoubtedly it was another Christian woman, this time unknown, who served as a model for the artist. But in any case, Swann visits the features of the non-Jewish Jewish woman (i.e., the Christian, serving as a model for the Jew) on Odette, who disappears behind the features ascribed to the Jewish woman: "He placed on his worktable, as if it were a photograph of Odette, a reproduction of Jethro's daughter" (1:221). It little matters what the real Odette looks like, Swann has a picture of Zipporah to figure this Jewish, non-Jewish woman for him.

The very images collapse, the distinctions disappear, and the alternation between Jewish and non-Jewish women amalgamates into one issue of the somewhat Jewish woman. Swann places a "reproduction of Jethro's daughter," not of the "figure of Jethro's daughter," on his worktable. Like Swann, who has made Odette into a Jewish woman through his comparison, Zipporah herself becomes Odette's Jewish mother. Elsewhere, Swann repeats the same gesture. At one point, the narrator notes in "Un Amour de Swann": "Or she would look at him broodingly, and he would see a face worthy of figuring in Botticelli's *Life of Moses*" (1:234). As if to prove that the infection by Judaism is never wholly absent from the figuration of the woman, even the ultimate analogy with the episodes of Christian women is tainted by a Jewishness hard to deny. Though starting with the pagan (and presumably safe for Christians) allegory of spring, this point is a touchstone to identify Botticelli for us. The narrator moves us toward a reverse figuration of Jesus, or more specifically, Mary and Anne:

She thus recalled even more than he usually thought, the figures of women by the painter of the Primavera. At that moment she had their beaten, bereft faces that seemed to succumb under the weight of a burden too heavy for them, simply when they let the baby Jesus play with a pomegranate or watch Moses pour water in a trough. (1:276)

Odette's real origin is hidden behind a sea of comparisons that identify her as a Jewish woman. All the marks are there: her daughter is Jewish, according to one theory; her son-in-law is Jewish, according to another.

Yes, but in specific, what is the nature of this first comparison between Odette and a Jewish woman, the one to which all others implicitly refer? As if by chance, she is compared to a representation of Zipporah, Jethro's daughter. Although she is first identified as someone's daughter, she is even more well known to any reader of the Bible as being someone's wife and someone's mother: for she is Moses' wife, and she bears him a son. Of no distinct identity herself, she is the Jewish Ur-mother who insists, who remarks her son as Jewish, as a child of the covenant, even before the law is given: "Then Zipporah took a flint, and cut off the foreskin of her son, and cast it at his feet; and she said: 'Surely a bridegroom of blood art thou to me.' So He let him alone. Then she said: 'A bridegroom of blood in regard of the circumcision" (Ex. 4:25–26).[8] It is Zipporah then who reinscribes the covenant between God and the Jewish people by performing a ritual circumcision that comes close to a castration scenario and by making her son her husband. It is surely a scenario to give pause to all readers of Proust: if all Combray comes out of a cup of tea, surely all the chains of Oedipal drama and identity relate to this startling image of Odette as Zipporah the mother-and-circumciser.

The image of Odette as Zipporah helps make the Oedipal crisis a literary construct: Proust's writing is the manifestation of Oedipal trauma not only because the author/narrator/character has Oedipal trauma (ultimately a banal statement) but also, and more importantly, because the story of circumcision is a literary trauma within the novel. By Judaizing Odette through the intermediate of aesthetics, Proust-Swann invests her with a fantastic power and makes her the fantasized other mother of a precocious Oedipus who succeeds in becoming his mother's husband. Odette replaces the real, Jewish mother (Madame Proust) who is dead, the melancholic and mourning-inspiring figure, now absent in the real world, who is the ultimate addressee of the author's writing. Odette replaces the de-Judaized, bourgeois mother of Marcel, she who does not answer his plaintive notes, she who refuses the Oedipal drama's resolution in his favor. Neither bourgeois nor Jewish at the beginning of the *Recherche*, Odette is made Jewish by the insistence of a Jewish man (Swann) that she is like a Jewish woman.

Zipporah is the embodiment of the Jewish woman who can reaffirm her blood, her child's blood, and their Jewishness by the act of circumcision. Zipporah *is* the circumcision of which Odette becomes the eventual incarnation. If the Jewish woman silently marked or unmarked as Jewish passes unnoticed, it is now the Jewish woman or her avatar who becomes the very *being* of the circumcision. Made Jewish by Swann, Odette is before the law, the law of the book, the law of production that will be the rest of the *Recherche*. It is Odette as Zipporah who is the minimal and the sufficient, agent of the law, even before it is detailed. The Jewish woman ensures that others become Jewish; Odette ensures the continuation of the inscription of the mark, the inscription of the writing, and the maintenance of the covenant.

Two images then form the cornerstone of the representation of the Jewish woman in this novel. Two images tell us a way to read the novel, a way doubly marked by naming and by the act of circumcision. The Jewish woman, then, who cannot stand alone is the one who ensures continuity and separation, marking and difference, the nondisjunction of opposites, and the endless difference of the writing from itself. Rachel or Zipporah, Odette or "Rachel quand du Seigneur," the Jewish woman is one of the singular motive forces of a novel that depend to a great extent on those acts of nomination and separation. In the end then, it is she that remains one of the primary motors of textual production in this most and least Jewish of novels.

With Proust's figure of the Jewess comes the final turn of the realist kaleidoscope. The figure is no longer assimilated or controlled fully by the whitening, homogenizing, and straightening of the realist machine. While the Jewish figure maintains a heterogeneity never fully submitted to the system, in narrative terms, this heterogeneity means that what is figure and what is narrative are never fully distinguished from each other. Instead of an analysis of the construction of homosexuality in the *Recherche*, it is fitting to close this book with an analysis of the other great construction of homosexuality of the time, as found in the work of André Gide.

## II.  Following Gide

The trajectory of this book starts with the creation of a new, modern woman, one who can somehow participate in the same system of consummation and hence have a similar "effet de sujet" as the subject of a phallocratic order, even if she is still deemed secondary when related to him. After that, the fulfillment of realism occurs in an extension to the transcendental figures that serve as parameters that come under challenge and that are themselves ultimately seen as immanent and not transcendental, the *sine qua non* for the realist model of the universe. Time and space, and good and evil, must themselves become figures that realism can produce within its aesthetic and its system of production. Realism turns to decadence: having extended itself as far as possible, realism slows to stasis in time: the other takes longer and longer to explain. In the return of realism, away from the decadent, and toward a renormalization of the other, there are two final figures, figures that were always there but that were somehow eclipsed in the search for acclimating the exotic. These figures are the Jew and the homosexual. Hence this final chapter. Significantly, it will not be after realism has been fully transformed into a modernist aesthetic that the last great other, the non-Caucasian, will ever be dealt with.

For André Gide, finally writing his one novel, *Les Faux-Monnayeurs*, a quarter of a century after his "récit," *L'Immoraliste*, narrative forms themselves seem resistant to certain strains that one might otherwise have expected to fashion his work in a more radical manner. In specific, given the subject of *L'Immoraliste* and its subsequent retellings, given the daring of *Corydon* and the flirting with homoerotic imagery in his *Les Caves du Vatican*, one might have expected figures of homosexuality to loom far more largely than they do in *Les Faux-Monnayeurs*. While material is obviously there in the character of Oncle Édouard, the figure does not, for example, match what Proust was doing at roughly the same time, and this, despite the rendering of the character as the figure of the novelist in a Gidean *mise-en-abyme*.

While not directly discussing *Les Faux-Monnayeurs*, Naomi Segal constructs her reading of "the utterance of homosexual desire" on the elision of women in *Les Nourritures terrestres*, *L'Immoraliste*, *La Porte étroite*, and *Et nunc manet in te*. For Segal, there is an "endless chain of male doubles"; the woman must "die so that the male narrator can tell 'his' story"; and there is the "desire to absorb what is the woman's especially her voice, to destroy it in her and reproduce it as Gide's own authorship" (62). How then does one account for the difference of *Les Faux-Monnayeurs*? There is a second set of homosexual works, starting with other scenarios in *L'Immoraliste*, running through *Si le grain ne meurt* and *Les Caves du Vatican*, and especially illustrated by *Les Faux-Monnayeurs*, which depends neither on murder nor on throwing one's voice. Each in its own way celebrates a discourse that cannot yet fully exist but that comes to exist through these praxes. While respecting the categories of realism, Gide still seeks to expand them here, in which the vocabulary of a free homosexuality, nonmisogynistic in nature or origin, is about to happen.

It is my hypothesis that Gide found the structures of narrative themselves so infused with the paradigms of normative heterosexuality that two things occurred as he wrote both *Les Caves du Vatican* and *Les Faux-Monnayeurs*. First, the writing itself is an act of resistance to or a struggle against these norms. Gide's own belatedness in his novel writing may be a recognition of that situation: until Gide himself felt comfortable with the usual fictionalization process that takes an uncomfortable truth and makes a novel of it, homosexuality could be told only as a confession, as a "non-novel," albeit still with all the attendant parameters of fiction. And, second, the eruption of figures of homoeroticism and homosexuality in the Gidean narratives mentioned produces a strain in the writing, a folding-over, and a resistance by narrative to these eruptive figures as well as a site of narrative irritation.

One could argue the converse too: having said all there is to say about the subject of homosexuality in *Corydon* in an apologistic mode and having himself "come out" in *Si le grain ne meurt*, there is no need to dwell on Édouard's homosexuality in *Les Faux-Monnayeurs*. This is a seductive position: Édouard is just homosexual, no more no less. It is uncomplicated and straightforward. But, as appealing as this is, it does not work: Édouard is not homosexual alone: he is opposed by Gide to the bad homosexual, the corrupter of souls, given in the character of Robert de Passavant, whose punning last name could mean "precursor" and could thus allude to Wilde on a semiotic level as much as the character seems to allude to him on a semantic one. Édouard's purity, though never challenged directly, is certainly threatened by exposure: at the end of a scene in which he has been spying on his own nephew, the nephew, on meeting him officially, threatens to accuse his uncle of having made advances. Finally, there is a compelling textual reason: Gide originally intended *Les Faux-Monnayeurs* to be built on the continuation of the character of Lafcadio from *Les Caves du Vatican*. The homoerotic subtext of that work will become sublimated as Gide transforms and whitens his novel.[9] The key figures of desire in these works, Lafcadio and Édouard, negotiate the various figures of resistance to a heterosexual norming and how they engage questions of alternative sexuality and alternative narrative. As two characters among many in Gide's writing who question the role of reproduction, the figure of paternity, the nature of the truth, and the sense of the self, all these expressed through a narrative that must conform to some extent to external norms, Lafcadio and Édouard incarnate the Gidean figure of resistance to the "problem of heterosexuality."

### III. On the Wilde Side

André Gide starts off the new year in 1892 with an extraordinary statement in which he writes that "I believe that Wilde did me only wrong. With him I unlearned how to think" (*Journal 1887*:148). A chilling statement three years before the scandal erupts in which the Marquis of Queensberry will, in one of the most famous illiterate moments in literary history, accuse Oscar Wilde of "posing as a somdomite" [sic]. Wilde's influence must have been extraordinary, for the two had met only five weeks before, on 27 November 1891. In the ensuing month of December, Gide and Wilde seem to have gotten together eight additional times. Such were Wilde's talents that, in these nine meetings, he had so fully corrupted Gide that the latter managed to forget all his years of learning, training, and discipline. Over three years before the Wilde scandal, it was also a year and a half before Gide's first trip to North Africa in the fall of 1893. Significantly, while Wilde and Douglas had met briefly in the fall of 1891, they were not at all good acquaintances, and their real contact began only in the spring of 1892 (Dollimore 3–18).

So the Wilde that Gide meets and who initially impresses him, as a Wilde without "THE" scandal, a Wilde without a flagrant love affair with Bosie, a married man riding toward the pinnacle of success with both *Dorian Grey*, which had appeared in 1891, and *Lady Windermere's Fan. Salomé* was on the writing table; *The Importance of Being Earnest* was in the future. The Wilde whom Gide meets is a modest success but not the darling of the London theater. He was also nominally the married, heterosexual Wilde, a person given to aestheticism (but certainly not alone in that in the gay nineties), posing (in the sense of *poseur*), and outrageous remarks. Taking all things into consideration, Wilde was certainly less scandalous than Paul Verlaine, for example. Yet Gide moves from adoration to accusation in five short weeks.

What happens? Did Wilde, one wonders, make a pass at Gide? Indicate morals other than upright Victorian ones? Seduce a waiter? Not as far as anyone can tell. Writing of a later encounter in Blidah,

Gide attests to Wilde's propriety: "With me, Wilde had completely kept his guard [*Wilde avait observé jusqu'à ce jour vis-à-vis de moi une parfaite réserve*]" (*Grain* 299). Wilde was certainly not yet the satanic figure painted during the trial and in the general opprobrium that surrounded it. At the moment of which Gide is writing, things had been stirred up, and Wilde, according to Gide, was the subject of gossip in literary circles in Paris. The earlier encounters seem to have been perfectly correct. Still, Gide turns.

What could he have seen in Wilde, three years earlier? What is there for which there are no name, no language, and no justification? Obviously there was some language, the language of gossip, but no official language or any literary discourse *à la hauteur* that could say what was being said. For Gide, it would appear, the only valid discourse was that literary one; knowing what was being gossiped about, half-said and half-understood, both informed him and deprived him of information. There was nothing to read in that month, at least not for Gide, for Gide could not read English. As late as this encounter in Algeria, several years later, Gide says that he did not know a word of English (*Grain* 301). If in the later encounter, Wilde chose to break the rules of propriety or *bienséance* by making comments (in French, with a slight accent that, according to Gide, he affected) about young Arab men, nothing of the kind seems to have taken place in the first set of encounters at the end of 1891.

At the later date, and this despite his earlier belief that Wilde had done him wrong, Gide accepts Wilde's company, though not without criticism, his mores, his adventures, and his tutelage. As Gide says in a general sense, "the great pleasure of a debauchee is to bring [others] into debauchery" (*Grain* 308). Or, as Emily Apter puts it, "Gide's homosexual initiation in North Africa was under the tutelage of Oscar Wilde" (27). Let us look at the apprenticeship. Wilde overtly proposes a young man to Gide:

—Dear [in English in the text], do you want the little musician?
Oh! The alley was dark. I thought I'd lose heart; what a stiffening of courage was necessary to answer: "Yes," and in what a strangled voice. (307)

Gide says yes, or "oui," for they are speaking in French, but he can barely say it. The admission, the assent, strangles him; he cannot manage to open his mouth or throat, as if, through the absence of language and light—the dark alley, the instant aphasia—the yes would disappear. But courage was stiffening, even if nothing else was, though the stirrings were there. Wilde seduces him into the arms of another and makes him hear himself as a homosexual (or pederast, for it little matters at the moment). Every other sexual encounter, at least according to the older Gide writing his memoirs, was a search for repetition of this one (*Grain* 309). Other adventures follow, but none is as good. The same love object, Mohammed, continues to occupy a strange position with Gide, long after the Wilde affair is over. Two years later, Gide, Mohammed, and Gide's friend, Daniel B., check into a *hotel de passe*, and Gide signs the register, most oddly, with a Jewish name: "Cesar Bloch." In the hotel room, Daniel takes Mohammed in his arms and proceeds to have his way with the Maghrebin youth, as Gide looks on (311).

For André Gide, the importance was in not being Oscar. Encountered more than the Frenchman would like, fled when the notoriety became too outrageous, Oscar Wilde was the repository of both seduction and evil, the artist of what would today be called a "lifestyle" that both called to Gide and repelled him at the same time. Wilde was the immoralist, the one who dared to be different, but the one who, for all his difference and all his outrageous excess, became not so much a martyr to the cause of homosexuality but a figure, even before his incarceration, whose very presence was dangerous. Only half a generation older than Gide, Wilde was, perhaps, already dissipated when the two authors first met and already on his spiral toward dissolution, prison, and an untimely death. Gide, in contrast, struggling to free himself from an armoire full of monsters had barely written his first important pieces, had begun to be known, but would not publish *L'Immoraliste* until after Wilde's death.

Fryer's book on the Wilde-Gide friendship tells readers that there really was not much there: much of the book has them going their separate ways and having a chance meeting here and there, such as the encounter that took place in January, 1895 in Blidah. Supposedly friends with Wilde, Gide found himself checking out of a hotel in Blidah in January, when he discovered that Wilde and Douglas were recent arrivals at the same hotel. Erasing his name from the list, he headed toward the station, had second thoughts, went back, and spent the evening with the two (Fryer 110–13). Immediately recalling the occasion, Gide writes a letter to his mother in which he notes that Wilde and Douglas are on "the Index" in London and Paris and in which he compares Wilde's relationship to Vautrin's, but not in *Le Père Goriot*.[10]

There also seems to be a strange ambivalence and ambiguity about the physical nature of the relations in which the three main characters are involved. As Fryer notes (46), "Douglas was an active sodomite, who practised buggery with rent-boys; Oscar was not. Nothing of that kind appears to have taken place between the two of them." Fryer's language may be taken at face value: Douglas participated in anal intercourse. In February, 1895, Gide and Douglas are at Biskra at the same time, and Douglas has an effeminate (pre-)adolescent, named Ali, in tow. Ostensibly, the active/passive relations are the same. Douglas tolerates Ali's trysts with a local shepherd boy but flies into a rage when he goes to bed with a woman (130). So Ali functions perhaps as the passive sodomite, to use Fryer's terms, for Douglas but manages to get it up for the shepherd (or perhaps it is the other way around) and Mériem, "whom André, Paul Laurens, and Pierre Louÿs had all enjoyed" (130). If "Oscar was not" an active sodomite, he was certainly not a passive sodomite, so perhaps he did nothing. Rather than being offended then at having been accused of "posing as a sodomite," he should perhaps have rejoiced.

This fuzzy language is visited by Fryer on Gide, in a discussion of Gide's bedtime adventures. As Fryer remarks (73), "Most of André's and Paul's little visitors were on the wrong side of puberty, as moralists these days would view it. Not that André's paedophilia seems to have taken on any physical dimension. Many of his future sexual partners would range between the ages of fourteen to seventeen, with the initiative coming from the adolescent himself." What could this mean? There is certainly a distinction to be made between "the wrong side of puberty," which one would understand as someone who is still biologically a child, and someone who has not reached the age of majority, i.e., someone who is biologically a man but who is still legally a minor. In many cases, there is a third category, between the age of consent, which in contemporary Europe, often is at 15 or 16, and the age of majority, still set at 18–21, depending on the situation and the country. Maybe Fryer means just that, that there were a number of prepubescent boys whom Gide took pleasure in looking at and not touching. But as he got older, Gide often chose someone who was the right side of puberty but the wrong side of the age of majority, according to prevailing Western standards of the time. In any case, Gide finally figured things out. Ten years later, he has graduated from prepubescent boys to an adolescent young man and moved from the sotadic zone in which anything goes, in which people routinely remain undefined along sexual lines, to Europe, where things are clear. As Fryer says, "The affair with 'M' ["a tennis-playing teenager" in 1905] helped André to understand that there was more to homosexuality than physical lust for boys. As Oscar had done before him, André now read more widely classical Greek and Roman authors to find clearer definitions of and justifications for man-boy love" (229).

The words are there if only they can be read. In his letter to his mother, Gide uses loaded vocabulary like "the Index" and a reference to Balzac's Vautrin. The latter is extremely clear: if it is not the Vautrin of *Le Père Goriot*, in which the character entertains a fond but chaste relationship with the very heterosexual Eugène de Rastignac, it is the Vautrin of *Illusions perdues* and *Splendeurs et misères des courtisanes*, in which the hapless hero, Lucien de Rubempré serves as catamite to the older man. Never mind that Lucien also has what would today be called heterosexual relationships. Gide knew that his mother would understand the references. Wilde and Douglas are like the active homosexuals—i.e., homosexuals who act on their desires in a physical sense—that Balzac has described in Vautrin and Rubempré. Gide does not need to spell it out; it would be considered vulgar, crude, and inappropriate, not only to one's mother but also to almost anyone at all. Gide has simply said that Oscar and Douglas are what everyone knows they are; he has done it obliquely and, given the *gravitas* of the situation, with some taste. As Marcel's grandmother always knew, an added aesthetic layer always adds value to an object.

So when Fryer says that the affair with "M" helped Gide, he is right in a way: Gide starts to look for language to explain his desire. Never mind that burnooses had dropped, ropes serving as belts had been slit, and orgasms had occurred ten years earlier; that was Africa, this is France. Never mind that he already knew that literature. Gide was looking for a language in which the desire of one white man for another could be expressed. That he chose a classical tack, as Wilde

had chosen aestheticism, is almost beside the point. For Gide, starting to write *Corydon*, homosexuality begins as a search for language.

We now move from episodes in Gide's life to his work. Homosexuality seems the central matter in Gide, the fundamental problematic preceding all others and giving rise to each supposed transcendental value of directness, forthrightness, truth, frankness,
confession, *disponibilité*, and the *acte gratuit*. Yet no subject in Gide
has led to more readings that seek to explain the homosexuality as
something else, as something other than what it is. If any radicality
is to be understood in Gide, a radicality found in *Corydon*, *Si le grain
le meurt*, and especially, *Les Faux-Monnayeurs*, this will occur only
through a radical rereading of homosexuality in his work.

The question of homosexuality in Gide's work has been set out as
a field in which numerous recent scholars have contributed invaluable
work. Naomi Segal has shown the intimate relations existing in Gide's
writing between the representation of homosexuality (pederasty) and
the scenes of learning (pedagogy). Elsewhere, the *mise-en-scène* of homosexuality has been related to the *topos* of travel in the so-called sotadic zone of the Maghreb (Schehr *Alcibiades* 113–54). Emily Apter
reads the rhetoric of truth and figures of speech in what she calls the
"displaced journal," which includes *Paludes*, *Les Nourritures terrestres*,
*La Porte étroite*, and *L'École des femmes*.[11] And Michael Lucey reads
Gide with and against queer theory.[12]

What all these readings have in common is a relation of homosexuality to textuality: a rhetoric and a poetics are associated with homosexuality that destablize it and the narrative. Homosexuality is a
figure that interrupts the narrative.[13] With Gide, the fertile period in
which he most directly grapples with the question of homosexuality
as that destabilizing figure includes the production or publication of
*Les Caves du Vatican*, *Corydon*, *Si le grain ne meurt*, and *Les Faux-Monnayeurs*, four very different kinds of writings with different generic
constraints and different codes of production. In his writing, Gide
repeatedly returns to figures in his elaboration of a personal textual
mythology: the encounter with an Arab boy, endlessly repeated in a
variety of textual climates, is the best example that comes to mind.

How does one read homosexuality in Gide? It would be very
easy to lean not only on the insights afforded by the optics of
contemporary debates in queer theory but also on its two clichés: the

infamous closet and the "label" of homophobia.[14] But the context is far more subtle, far less easy. Gide develops a rhetoric almost by fits and starts, and the Gidean vision of homosexuality, its propriety and its discourses, is not to be found at any one spot but at a combination of hypertextual loci from his production of the twenties. Moreover, what may appear as a homophobic discourse is more a reflection of the incomplete nature of the position from which one may speak or write. *Corydon*, then, is a reflection of the dialectical tension involved in producing a coherent position and discourse where none previously existed. Only when the other is completely silent might one invoke a discourse already present: I have discussed this in my reading of the role of the Maghrebin adolescent who is deprived of a voice.[15] Third, what Gide invokes in the persona of Oscar Wilde is capital: there is a figure of homosexuality that erupts, interrupts, simultaneously completes the heterogeneous nature of the textual space.

So, in a way, the Marquis of Queensberry was right, at least in Gide's mind: Wilde was posing as a sodomite, confusing the categories of good and bad homosexuality, corrupting the youth of London or North Africa, if not of Athens, not being true to himself but to his words. The question of posing, as opposed to being who one is, comes up in Gide, in *Si le grain ne meurt* (235): "Since I had posed for Albert (he had just finished my portrait), I devoted a good deal of time to my character; the care of appearing precisely what I thought I was, what I wanted to be: an artist, went so far as to prevent me from being [*empêcher d'être*] and made me what one calls: a poser." What is this posing? The initial reaction is that posing is a performance, a factitious creation of a false self opposed to some reality of being. Posing is a figure of repetition, of copying, and of the mimetic, instead of the essence of self that is the purity of one's independent ego. So when Gide is posing for Albert, Albert reproduces that posing (at a second degree). Posing is not only a falsity, a studied difference from the truth and the immediacy of that truth to all who care to see it (as opposed to reading it) under the hot sun of the tropics. Posing is also a copying: in short posing is the "je suis" of following, as opposed to the "je suis" of being.[16]

The final chapter of the first part of *Grain* is a point of transition between a past recounted at length and a future of which readers are already aware, the public life of André Gide, including the events of his life that had figured thinly disguised in his works, as well as his public or official biography. The chapter starts with a reflection that the period after the publication of *André Walter* began "the most confusing period of my life, dark forests [*selve obscure*] from which I only was separated when I left with Paul Laurens for Africa. A period of dissipation and uncertainty" (250). Gide would willingly skip telling his readers about it, but it helps, he says, illuminate what follows. What follows is what one already knows: the opening of Gide's mind, heart, and body to and by Africa, the encounter with same-sex love or at least physicality, and the firm rejection of the bourgeois existence that had kept him down so long. The transitional chapter of *Grain* ends with a metatext: Gide had given these pages to his friend Roger Martin du Gard, and the latter reproaches them (not him) with never saying enough. And this despite Gide's best intention, which "has always been to say everything" (267). "Perhaps," Gide concludes, "one nears the truth more closely in the novel."

## IV. Among the Writings

Gide wavers. During the long process of writing that will bring about *Les Faux-Monnayeurs*, Gide intends for the longest time to make Lafcadio one of the focal characters of the novel. At first, it seems like an idea worth exploring, a chance to link the two works, and a means of insisting on the stylized art of the novel to be. The first line of the *Journal des Faux-Monnayeurs* tells it all: "For two days I have been hesitating on whether to make Lafcadio tell my novel" (11). This strategy will go on for a while, and it will be around (or behind) Lafcadio that the whole plot of counterfeiting takes place: "This spot in the garden where the exchange of false gold pieces takes place, behind Lafcadio's back and without him suspecting" (17). Now the reader of both finished prose works should immediately have questions. On the one hand, why should a character as astute as Lafcadio in the earlier work suddenly become a dupe or a patsy in the latter one? On the other hand, what happens when Gide finally abandons the idea of using Lafcadio?

In this journal that parallels the writing of the novel itself; as late as 1921, Gide is still intending to use Lafcadio in the novel and proposes nothing short of a homosexual encounter between him and Édouard: "In truth, Édouard feels that Lafcadio, although having returned all the letters, has an advantage over him; he feels the most elegant way of disarming him is to acquire him for himself. And Lafcadio delicately makes him understand this. But soon this forced intimacy makes way for a true feeling. After all [*au demeurant*], Lafcadio is among the most attractive (he does not know this yet)" (*J FM* 33–34 [3 May 1921]). It is immediately following this passage that Gide gives us the tale of the pilfered book that will crop up again in *Les Faux-Monnayeurs*. Gide sees the "kid" [*gosse*] take the book, and the "kid" realizes he has been seen. The book is a guide to Algeria (1871), which Gide gives him money for. It turns out (36) that the "kid" is 15–16 years old and not just the kid that he will become in the form of Édouard's youngest nephew in the novel, the same nephew who will threaten to expose the uncle for having made indecent advances, if the uncle tattles on him.

The theft aborted through his intervention is inscribed in the novel more or less as it is recorded in the *Journal* but with several telling changes. First of all, the characters are related: the thief is Georges, Édouard's nephew, and he is somewhat younger than the adolescent Gide sees. Second, if the original thief is common, Georges is not, but he nevertheless puts on vulgar tones when talking to his uncle, as if he were parading a character. Since it will be Georges who is central to the counterfeiting ring, he is already trying out his outlaw status. Third, while the initial scene and the reinscribed one can have homoerotic overtones because of the invocation of the standard Gidean imagery of espying a youth and following him, such overtones are left in the realm of the intersubjective in the original incident. Georges threatens to turn that intersubjectivity into something vulgar: as opposed to the silent, intersubjective ephebophilia that characterizes noble pederastic love for Gide (and by inference, for Édouard), Georges threatens to tell his parents that the uncle is a would-be child molester. Georges threatens to call homoerotic behavior homoerotic behavior: he threatens to make his uncle's homosexuality real, by saying it in the language of the other.

As soon as he has threatened to unveil the homosexual Édouard as a homosexual, Georges offers his uncle his own schedule, i.e,. when he would be free after school. To say the least, Georges is offering to participate in a homoerotic game. In so doing, Georges picks up a piece of the original story: the acquisition of Lafcadio that Gide proposes for Édouard is now sexually put on Georges, but it is not only on him. For Gide divides the ephebic love object among three characters in the novel. Aside from Georges, there is Olivier, the middle brother, who will not be acquired by Édouard but by the Wildean homosexual alter ego, Robert de Passavant. Then there is Bernard, the illegitimate child of Madame Profitendieu, who replaces Lafcadio in the novel, for he is the one who steals Édouard's suitcase, and whose illegitmacy is shared by Boris and by Laura's unborn child. And again, the strain or leitmotif of Lafcadio's illegitimacy in the earlier *Les Caves du Vatican* is split in the novel between the illegitimate Bernard, who will ultimately return to the fold, for families, false or true, have endless sway, and Boris, who takes from Lafcadio the multilingual trait that the latter inherits from a series of false "uncles," i.e., the lovers of his mother, one of whom is his own father.

Gide goes back to the classics to find an idea in classical language not predicated on the silence of the moderns about homosexuality. Silence is that which follows, that which, in specific, follows death, whereas Gide necessarily views homosexuality as a means of finding life, a road to salvation, and a commitment to renewal. To say "silence" is to move quickly, for as Michel Foucault has so eloquently shown in *Histoire de la sexualité*, when nineteenth-century sexological science was not talking about feminine hysteria or the perils of (male) masturbation, it was busy producing long disquisitions on the perversity or perversion of (male) homosexuality. Differences abounded depending on national cultures, and while male homosexuality remained unpenalized in the legal sense in France, for example, it came under the letter of the law both in England with the Labouchere Amendment and in Germany with Paragraph 175. In those two countries, though more extensively in England than in Germany because of the *cause célèbre* that the Wilde case was to become, the discourse of scientific perversion was seconded and supported by this legal discourse, in a move toward a multiple echoing of the truth through its representation in plural discourses. It is no small irony that the Wilde event comes out of the same *Zeitgeist* as the penal discourse that will repress it, and one could argue that the so-called homophobia of Victorian England and the pose of aesthesis degenerating into the dangers of buggery were part and parcel of the same discursive episteme.

In France, the relative legality of the private act performed between two consenting adults left a place for a different aesthetic to develop. This comparative freedom does not produce, as one might have otherwise expected, a *foisonnement* of textual positions or even figural images by the time that Gide himself is sitting down to write. At one point, serving as Corydon's interlocutor, the narrator puts his finger on the matter, much as schoolteachers might put their fingers to their mouths to ask for silence. He is astonished that "this taste, this penchant, which everything hides and which everything opposes, which does not have permission to appear [*se montrer*] either in the arts or in books or in life, which comes under the force of the law as soon as it affirms itself and which you immediately nail to a pillory of infamy, the butt of jokes, insults, and almost universal disdain . . . " (39).

When Gide first starts to consider writing his *apologia pro vita sua*, he has the same image of Wilde, that which he will not be or follow, and a more benign, if more distant, image of Walt Whitman, clad in old age and an almost childlike belief in the immeasurable nature of the human spirit, which includes, because it neither names nor excludes, a homoeroticism that many took for homosexuality. Thus, at the very beginning of *Corydon*, Gide presents us iconically with that other figure: "On his work table, the portrait of an old man with a big white beard, whom I immediately recognized as the American Walt Whitman" (*Corydon* 16). Just as image precedes and permanently interrupts writing in the case of Wilde, image precedes writing here, even if the image is a reinscription of a moment of writing. The narrator recognizes the picture as being that of Walt Whitman, because that very picture is the frontispiece for a recent translation of Whitman's work. For the Gidean reader, the image, be it good or bad, precedes the construction of a cogent textual position. The discourse that follows that emblematic positioning of the picture consists of two syllogisms in which first Whitman is proven not to be a pederast, and then, Whitman's pederasty being given as the minor of the second syllogism, pederasty is taken to be normal.

These strange peremptory arguments, born out of tongue-in-cheek syllogisms, could be part of the reason that some critics have reacted negatively to some aspects that seem to be excessive, disquieting, or even, "homophobic." Apter points to the "rather hackneyed use of Platonic dialogue" (82) in the book, and Lucey says:

But as for *Corydon* . . . being Gide's most important and socially useful book, a claim he made several times late in his life, such a claim seems a little hard to swallow. How could a declared homosexual writer who had, while still somewhat closeted, written as apparently homophobic and misogynistic a book as *Corydon*, later in life claim that book as his most important for the good it might do for gay men?[17] (69)

These readings are symptomatic of Gide's problem: he has no language but silence. All writing is infused with a picture that looms large and, significantly, has no unified position from which to speak. Hence, Gide's double turn: on the one hand, to the classics, and especially to Virgil, on the other, to the image of the adolescent untouched by textuality, the pure image that will lead him further, not the image of the *erastos* tinged with Wildean overtones but that of the *eroumenos*, who somehow will never be blanketed by writing. It is not for nought that, late in *Les Faux-Monnayeurs*, Bernard says that the only poet who satisfies him nowadays is Rimbaud (1150). At least that is the ideal; the textual reality is elsewhere.

Gide mines Virgil's *Eclogues* throughout his career, and characters like Tityrus, Menalcas, and Mopsus, and quotations from and allusions to those books are a leitmotif in Gide's personal intertextual library. While the odd-numbered *Eclogues* tend to be cast in dialogical form, the even-numbered ones are more or less monological; this difference of form will come into play in a moment. No work looms as large as Virgil's *Second Eclogue*, the story of Corydon's love for Alexis. The same figure of Corydon survives and, in the *Seventh Eclogue*, will participate in a poetry contest with Thyrsis: "ambo florentes aetatibus, Arcades ambo, et cantare pares et respondere parati [both in the flower of life, both from Arcady, ready to sing and answer]" (ll.4–5). In the *Second Eclogue*, after five lines in which the poet describes the situation, Corydon speaks and implores for much of the poem (ll.6–55). The last eighteen lines are Alexis's somewhat lighthearted rejection of Corydon, whom he accuses of being a "rusticus [rube]" (l.56). In the *Second Eclogue*, Corydon is not so happy: he was burning ["ardebat"] with desire for Alexis, who already was involved with another, his master: "delicias domini [the master's favorite]." Ever spurned by the "cruel Alexis," Corydon repeatedly goes to the hills and empties his heart out to nature by addressing Alexis. Corydon, plaintively singing his songs of desire, concludes that, as is the case for animals, the passion he has for Alexis is both natural and inevitable: "trahit sua quemque voluptas [everyone is pulled along by his pleasure]" (l.65). The poem ends with some solace: "invenies alium . . . Alexim [you will find another Alexis]."

Let us look at the Gidean rewriting of Virgil's poem. Significantly, the monologue of Virgil's poem is split in Gide's version:

—What! You don't know that Alexis B. killed himself?
—Would you dare to claim that [Oseriez-vous prétendre que] . . .
—Oh! I claim nothing [Je ne prétends rien du tout]. . . . But here is the letter that at the foot of my bed I found [Voici la lettre qu'au chevet de mon lit je trouvai] [ . . . ] No, I shan't read you this letter. (26)

A seemingly simple situation that has not received much notice by literary critics. In three key areas, this passage helps illuminate the Gidean representation of homosexual desire. First of all, whereas Virgil's Alexis was safe, happy, and alive, Gide's Alexis is dead, in an act of suicide. The whole of *Corydon* is thus predicated on the impossibility of a dialogue with the beloved, predicated on the other always already being dead and always already having written. For Alexis leaves a letter that has been read but that will not be reread, introduced as evidence or testimony. Alexis will not provide testimony on his own behalf; Gide's Alexis will not be able to justify such love with a statement like "trahit sua quemque voluptas." Alexis's letter therefore becomes an object to be seen rather than a narrative to be read; the writing of the other, in this case, the dead Alexis, becomes an image that strangely rejoins the unreadable writing of the other that has been transformed into image: Wilde's work or that of Whitman. At the same time, Gide fulfills a Wildean prediction as if, when Wilde's words were allowed to be heard or read, they could confirm the act that Gide sets up as the emblematic vision of the narrative, the suicide of one too young: in the *Ballad of Reading Gaol*, Wilde poignantly points out that each man "kills the thing he loves."

Gide recalls Virgil's poem through a distortion of normal French syntax. Gide writes: "Voici la lettre qu'au chevet de mon lit je trouvai."

It will be remembered that in Virgil's poem, it is not something or someone that was found in a preterite but another Alexis that will be found: "invenies alium . . . Alexim." For Gide then, writing substitutes for the dead body, and there will be an endless inscription of that dead body, that unreadable letter, in the place of the beloved other, who is, for all the joys of the moment of bliss, ever absent. Gide writes so as not to have to say that the live body is no longer there; it is easier to have dead writing instead of a dead body. In *Si le grain ne meurt*, this is poignantly stated: "Why do I tell all this? Oh! Simply to put off what is going to follow [*ce qui va suivre*]. I know it is without interest" (277).

The third point is another one of intertextuality. In his writing relating to homosexuality, Gide employs a specific vocabulary that comes back at strategic moments and, this vocabulary is in evidence here in the phrase "Oseriez-vous prétendre?" Both words reflect Wilde, in a lingering textual strain or remainder that recalls him, but as described by others, specifically the Douglas family. Lord Alfred was the author of the line "the love that dare not speak its name" and his illiterate father, the penner of the misspelled expression "posing as a somdomite." Gide's line, predicated on the dead Alexis, who has left a letter (that will remain unread), collapses both into one. Whether interesting by chance or by willful act, Gide's line bears further investigation. For Gide, "daring" is, and will always be, daring to be oneself, himself, and the unrepentant pederast who celebrates his freedom and who dares to be different from that which others expect of him.

A word first about "prétendre," which means different things in English and French. In French, "prétendre" has no pretense or pretend in it but means "to claim" with no malice aforethought. Did Gide understand the difference between the words in French and English? When he uses the word "prétendre," it always seems to be tinged with the English meaning of the word, so there is often a measure of falsity. It is thus opposed to the daring that for him is an act of self-enunciation. For Gide, what the word winds up meaning, in both languages, is "to pose": one should not claim to be a sodomite, pretend to be a sodomite, or pose as a sodomite. One should simply be a sodomite or dare to be one. For Gide, it is a question of making a clean break, of being oneself, of being sincere, and of letting the masks fall. It is not that he takes the word "sodomite" at face value. But one must become what he calls a "pederast"; one must accept this noble love if it exists in one's heart. To pretend no longer: to dare to do everything.

These two words are found throughout Gide's writing, but they are never more clearly juxtaposed than in *Corydon*. For example, there is a short exchange between the narrator and Corydon, the former astonished that the latter is thinking of publishing a *Defense of Pederasty*: "'And you dare to publish that?' 'No; I dare not ['Et vous oserez publier cela?' 'Non; je n'oserai pas']'" (19). Later, at the end of the first dialogue, are the following words: "'I claim [Je prétends] that far from being the only 'natural' act, the act of procreation . . . is most often only a fluke [raccroc]'" (32). If the word *prétendre* is understood in its double French and English meaning, the sentence is as radical as it is meaningful. If the words are ambiguous, it is because Gide maintains a complex strategy to tie narration to elucidation: if Corydon is the spokesperson for the author most of the time, the narrator (curious, but not wholly convinced) formulates the objections and contradictions always found in the ever-ambiguous Gide. It is for that reason that the word *prétendre* has such amplitude and ambiguity. As Gide cannot yet make the clean break he desires, as he, while writing *Corydon*, cannot yet dare to do everything, cannot stop pretense, the singular semantics, contradictory as it is, split between the narrator and Corydon, remains fundamental to readers' understanding.

Through Corydon, the author affirms that this defense and apology, or this argument, will not fully convince the other without the sophistry that naturalizes nature and makes nature something artificial, something linguistic, when all is said and done. This Gidean nature—in which the author believes only to the extent that it is useful to him—is the same invoked in the expression "contre nature," when it is a question of speaking of Whitman's mores. This nature, for which homosexuality is "against nature," is thus a nature in which the predominance of heterosexuality is also a dominance of and domination by heterosexuality. In *Corydon*, Gide seeks to replace that nature with another nature, in which this predominance does not become domination. He creates this second nature by using logic and language to make the first burst at the seams.

Thus the narrator, playing his role of interlocutor to the hilt, asks: "'Do you claim [Prétendez-vous] that heterosexuality is simply a matter of custom?'" (37). The negative answer is modulated: "'Not at all! But let us judge according to custom in taking only heterosexuality as natural'" (37). Thus he claims, disclaims, and pretends at the same time, for custom, like nature, is a heterosexual representation. There does not seem to be a way of escaping the system of thought promoted by (and that promotes) heterosexuality. What metaphysics becomes for Jacques Derrida, heterosexuality is, fifty years earlier, for Gide in *Corydon*.

In his discussion of *Les Faux-Monnayeurs*, Lucey writes against what one might call a condemnation to homosexuality, a preordained *coup* (to use Lucey's *trouvaille* [121]), such as that characterized by Delay in his psychoanalytical reading of Gide. As Lucey puts it, summing up Delay's reading: "Gide's homosexuality is for Delay the consequence of three things: too much masturbation; weak nerves . . . ; and a meeting with Oscar Wilde" (120–21). For Lucey, there is another logic at work, almost a dream-state, a sleepy discourse—he provides a lengthy study of people waking or falling asleep in the novel—one that unties the novel from a determination or intention toward a specific sexuality. Gide's sleep states are the loci where heterosexual logic does not apply and where there is a freedom to follow a different path, not necessarily the Freudian "royal path" to the unconscious but a path to selfhood. One could add to Lucey's observation a significant moment in the later *Si le grain ne meurt*, when Gide says of himself: "I repeat: I was still sleeping; I was like one not yet born" (64). The very next sentence is the clincher: "It was shortly after that that I was sent away from school, for reasons [motifs] that I shall try to dare [oser] to say."

Daring to be oneself, as described here, means being involved in an act of self-pleasure, one of the acts of masturbation that mark that work. It is meet to look at the Gidean figure of masturbation for a moment, if only because of the condemnation visited on that activity by the nineteenth century. Despite the "decriminalization" by Freud of such activities as masturbation and male homosexuality, the underlying logic of association of perversions remains in the minds of many: one necessarily leads to the other, perversions are all interlinked, and anything other than the straight and narrow is the path to a whole host of evils. Hence, the condemnation to homosexuality (condemnation in a very non-Sartrean way) in the psychoanalytical reading of Gide just mentioned.

If daring to be oneself is the ultimate act, it can be accompanied by only a few words, for there is still, despite the thousands of pages of writing, no language that fits. Daring means not speaking, not writing, and giving oneself a moment of freedom in an act of self-arrogation that precludes the imposition of another tongue, the writing of the other, a writing that sees any act as posing, pretense, or pretending. How can one avoid the pitfalls? To write one's homosexuality means to refer either to the figure of homosexuality that always looms large or to find oneself endlessly bent (as Michael Lucey so aptly puts it) toward or under the weight of heterosexuality. Gide's Édouard opens a gulf in which homosexuality can be written by making a distinction and by finding a space uninformed by seemingly ubiquitous heterosexuality. Édouard says that what he wants to do in the novel is to present reality and make the effort to stylize it: "To obtain that effect, follow me, I invent a novelist-character, whom I place as a central figure; and the subject of the book, if you will, is precisely the struggle between what reality offers him and what he intends [prétend] doing with it" (1082).

Édouard opens up a space for writing, first by placing it in an infolded position and then by allowing that folding to open up a locus where writing can occur. Let us return to the figure of masturbation, which is itself the paradigm by which that infolding of the textual body on itself will take place. The masturbating subject is caught in a homoerotic model, although masturbation and homoeroticism are neither coterminous nor necessarily related. Gide makes readers respond to the masturbating subject, as if to a homosexual one, by delivering an example in which the act of spectatorship and the act of self-pleasure are intimately entwined by a homoerotic gaze: masturbation is fun if done with a friend. Thus, at the beginning of *Si le grain ne meurt*, the young André gives himself over to guilty pleasures: it is what he calls "bad habits," which he later learned were called thus: "Which of us had instructed the other?" (81). Significantly, it is school that gives the name "bad habits" and that chastises him for guilty pleasures (120). Thus society, rejecting the act, does not permit the possibility of his homoerotic bonding and an integration of the self, even if the threat is so outlandish as to be amusing. For his devotion to masturbation, Gide is threatened with thinly veiled castration, specifically, an "operation with "Tuareg lances" (121), a threat he finds too obvious to be taken seriously.

So the infolded body of the sexual self identified with the sexual other becomes a locus that cannot be integrated through action, or even through language. It is thus not surprising then that the moment of self-reflection given in a generalized economy of writing on the self is a moment of what Apter calls "negative writing of the body" (69), the scene in which Lafcadio, in *Les Caves du Vatican*, inflicts wounds on himself for various peccadillos. Lafcadio's space, which is that of his body, his writing (in a general sense), and his possessions, invaded by the look of the other, who seeks to possess through his knowledge and his writing. Lafcadio's space of self-gratification becomes one of self-scarification. Lafcadio turns the knife on himself to write on his body because writing elsewhere, as independent narrative, was and will be a betrayal of self. At least at this point for Gide, writing always forces the writer into a compromise with the discourses of paternity: Lafcadio has calling cards made that are true, in the sense of biology and bloodlines, but false in the sense of honesty to himself and to who he is. In the same way, in *Les Caves*, part of the plot hinges on tickets and hats that identify the bearer as someone who he is not. Writing makes one out to be that which one is not, that who one is not.

In *Les Faux-Monnayeurs*, Gide turns the space of infolding into a literal or literary one. Whereas Lafcadio turns the knife on himself to write on himself, since all traditional textual space is marked by the paternal signifiers, Édouard can open up the space of writing, as he creates both a breach and a locus in which the discourse can occur. Let us consider the turning point in the plot that brings about this space. Édouard has received a letter from Laura in which she avows her pregnancy and the question of paternity: nothing could be more heterosexual or family oriented. Having read the letter, Édouard decides to put it "among" his own writing, as if, instead of homosexuality being carved out in a niche within the walls of heterosexuality, the latter could, in reverse, be folded into a generalized homosexual space of writing: "The place of that letter [Laura's letter to Édouard] is not between a vest and shirts; under the clothes, he reaches a cardboard notebook half filled with his writing; looks in it, at the very beginning of the notebook, some sheets written last year—which he rereads—between which Laura's letter will take its place" (986). Gide transcribes the pages from Édouard's journal from the previous October, ostensibly for us to read as Édouard rereads them. Édouard shrugs his shoulders, closes his diary on the letter and puts everything in the suitcase.

He also puts his wallet in the suitcase, after having removed a 100-franc note, which will certainly do him until the moment that he re-cuperates his suitcase, which he intends to leave at the *consigne* on ar-rival (989). Bernard, who has been following Édouard and Olivier in the Gare St. Lazare and outside, sees the two together and is some-what jealous: "a bizarre feeling both made him follow [suivre] the couple and prevented him from showing himself" (994). He feels too much yet wants to slip between them, in a desired movement that not only is an act of jealousy that would invade and yet confirm the male-male couple but also is an action that would repeat (though Bernard could not yet know this), the act of "slipping between" that Édouard has accomplished by inserting Laura's writing into his own. At that moment, Bernard sees the *bulletin de consigne* drop from Édouard's hand, picks it up, and sees it as the pretext he needs to meet Édouard. Hamlet-like (the comparison is Gide's), Bernard wonders about his actions but remains steadfast, for he has promised his friend to "dare to do everything/anything [tout oser]" (995). He thus goes and recovers the suitcase.

To dare to do everything or anything means not only following the couple and spying on them; it also means finding an excuse somehow to fit into that life that he perceives as homosexual, with-out yet knowing it. He does so by recuperating a scrap of paper, the merest shred of evidence, that will turn into other papers. For Gide, then, placing Bernard in this situation means that homosexuality will be described through a multiplication of discourses, a panoply of writing: homosexuality is its inscription. In Édouard's journal, Ber-nard will read of the scenes between Georges and his uncle, first at the bookstore and then in the Molinier apartment (997–1003). It is also there that Bernard will read Édouard's remarks about Olivier holding his hand in church. Olivier, for Édouard, "resembles the sleeping shepherd from a bas-relief from the Naples museum," a photograph of which Édouard has on his desk (1008).

Bernard is the recipient unforeseen by the sender.[18] The reader doubles the position of Bernard, as she or he follows all the characters through the novel by picking up scraps up paper and turning them into a set of discourses, which is the novel itself. The perspective that Bernard has on Édouard and Olivier is echoed by the one that the reader has on Bernard. For there has already been a scene of male intimacy in the novel that marks the homoerotic elements of the narrative as being related to both a proxemics of touching and to a rejection of women. It is somehow appropriate for Olivier and Bernard to be in bed together when talking about sex:

[Olivier to Bernard]: "I want to tell you something, but I can't unless I feel you next to me. Come into my bed." And after Bernard, who got undressed in an instant, joined him, "You know, what I told you last time . . . That's it. I was there." Bernard only half understands [comprend à demi-mot]. He presses his friend against him, and Olivier continues: "Well, old man, it's disgusting. It's horrible . . . After, I wanted to spit, to vomit, to tear off my skin, to kill myself." (953)

Yet this misogyny is not typical of the Gidean ardor in homosexual pursuit. In general, women are far more invisible than they are objects of either lust or resentment. Gide offers a focal point for the plot of the novel, which is Laura's pregnancy as recounted in the letter that Bernard reads as the last chapter of the writings with which he has absconded (1038). A forceful rejection of women is not possible, and Olivier's reaction is really not acceptable in the Gidean universe.

For Gide, the need is not only to tell the truth but also to refuse both the *béance* of negation and the pose of falsity. Again, whereas Édouard is willing to state that he finds Olivier's poetry very bad, except for two lines, the latter appreciates his criticism, so much so that he wants to kiss him (958). However, even without having read it, Robert de Passavant is sure that he would find Olivier's poetry good (963). The latter, Édouard's alter ego as writer and adult homosexual, is almost everything for Gide that is reprehensible in the predatory stance of the perverse. Édouard considers Passavant a counterfeiter (1085). If not among the race of inverts for whom Gide has no use, because they are the all too palpable and visible introduction of the feminine, Passavant still falsifies the homosexual couple by feminizing the other. Olivier writes a letter to Bernard from Corsica, where he has traveled with Passavant, who has started to call Olivier by the definitely feminine name of "Olive" (1103). In *Corydon* (16), Gide specifically associates the idea of inversion, not only with effeminacy but also with the detail that marks: "In the room in which he introduced me, my eyes sought in vain those marks of effeminacy that specialists find in everything that touches inverts, and in which they claim [prétendent] never to be in error." Needless to say, that detail involves pretense and falsity.

How then does one become truly and honestly homosexual? Bernard has given us the clue to following one's heart. In part it is a play on the Cartesian cogito, in part, it is a pun: *je suis parce que je suis*. At the same time, *je suis par ce que je suis*. Or in English, "I am because I follow" and "I am by what I follow." As Gide writes in *Si le grain ne meurt*, "In the name of what God, what ideal, do you forbid me to live according to my nature? And that nature, where would it lead me, if only I followed it [je la suivais]?—Up to that moment I had accepted the morality of Christ, or at least a kind of puritanism that I had been taught as being Christ's morality" (269).

Extraordinary are the number of scenes in which following leads to an encounter or even the merest reflection on masculinity.[19] It is certainly not cruising in the banal sense of two hunters seeking each other as prey. For Gide, following is an art but is also the echo of the most profound part of his being. Take an entry from his diary, a scene in Rouen on 29 August 1904: "Then an Arab passed by; I followed him; I accosted him at the fork in the road. He was big, well developed, young, admirable. . . . The conversation flagging, I left him in giving him ten sous. His gratitude seduced me so much that I could not stop following him" (*Journal 1887* 429). The cause for an erotic fixation leads Gide and makes him follow. Ever bewitched, as if by a siren song of male masculinity, Gide is given to following, as Bernard will do in the Gare St. Lazare. Following means becoming and then being, but it also means making up for a lack of immediacy. To follow is to increase the relation between the bodies, whether or not a homosexual encounter actually ensues. To follow is to possess either with the body or with money. To be possessed by the very act of captivation: following means getting caught in an erotic situation regardless of the status of the other, his availability, or his knowledge. To follow means to bring the object permanently into view and to possess it visually, even if nothing else ensues:

The most unhealthy curiosity keeps me at the window, behind the shutters, and spying on the windows facing us, on the other side of the street, the boys working at the grocery store. In this great heat, the windows remain open; my look goes down; in the shadow of the room one can vaguely make things out. And I do not decide not to see any more. A dozen times, before going to bed, I take up my watchpost again, even in the middle of the night, I get up again (3 June 1905). (*Journal 1887* 463)

Finally the following suffices, and in old age, it is all there is. Possession is always in the eyes of the Gidean beholder: As he writes in the *Carnets d'Égypte* on 3 February 1939:

No, I no longer have a great desire to fornicate; at least it is no longer a need like in the good old days of my youth. But I need to know that if I wanted to, I could; do you understand that? I mean that a country pleases me only if multiple occasions to fornicate are present. The most beautiful monuments in the world cannot replace that; why not admit it frankly? This morning, finally, going through the native quarters of Luxor, I was rewarded. With my eyes, I caressed ten, twelve, twenty charming faces. It seemed to me that my gaze was immediately understood; as an answer, it got a smile that could not be misunderstood. (*Journal 1939* 648)

Turning back the clock is perhaps the last nostalgic desire, in which he may recover a first moment of pure bliss, a first encounter, or a silence of the voluptuous before God and everyone else. Let us look at *Si le grain ne meurt*: Ali in the dune invites Gide, Gide "waits," and Ali says "Adieu." Gide seizes his hand, Ali cuts the cords of his burnoose, and that is that: "In the adorable splendor of the evening, in what rays was my joy clad!" (280). That is the bliss: to be clad only in the joys of the moment and to have followed perfectly and become who one is, separate and apart from the one that one has become through work and efforts, writing, and knowledge.

Consider this wish: "I want to forget everything; live a long time among naked Negroes, people whose language I would not know and who would not know who I am; and fornicate savagely, silently, at night, with anyone, on the sand" (*Journal 1926 556* [13 May 1937]). In the end, the other is in his place, the place Gide has marked for him, even if, nowadays, this line would be understood as somewhat racist. The other is the one who will have helped Gide, in more than an ancillary fashion, though never credited enough, to pretend no longer, to dare to do everything, to make one verb, finally of *suivre* and *être*.

Reference Matter

# Notes

INTRODUCTION: THE PLACE OF THE OTHER

1. De Man's idea of an "allegory of reading" implies an "allegory of writing." This does not really need the rhetorical support of Yale deconstruction. Roland Barthes's entire project, especially *S/Z* and *Le Plaisir du texte*, is an allegory of writing.

2. The letter has often been quoted. Engels received a "naturalist" and socialist novel from a writer named Margaret Harkness. In his letter to her, he tries to explain that Marx's favorite writer was not someone who was sympathetic to the plight of the working classes, like Zola, but rather the fiercely conservative Balzac who was better than all the Zolas "passés, présents, et à venir" (in French in the letter). Engels's justification for Marx's literary opinion, as opposed to his personal taste, is grounded in the extraordinary irony they perceive in Balzac's treatment of those whom supposedly he holds in highest esteem.

3. Parenthetically, one wonders to what extent a deconstructive reading could be anything but an allegorized reading of a weak work such as a *roman de gare*, one that does not implicitly or explicitly problematize itself and its own inscriptions.

4. In a recent strong reading of this kind of argument, grounded in a thorough knowledge of Barthes, Armine Kotin Mortimer insightfully shows that there has "often" been realist writing, both before and after "realism" itself.

5. Giving a discourse about heat when there is no coal to be had, is, on the other hand, not necessarily acceptable on a human, humane, or humanistic level but is certainly acceptable realism, as long as the discourse corresponds to some potential logic of reality in the real world. Zola's *Germinal* is about this, among other things.

6. The future tense of fashion seems to develop along with the possible high-speed transmission through language and pictorial representation of things that are *à la mode*. Thus, rather than being a reflection merely of what Parisian women have been wearing—one used to get Paris fashions after they had been fashionable in Paris—with the advent of fashion photography, women are told what they will be wearing.

7. Picking up Richard Dawkins's term, Susan Blackmore defines a meme quite simply as "an idea, an instruction, a behaviour, a piece of information" that can be imitated and passed on "again, and again, and so take on a life of its own" (4).

8. On the concept of freeplay, see Derrida ("Structure"). Along with the rejection of the centeredness of structuralism, the structures of structuralism, Derrida's positing of freeplay at the "heart" of any system was, along with Barthes's *S/Z*, on a completely literary level, the double transition between what was retrospectively known as structuralism versus poststructuralism. Freeplay is important: it is a figure that surges up in the Lyotardian sense to upset the structures (*vide infra*); it is also the figure that most lucidly accounts for the ways in which the autonomous status of the secondary modeling system puts direct representation into question.

9. For Lyotard (*Discours, figure* 248), "figurability" or, what Freud calls the *Rücksicht auf Darstellbarkeit* ("the glance at representability") is one of the four primary processes of dream representation. Here, what obtains for the dream work as Freud and Lyotard define it also obtains for the literary work, although I am not likening the latter to the former in any way other than the concerns for representability and the means of representation (literality and figurality). On the relation of sense and nonsense in the literary, see Deleuze.

10. For example: literature as revealed truth (religious writing) or certain aspects of the supernatural or the nonrealistic. In the latter category would be certain metaphysical stories by Borges, including "La biblioteca de Babel" and "Tlön, Uqbar, Orbis Tertius," with its discussion of what Borges names *brönir*. All Borges's stories with metaphysical objects, including "El Libro de arena" and "El Disco," would fall into that category. Arguably a good deal of Kafka's narratives, including *Der Schloß* and "Die Verwandlung," would also come under this category.

11. Two caveats here. First, this is not a socioliterary critique of realism in its relation to the ever-expanding world of capitalism. The expansionism

and the acquisition associated with one benefits the other. Second, that realism fits capitalism does not imply exclusivity. Expansion, associated not only with capitalism but also with the dominance of various kinds of imperialism, often modified the literary to give it a messianic mission. The world was, after all, the "white man's burden."

12. This kind of representation without explanation will go on as late as authors such as Conrad (in *The Heart of Darkness*, for example) and Thomas Mann, both of whom will try to demystify alterity while leaving an *Unheimlichkeit* fully in place.

13. For an excellent study of this painting, see Grigsby.

14. It is unfortunate that this ground-breaking work, one of the most important in Lyotard's *œuvre*, has never been completely translated into English. In *Discours, figure*, Lyotard distinguishes three kinds of figures that interrupt: figure-image, figure-form, and figure-matrix. Bennington (22) among others rightly finds it difficult to defend the differentiation of the figures into those three categories. Yet, even despite that flaw, the concept of the figure as the means of interruption, or as the mark of deconstruction still seems an extraordinarily powerful notion.

15. Elsewhere, I have argued that for something to be a theme in a realist narrative, a certain degree of closure is necessary (*Shock* 63–65).

16. In "The Unknown Subject," I have discussed possible literary meanings of the word subject.

JUST BALZAC

1. For obvious reasons, most of the *Études philosophiques* are excluded from this generalization.

2. This phrase, "*quibiscum viis*" comes up at an important juncture later in the novel, when the narrator uses it to describe Charles's determination to succeed by any means possible. See the discussion below.

3. Writing about "Ferragus," Michele Hannoosh notes that Balzac's *modus operandi* is "to use the cultural code ironically to reveal its limits and its foundation in the phantasms of an individual or a class" (141).

4. In addition to the slave-based plantation that Vautrin envisions for himself, Rastignac, in a moment of *discours indirect libre*, is marked by the infamous *traite des blanches*: "Il avait ainsi quinze mois de loisirs pour naviguer sur l'océan de Paris, pour s'y livrer à la traite des femmes, ou y pêcher la fortune" (1:122). In this case (and despite the mixed metaphor), the expression is a metaphor for amorous conquests instead of being a representation of the reality of slavery envisioned by Vautrin or practiced by Charles Grandet.

5. As an illustration of this belief, the United States believes that it is

exporting freedom and democracy, whereas others may believe that the
United States is exporting globalization (American goods) and servitude.

6. In the real world, well into the twentieth century, some Europeans argued for the expulsion (the "repatriation") of the Jews, just as some Americans argued the same for blacks. The status of seropositivity is technically a
means of refusing entry today at the United States borders. That this shibboleth is unequally applied is manifest, for given the fact that people from
many "white" countries do not need visas nowadays, the law would undoubtedly fall more on seropositive individuals from nonindustrialized and/
or non-Western countries.

7. As P. M. Wetherill says (169), Grandet is "a balance sheet on the
move," and as Alex Fischler rightly suggests, the name Grandet can be read
as an anagram for "d'argent."

8. Characters such as Villiers de l'Isle Adam's Ève and other mechanical
women in decadent writing are partly a result of Eugénie. Certainly the mechanical woman is in part a phantasm in the classic sense: both the incarnation of the fear of the feminine and a means of containing that fear. The mechanical woman is also a construction and a rival generation of the feminine
from within an androcentric universe: she is made from available and safe
material controlled by men.

9. Henry James took this aspect of *Eugénie Grandet* to heart in preparing
*Washington Square*, a work in which he moves the character from being a reactive female to being an active one who finally rejects her suitor.

10. Part of Balzac's project (without any necessary intentionality) is to
open up the narrative to "two sexes and others." In *Le Père Goriot*, he breaks
open the bivalent gendered opposition by the introduction of Vautrin, as
well as by the collection of nonproductive (in an engendering sense) figures
who people the boarding house.

11. Various critics have addressed this matter in Balzac's writing. David
Bell (*Circumstances* 111–93), for example, has engaged the representation of
chance in Balzac's work; Franc Schuerewegen, the question of the position
of the reader; Richard Terdiman, the construction of ideology. In these cases,
the critic shows how various categories, interests, and constraints affect the
construction of verisimilitude.

12. Furst seems to recognize the importance of description but evinces
some frustration with Balzac's "overdescription whose impact can be dizzy-
ing" (152–53). She seems to rebel at the extent to which Balzac casts things
in narrative instead of just presenting the characters and seeks the collusion
of her readers in this endeavor. For example: "*Eugénie Grandet* has a packed
thirty-page overture, which tends to exasperate most readers eager to hear
her story" (82). Or again: "At one end of the gamut Balzac insists on telling

readers more about Saumur (in *Eugénie Grandet*) than most of them care to hear" (99–100).

13. With what seems to be her valence about this novel, Furst remarks: "In *Eugénie Grandet* a full nineteen pages elapse before the titular heroine makes her first appearance. Meanwhile, the exterior of the house, the street, the town of Saumur, its commerce, its leading citizens and factions, and the economic and social prehistory of Eugénie's parents is unfolded with an expansiveness that amounts to 'the sublimation of details'" (152–53, quoting Schor, "Details").

14. This is a sexist or misogynistic remark on the part of the author/narrator, but also the symptom of a (phallogocentric) system that considers women tyrannizable. This is further underlined by the narrator's recourse to one of his stylistic clichés, "one of those . . . " the use of which, thanks to the deictic demonstrative, inevitably implies the tacit agreement of his readers, the *captatio benevolentiae*, in terms of the general will and the dominant ideology.

15. As Dufour points out, silence appears in *Eugénie Grandet* and becomes "brusquely omnipresent" at the death of Charles's father. That silence corresponds to "the eruption of feeling . . . in the cold house" (50–51). Silence is also what is not marked by language and what is as yet unfilled by figure. Here, the silence that appears at Charles's father's death is the mark of a locus for which there is no language. This would mean that either there is ultimately no vehicle in this world for the transportation of desire or that the preexisting vehicle of which Lotringer writes does not work here.

16. The words "read everywhere" recall the writing on the wall. On the figure of characters in Balzac reading other people's mail, see my discussion of *La Cousine Bette* in *Rendering French Realism* (118–46).

17. The editor of the novel in this edition, Nicole Mozet, glosses: "M. Castex is quite rightly astonished that Charles Grandet could sell artists. Maybe Balzac thought of singers, be they castrati or not" (1736). Perhaps unconsciously Mozet is referencing the topos of castration/eunuchs/virginity/circumcision discussed above.

FLAUBERT'S FIGURES

1. Flaubert's perspective on his own writing is not essentially a privileged one; he does not somehow read *Salammbô* "better" than Sainte-Beuve. The letter is an insight into what Flaubert considers to have been his own project in writing the novel.

2. As Catherine Lowe (88) points out in her Lacanian reading of the work: "C'est donc là, dans l'ordre du langage, où il n'y a de réalité romanesque que dans son absence, que le roman porte son propre achèvement."

3. The reader "with a white hand" is implicitly Parisian, even if in a far-flung outpost of France. Thus Balzac does submit his provincial writings to Parisian scrutiny and values.

4. For Gautier, Jules Verne, or Loti, to take three disparate examples, the gesture of assimilation consists of an un-Shklovskian "familiarization" of the unfamiliar. The exotic (or different or ancient) is really a theater production of *Our Town* in strange costumes. The best—or worst—example of this writing would be the Victorian-era novels of authors like Edward Bulwer-Lytton, who, in works such as *The Last Days of Pompeii* and *Harold, the Last of the Saxon Kings*, makes the unfamiliar familiar by imposing Victorian ethics and parameters, unhistoricizing the so-called historical novel to the extreme.

5. Lukács discusses it as a historical novel (*Historical* 218–27) but finds that it comes up short, precisely because there is no verifiable material base. Other investigations into historicity include Anne Green's perceptive study and Patrick Brady's article on plot and conflict, while Peter Starr presents a political reading of closure in the novel. Perhaps because the work seems to be at such a distance from realism, Frier-Wantiez relates *Salammbô* to the genre of the fantastic. More on a stylistic level are studies by Jean Rousset, J. R. Dugan, and Marilyn Gaddis Rose. More directly theoretical studies deal with the establishment of methods of reading the narrative. See Jacques Neefs's ("*Salammbô*") brilliant discussion of the question of representation in the work and Sima Godfrey's excellent reading of the *zaimph*.

6. Lowe's position is difficult to maintain, except insofar as every realist novel would conform to some extent to the creation of the trap of the Lacanian imaginary.

7. Bem is certainly right to see a parallel between the world described and the violent nineteenth century; nothing in Flaubert's novel compels the reader to produce an allegorical interpretation. In a related troping of the novel, both Forrest-Thomson (787) and Barnett (73) underscore the difficulty, if not to say the impossibility, of interpretation in *Salammbô*; the reader seeking pattern, symbol, or imagery will try to organize the work so that it can be interpreted. This is the general pattern critics have had in doing an interpretation of the novel. Interestingly many of the readings seem to use a psychoanalytical model to ground what may appear to be a dreamlike work. Elizabeth Constable's reading depends on an economy in which fetishism is a determining pole. Constable says: "To summarize, where Orientalism relies conventionally on a restricted economy of fetishism, *Salammbô* generalizes the untranscended, or irreducible, materiality associated with the fetish, showing it to be ubiquitous: we all, readers and protagonists, find ourselves 'primitive' fetishists struggling to interpret textual and phenomenal materiality on a case by case basis" (636). If everything is a fetish, no progress has

been made in interpretation, for the latter relies on the establishment of difference, which the ubiquity of the fetish cannot support. In *"Salammbô,"* Jacques Neefs demonstrates the alterity of the book not only to the world in which it is written but also, and perhaps more tellingly, to interpretation and representation: the writing brings "the impossibility of representation" to representation (62).

8. The late Naomi Schor (115) for one, feels that synecdoche becomes more important than metonymy in the novel. It is undoubtedly true that there are more synecdoches than metonymies in the work, but the synecdoche never becomes a master trope, as it is never capable of signaling anything but what is stereotypically known.

9. For the sake of brevity, I am leaving to one side the later developments of this praxis, which, largely beginning in the 1870s and 1880s, more and more severely recast the other in terms of the self, a practice especially beloved of the Victorians—witness Gilbert and Sullivan—and the writers of the exotic, such as Loti.

10. While this may seem a singular example, it is really the most common, even in the most literate societies. In Thailand, for example, it is traditionally forbidden to have one's head higher than that of the king. In essence, though it is a sign of respect, this means the distribution of space is perceived as heterogeneous: the space around the king is higher/larger than that around an ordinary person. But in the studio system of the golden age of Hollywood, many a short actor was placed on a box or a platform to appear taller than his female costar when the actress herself was not just placed in a trench to effect the same result. So the inscription of such as actor is as someone taller than his costar regardless of the objective, measurable reality.

11. Her reading is elegant and admirable, though it does not quite seem to take into consideration the parameters of signification for an object or its representation in the novel. But her demonstration is most noteworthy as she develops the idea of the *zaimph* as the metaphor and the metonymy of the novel as a whole.

12. I would not insist too much on what would amount to a strawperson argument here. No one would confuse Proust's *A la recherche du temps perdu* with a lost farmer's almanac. Still, there is an insecurity in the time given to Flaubert's characters, a disquieting untimeliness that bears investigation.

NATURALIST ULTRAVIOLENCE

1. See Susan Harrow's excellent articles on the function of fabric in Zola. As she puts it: "Like Gervaise (like Zola) Lantier knows that clothes tell a story" ("Dressed" 150).

2. This is a topos known in fantastic literature: a knife that remembers materially the murders that it has committed. Zola flirts with that topos that has become somewhat banal but does not spend much time on it; the bed is a far more propitious site. The well-known song from Kurt Weill's and Berthold Brecht's version of *The Three-Penny Opera* says it well: "Oh, the shark has pretty teeth, dear / And he shows them, pearly white / Just a jackknife has MacHeath, dear / And he keeps it out of sight / When the shark bites with his teeth, dear / Scarlet billows start to spread / Fancy gloves, though, wears MacHeath, dear / So there's not a trace of red." There is no trace on the gloves, but the knife is hidden because it is always readable. The violence in which it might be used remains as a memory of the past and a potential sign of the future. The German text is even clearer, with the repetition of the verb "tragen," which ties the actions of Mac and the shark together, and the presence of the verb "lesen," where the English translation offers only "there's not": "Und der Haifisch, der hat Zähne / Und die trägt er im Gesicht / Und MacHeath, der hat ein Messer / Doch das Messer sieht man nicht. / Ach, es sind des Haifischs Flossen / Rot, wenn dieser Blut vergießt! / Mackie Messer trägt 'n Handschuh / Drauf man keine Untat liest."

3. As Jean-François Lyotard reminds us, the Romans made a distinction, one worthy to retain for the purposes of this chapter: "But there is blood and blood, *sanguis* and *cruor*, the blood of life in the arteries and veins and spilled blood" (40). Zola's *coup de génie* is to make the *cruor* circulate like *sanguis*.

4. The seeming glorification of violence for its own sake may lead some readers to see this as a moral tale, instead of as an amoral one. For Solda, the novel is a story of an initiation, or a sort of transcendence, rather than being only a story of "erotic and sadomasochistic events" (61), and the Chinese that Mirbeau depicts are "degraded beings who have lost their humanity" (64). And again, the prisoners are "dehumanized" (68). Finally, Solda sees the novel as a denunciation of what is permitted by French and European institutions (80) and concludes by saying that China and Europe "are not as far away from each other" as one might think. Reading the novel as a moralizing tale that condemns what is depicted is tantamount to asking us to avert our eyes when we read the detailed description of the supplices. If the novel is not a sadomasochistic scenario, it is certainly one that encourages a form of voyeurism that, even stripped of its erotic components, asks us to look and to revel in our looking.

5. Pierre Gobin speaks of the social region, the intermediate zone between the observer or witness and the cosmos whose powers are embodied in the woman. "It is the region of the 'they' . . . where the human individual is both the agent of order and its victim" (195).

6. Mirbeau's tortures are not the eternal tortures of the damned that include the tortures of Prometheus or those of Ixion, much of Dante's *Inferno* typified by the tortures of Ugolino, or Hieronymus Bosch's triptych *The Garden of Earthly Delights*. Nor is Mirbeau exactly the metaphysical forerunner for the Sartrean hell of *Huis-Clos* where the characters seem to expect the instruments of torture but find out that "L'enfer, c'est les autres." Of Ixion, Ovid writes: "volvitur Ixion et se sequiturque fugitque [Ixion revolved, both following and fleeing himself]" (IV: 461). Other tortured victims mentioned in the same part of the *Metamorphoses* include Tantalus and Sisyphus. I mention the torture involving Ugolino because of its strikingly modern economy. As Dante describes it, "I saw two frozen in one hole so close that the head of the one was a hood for the other; and as bread is devoured for hunger, so the upper one set his teeth upon the other where the brain joins with the nape" (*Inf.* 32:124–29). Dante's torture of Ugolino will be taken up in an economy of supplice as described in the last supplice in Mirbeau's novel, that of the bell, in which both the victims and the torturers are condemned. In an excellent article, Julia Przybos elegantly shows the formal structures and similarities between Mirbeau's triptych and Hieronymus Bosch's painting, *The Garden of Earthly Delights*. She also underlines the equivalence between "supplices" and "délices," the latter word figuring in the French title of the painting: *Le Jardin des délices*. Here, I am merely pointing out that the kind of torture involved in the painting, i.e., eternal damnation, is not exactly the same as the kind of torture, i.e., supplice between judgment and death, that Mirbeau depicts.

7. Mirbeau's poetics are thus opposed to the operetta poetics of Gilbert and Sullivan who, in *The Mikado*, "make the punishment fit the crime, the punishment fit the crime."

8. This story, "Colonisons," contains two scenes of Western savagery that will find their way into *Le Jardin des supplices*. In one, some Indian princes are murdered by the British; in the other, some Maghrebin men are buried alive up to their necks in the sand of the desert ("Colonisons" 268 and 272; *Jardin* 189–90). In the *Jardin*, Clara points out that the British are stupid because they kill the princes without supplice. In the novel, it is a French explorer who admits to cannibalism in its literal sense: "Their were many people in our party, and mostly Europeans . . . Marseillais, Germans, Italians . . . a bit of everything . . . When we were too hungry, we killed someone in the party . . . preferably a German" (115). This is a far cry from the arbitrary world of the Chinese Garden of Supplices where one kills the victim with or without a reason: "'What crimes did these people commit?' . . . 'None perhaps, or something small undoubtedly'" (173). European cannibalism has a reason: hunger. It is a slave mentality, Nietzsche would say, and not that of the

expression of liberty of a superman who is exercising his freedom to act, to choose, and to watch.

9. This supplice is reminiscent of a series of *écorchés*, or flayed bodies, by Fragonard that can be seen at the Musée Fragonard d'Alfort (Grescoe).

10. According to Roland Villeneuve (70) following Father Gallonio, this supplice can be dated as far back as 1591, when Protestants first used dormice to torture Catholics.

11. As Deleuze and Guattari say of Kafka's social machines in their study of that author: "The machine is no longer mechanical and reified, but is incarnate in the very complex social arrangements that by dint of human employees and human parts and gears allow for effects of violence and inhuman desire infinitely stronger than those obtained through animals or isolated mechanisms" (*Kafka* 71–72). For Deleuze and Guattari, then, Kafka's novels become the apotheosis of the machine that is unfortunately falling apart in his novella, "In the Penal Colony." In Mirbeau's work, one could see the entire Garden of Supplices itself as being similar to such Kafkaesque machines.

PROUST AND GIDE

1. On the ramifications of the figure of Rachel, see the excellent article by Scott Lerner.

2. Then as now, things are pretty much the same: a modern audience, which in matters operatic means an audience familiar with the blossoming of opera in the late nineteenth century in the hands of Verdi, Wagner, and Puccini, would expect nothing less. The exact same trick used in Verdi's *Il Trovatore*, in which the dying gypsy mother, Azucena, announces that her son, Manrico, was actually not her son but the Duke's brother: "egli era tuo fratello. Sei vendicata o madre" [He was your brother. Mother, you have been avenged].

3. For Beryl Schlossman, the figure of this Rachel is set in opposition to Giotto's Charity and Halévy's Rachel (216). One might add that Giotto's Charity is herself refigured in the pregnant kitchen maid as the image of Charity. One of the operative figures of the entire *Recherche* is a process of inversion, often accompanied by aesthetic enrichment, whereby initial image and final incarnation correspond little, if at all.

4. A few pages later Proust repeats the word "kaleidoscope": "To return to the reasons that prevented Odette from penetrating the Faubourg Saint-Germain at this time, it must be said that the most recent turn of the worldly kaleidoscope had been provoked by a series of scandals. Women whom one visited in complete confidence had been recognized as prostitutes, as English spies" (1:510). Later in the novel, Proust associates the image of the kalei-

doscope once again with the Jewish question: "It is true that the social kalei-doscope was turning and that the Dreyfus Affair would send Jews plunging to the last rung of the social ladder" (2:487).

5. In her recent study of Proust, Julia Kristeva discusses the role of reli-gion in the novel (*Le temps sensible* 185ff et alibi) and in fact refers to the opera in question. But she does not seem to note the crucial point of inver-sion that the reference to the opera entails: the Jewish woman is *not* a Jewish woman.

6. Without actually using the word "shibboleth," Kristeva (*Temps* 188) points to one relative to Albertine, in which she discusses the importance of one "n" or two in the surname Simonet. For Kristeva, the single "n" Simonet recalls "Simon Macabee" in the Bible.

7. Gilberte is 3/8 Jewish because Swann himself has a paternal grand-mother who is Protestant. As this is on the paternal side, others would say that Swann is Jewish because his mother and maternal grandmother are Jewish.

8. I should add that the son is named Gershom. That name reinscribes otherness, as it means "stranger there."

9. Jean-Joseph Goux theorizes in passing that Edward's homosexuality could be "read as a symbol of this deficiency in the realm of the *imaginal*" (85n), i.e., the difficulty that the character has in imagining images in his mind. Goux sees this as a "defective relation both to the *feminine* and to the *image*" (85). Lucey (114) remarks Goux's minimal discussion of homosexu-ality as part of "continuing the tradition of keeping homosexuality in the margins." It is safer to upend Goux's approach: the idea of counterfeiting that repeatedly invades the book and that gives the book its title is the excess image for homosexuality, for the language of the latter has not fully devel-oped. Homosexuality is counterfeit coin, language, or writing, without the origin ever coming into question: it is another source, another version. Ho-mosexuality is the counterfeit of counterfeits: a deconstruction of counter-feits that puts the original legal tender (no pun intended) into question.

10. Fryer is perhaps not the most sympathetic reader of the situation, for he visits a whole moral dimension on the reading of the friendship, and spe-cifically on the kinds of homosexual relations, undertaken by his cast of char-acters. So Bosie, despite Gide's (and Wilde's) fascination with the "laird," has little to recommend him because, as Fryer (45) describes him: "Both at Oxford and for several years after coming down from university, Alfred Douglas was a shamelessly promiscuous homosexual. Moreover, he had a taste for rough trade: servants, grooms, street-boys and others whose ser-vices could be cheaply bought."

11. In her last chapter on gender and negation in the *récits* (105–50), Apter focuses on the idea of a Freudian slip of the tongue as a means of

revealing a truth. It is not what is said wrong, the unconscious error, that reveals truth in Gide's writing but rather the unspoken (106). For her, the clue, the rhetorical invitation to gloss in that way comes from the confessional nature of much of Gide's narrative, including *L'Immoraliste*, *La Porte étroite*, and *La Symphonie pastorale*, along with the later trilogy of *L'École des femmes*, which includes not only that work but also *Robert* and *Geneviève*. Missing from this analysis is *Les Faux-Monnayeurs*.

12. Michael Lucey's excellent study of Gide's writing, aptly entitled *Gide's Bent*, is an analysis of a double shift of that writing. First, while Gide gives clues to his own homosexuality in works such as *L'Immoraliste* and *Les Caves du Vatican*, it is only with the writing of *Corydon*, *Les Faux-Monnayeurs*, and *Si le grain ne meurt* that Gide engages the topic of homosexuality head on. After the twenties, for Lucey, Gide's turn to the political in his writing is a mark of "the complexities and particularities of the social forces that attempt to dictate the public/private behaviors of gay men" (9). I share Lucey's interest in this public/private division and have already written about it in *Alcibiades at the Door*. Lucey echoes the classic themes of Gide himself in works such as *Les Nourritures terrestres* (with its apostrophe "Familles, je vous hais!") to *L'Immoraliste*: liberation of the self means liberation for the self, a situation that will culminate in the liberation of the core sexual self. But it also means liberation from the social oppression and class pressures of bourgeois society (31). A trip to Africa is just what it takes, in an oft-recast scene of an African adolescent disrobing, a point at which Gide has both ecstasy and epiphany. It is only natural then that in his postcoital years, Gide should turn to a general liberation, espouse left-wing causes, and see the problems of the continuing colonial situation.

13. Opposed to these readings is one that treats homosexuality as an old-fashioned theme with neatly defined edges, a topos also subject to a moral reading: Pollard's study, *André Gide: Homosexual Moralist*. This 500-page tome promises much by its heft; one expects an exhaustive monograph on *Corydon*. The first part, some thirty pages, is a straightforward reading and summary of *Corydon*, the second and third parts, the bulk of the book, a summary of sources in history, science, sociology, and literature of attitudes toward and references to homosexuality. The fourth part consists of summaries of references to homosexuality in Gide's other writings and plot summaries strung together by this thematic thread. Pollard warns us that: "We should not make the error of assuming that a writer is merely the sum of the influences he has undergone. Nor should we believe that he is incapable of the imaginative feat of creating his own world of fictional characters and events. We must, however, recognise that Gide's homophile outlook often contributed an important element to what he wrote. Sometimes it is to be found

overtly expressed; at other times it forms a subtle and suggestive atmosphere. It may be limited to ideals of hedonism, of abnegation, of sin, of noble chastity or of true self-fulfilment. Nevertheless, it is difficult to escape the conclusion that a need for self-confession sometimes dictated the inclusion of scenes with strong pederastic undertones" (296).

14. I have already engaged the question of the closet in an earlier book and do not intend to revisit what I said there, except to note that the concept of the closet, whether or not one is an essentialist or a constructivist, is itself culture-specific, class-specific, and time-specific.

As far as "homophobia" is concerned, I am not denying that homosexuals (to use a reasonably neutral term for the sake of argument) have been mistreated, denied rights, or otherwise condemned. I am saying several things. First, the term "homophobia" seems as badly cast as the so-called "scientific" word "homosexual" itself, except that "homophobia" does not have a macaronic etymology. The word etymologically means "fear of the same," a meaningless word to be sure. But along the lines of semantics, the word implies a shift, an automatic shift, between violence done to homosexuals or exclusion of homosexuals and a fear of homosexuals. In a society in which everyone who is sad is "depressed," everyone who is fearsome is "paranoid," everyone who is energetic is "manic," it is natural to assume that everyone who does not like homosexuals or homosexual behavior is afraid of them. And yet, in a discourse—that of gay liberation and that of queer theory—that made one of its primary foci the psychological normalization of homosexuality, it seems a complete aberration to introduce this catch-all term that revives the psychological monster and demonizes both the so-called homophobe and his or her object of fear or hatred.

Second, there is the matter of historical, cultural, and class-oriented behavior. Even if there is some essentialist figure associated with same-sex desire, be it biological or simply achronic, the vehicle of that desire changes. In all societies, through seven thousand years of recorded history, there have been people of one biological sex who felt a desire for members of the same biological sex. My sneaking suspicion is that while this is true, it is *a fortiori* true for the *polis*, at least in a reflective sense. Even if such desire was always present, there is a recognition of that desire when the city develops as a place in which both property and desire are compartmentalized. Is this a Rousseauist reading of "Ceci est à moi"? Or is it a Freudian reading about anal behavior? In any case, the relative consciousness about such desire and the valorizing or demonizing of such desire, interrelate with a reaction thereto, what is wrongly called homophobia (Cf. Sartre on anti-Semitism). If this is true from an essentialist position, it is even more true from a constructivist position: to label anything homophobia in the light of the existence of homosexuality for only one hundred years (or so) is to paint with a broad brush.

15. Thus while it is unfair to visit the demon of homophobia on Gide, because "homophobia" is an inaccurate, catch-all term, I do not have a problem with reading him, in these works, as a colonialist.

16. Parenthetically, I would add an anecdote. Pollard makes a list of the "homosexual scandals" reported by the French press during the time that Gide was "gathering material for *Corydon*" (131). The first is perhaps the best: "An anonymous Englishman [Lord Alfred Douglas], who was enticed by two youths posing as homosexuals, and who was then robbed."

17. Gide makes this claim, as Lucey reminds us, in a journal entry from the beginning of 1946.

18. See my study of "misreading," or dyslexia, in Balzac, in *Rendering French Realism* 118–44.

19. Segal (*André Gide* 215–22) remarks a number of instances of this boy hunt, which she describes with the Gidean word *rôder*.

# Bibliography

Alighieri, Dante. *Inferno*. In *The Divine Comedy*. Translated, with a commentary, by Charles S. Singleton. Princeton: Princeton University Press, 1977. Volume 1.

Amossy, Ruth, and Elisheva Rosen. "Les 'Clichés' dans *Eugénie Grandet* ou les 'négatifs' du réalisme balzacien." *Littérature* 25 (1977): 114–28.

Apter, Emily S. *André Gide and the Codes of Homotextuality*. Stanford: Anma Libri [Stanford French and Italian Studies], 1987.

Arendt, Hannah. *On Violence*. New York: Harcourt, Brace, 1970.

Bakhtin, Mikhail. *Problems of Dostoevsky's Poetics*. Trans. R. W. Rotsel. Ann Arbor: Ardis, 1973.

———. *Rabelais and His World*. Cambridge, Mass.: MIT Press, 1968.

Barnett, Stuart. "Divining Figures in Flaubert's *Salammbô*." *Nineteenth Century French Studies* 21:1–2 (1992–1993): 73–87.

Barthes, Roland. *Le Plaisir du texte*. Paris: Seuil, 1973.

———. *S/Z*. Paris: Seuil, 1970.

Bauer, George S. "Gay Incipit: Botanical Connections, Nosegays, and Bouquets." In *Articulations of Difference: Gender Studies and Writing in French*. Ed. Dominique D. Fisher and Lawrence R. Schehr. Stanford: Stanford University Press, 1997: 64–82.

Bell, David F. *Circumstances: Chance in the Literary Text*. Lincoln: University of Nebraska Press, 1993.

———. "Effects collatéraux." In Bernard and Schuerewegen: 63–71.

———. "Zola's Fin-de-Siècle Pessimism: Knowledge in Crisis." *L'Esprit Créateur* 32:4 (1992): 21–29.

Bem, Jeanne. "Modernité de *Salammbô*." *Littérature* 40 (1980): 18–31.

Bennington, Geoff. "Lyotard: From Discourse and Figure to Experimentation and Event." *Paragraph* 6 (1985): 19–27.

Benveniste, Émile. *Problèmes de linguistique générale*. Paris: Gallimard (TEL), 1966. Volume 1.

Bernard, Claudie, and Franc Schuerewegen. *Balzac, pater familias*. CRIN 38, 2001.

Bernheimer, Charles. "The Decadent Subject." *L'Esprit Créateur* 32:4 (1992): 53–62.

Blackmore, Susan. *The Meme Machine*. Oxford: Oxford University Press, 1999.

Bourdieu, Pierre. *La Distinction: Critique sociale du jugement*. Paris: Minuit, 1979.

Boyer, Philippe. *Le Petit Pan de mur jaune. Sur Proust*. Paris: Seuil, 1987.

Brady, Patrick. "Archetypes and the Historical Novel: The Case of Salammbô." *Stanford French Review* 1 (1977): 313–24.

Brombert, Victor. *Flaubert*. Paris: Seuil [Ecrivains de Toujours], 1971.

Brooks, Peter. *The Melodramatic Imagination: Balzac, Henry James, Melodrama, and the Mode of Excess*. New Haven: Yale University Press, 1976.

Butler, Judith. *Gender Trouble: Feminism and the Subversion of Identity*. New York and London: Routledge, 1990.

Carr, Reg. *Anarchism in France: The Case of Octave Mirbeau*. Montreal: McGill-Queen's University Press, 1977.

Castle, Terry. *The Apparitional Lesbian: Female Homosexuality and Modern Culture*. New York: Columbia University Press, 1993.

Chambers, Ross. *Room for Maneuver: Reading (the) Oppositional (in) Narrative*. Chicago: University of Chicago Press, 1991.

Chambers, William. *A Dissertation on Oriental Gardening* (1772). London: Gregg International Publishers Limited, 1972.

Constable, E[lizabeth] L[ouise]. "Critical Departures: *Salammbô*'s Orientalism." *MLN* 111:4 (1996): 625–46.

Crary, Jonathan. *Techniques of the Observer: On Vision and Modernity in the Nineteenth Century*. Cambridge: MIT Press, 1990.

Culler, Jonathan. *Flaubert: The Uses of Uncertainty*. Ithaca: Cornell University Press, 1985.

Delay, Jean. *La Jeunesse d'André Gide*. Paris: Gallimard, 1956–1957. 2 volumes.

Deleuze, Gilles. *Logique du sens*. Paris: Minuit, 1969.

Deleuze, Gilles, and Félix Guattari. *Kafka. Pour une littérature mineure*. Paris: Minuit, 1975.

de Man, Paul. *Allegories of Reading: Figural Language in Rousseau, Nietzsche, Rilke, and Proust.* New Haven: Yale University Press, 1979.

———. *Blindness and Insight: Essays in the Rhetoric of Contemporary Criticism.* Minneapolis: University of Minnesota Press, 1983. 2nd edition.

Derrida, Jacques. *De la grammatologie.* Paris: Minuit, 1967.

———. *Marges de la philosophie.* Paris: Minuit, 1972.

———. "La Structure, le signe et le jeu dans le discours des sciences humaines." In *L'Écriture et la différence.* Paris: Seuil, 1967.

Dollimore, Jonathan. *Sexual Dissidence: Augustine to Wilde. Freud to Foucault.* Oxford: Clarendon Press, 1991.

Donato, Eugenio. "The Museum's Furnace: Notes toward a Contextual Reading of *Bouvard et Pécuchet.*" In *Textual Strategies: Perspectives in Post-Structuralist Criticism.* Ed. Josué V. Harari. Ithaca: Cornell University Press, 1979: 213–38.

Doubrovsky, Serge. *La Place de la madeleine. Ecriture et fantasme chez Proust.* Paris: Mercure de France, 1974.

Duchet, Claude. "Roman et objets : L'exemple de *Madame Bovary. Europe* 485–87 (1969): 172–202.

Dufour, Philippe. "Les avatars du langage dans *Eugénie Grandet.*" *L'Année balzacienne* 16 (1995): 39–61.

Dugan, J. R. "Flaubert's Salammbô, a Study in Immobility." *Zeitschrift für franzözische Sprache und Literatur* 79 (1969): 193–206.

Ellison, David R. *The Reading of Proust.* Baltimore, Johns Hopkins University Press, 1984.

Fischler, Alexander. "Show and Rumor: The Worldly Scales in Balzac's *Eugénie Grandet.*" *International Fiction Review* 8:2 (1981): 98–105.

Flaubert, Gustave. *Correspondance.* In *Les Œuvres de Gustave Flaubert.* Ed. Maurice Nadeau, Lausanne: Editions Rencontre, 1964–1965. 18 volumes.

———. *Œuvres.* Paris: Gallimard, 1951–1952. 2 volumes.

Forrest-Thomson, Veronica. "The Ritual of Reading *Salammbô.*" *Modern Language Review* 67 (1972): 787–98.

Foucault, Michel. *Les Mots et les choses. Une Archéologie des sciences humaines.* Paris: Gallimard, 1966.

———. *Surveiller et punir. Naissance de la prison.* Paris: Gallimard, 1975.

———. *La Volonté de savoir.* Paris: Gallimard, 1976.

Franchi, Danièle, and Roger Ripoll. "Douceur et intimité dans *La Bête humaine.*" *Cahiers naturalistes* 51 (1977): 80–90.

Fryer, Jonathan. *André and Oscar: The Literary Friendship of André Gide and Oscar Wilde.* New York: St. Martin's Press, 1997.

Furst, Lilian R. *All Is True: The Claims and Strategies of Realist Fiction.* Durham: Duke University Press, 1995.

Gasché, Rodolphe. *The Tain of the Mirror: Derrida and the Philosophy of Reflection.* Cambridge: Harvard University Press, 1986.

Genette, Gérard. *Figures III.* Paris: Seuil, 1972.

———. "Proust et le langage indirect." *Figures II.* Paris: Seuil, 1969: 223–94.

Gide, André. *Corydon.* Paris: Gallimard [Folio], 1924 [rpt. 1991].

———. *Journal 1887–1925.* Paris: Gallimard, 1996.

———. *Journal 1926–1950.* Paris: Gallimard, 1997.

———. *Journal 1939–1949. Souvenirs.* Paris: Gallimard, 1954.

———. *Journal des faux-monnayeurs.* Paris: Gallimard, 1927.

———. *Oscar Wilde. In Memoriam (Souvenirs). Le "De Profundis."* Paris: Mercure de France, 1989.

———. *Romans. Récits et Soties. Œuvres lyriques.* Paris: Gallimard [Pléiade], 1958.

———. *Si le grain ne meurt.* In *Souvenirs et voyages.* Paris: Gallimard [Pléiade], 2001: 79–330.

Gilbert, Sandra M., and Susan Gubar. *The Madwoman in the Attic: The Woman Writer and the Nineteenth-Century Literary Imagination.* New Haven: Yale University Press, 1984.

Girard, René. *La Violence et le sacré.* Paris: Grasset, 1972.

Gobin, Pierre. "Un 'Code' des postures dans les romans de Mirbeau? De l'esthétique romanesque à l'esthétique dramatique." In *La Lecture Sociocritique du texte romanesque.* Eds. Graham Falconer and Henri Mitterand. Toronto: Hakkert and Company, 1975: 189–206.

Godfrey, Sima. "The Fabrication of *Salammbô*: The Surface of the Veil." *MLN* 95 (1980): 1005–16.

Goulet, Alain. *André Gide, "Les Faux-Monnayeurs," mode demploi.* Paris: SEDES, 1991.

Gouyette, Jérôme. "Perspectives sadiennes dans *Le Jardin des supplices.*" *Cahiers Octave Mirbeau* 1 (1994): 83–93.

Green, Anne. *Flaubert and the Historical Novel: Salammbô Reassessed.* Cambridge: Cambridge University Press, 1982.

Grescoe, Taras. "Museum of Horrors." *Independent on Sunday* [London] (25 August 1996). Rpt. in *World Press Review* (December 1996): 42–43.

Grigsby, Darcy Grimaldo. "Orients and Colonies: Delacroix's Algerian Harem." *Cambridge Companion to Delacroix.* Ed. Beth Wright. Cambridge: Cambridge University Press, 2001.

Gruzinska, Aleksandra. "Structure in Octave Mirbeau's *Le Jardin des supplices.*" *Zagadnienia Rodzajów Literackich* 25:2 (1982): 65–73.

Halévy, Jacques Fromental. *La Juive. Opera in Five Acts.* Libretto: Eugène Scribe. Philips 420, 190–92. 3 compact discs plus libretto.

Hamburger, Käte. *The Logic of Literature.* Trans. Marilynn J. Rose. Bloomington: Indiana University Press, 1973.

Hamon, Philippe. "Un Discours contraint." *Poétique* 16 (1973): 411–45.

Hannoosh, Michele. "La Femme, la ville, le réalisme: Fondements épistemologiques dans le Paris de Balzac." *Romanic Review* 82:2 (1991): 127–45.

Harrow, Susan. "Dressed/Undressed: Objects of Visual Fascination in Zola's *L'Assommoir.*" In *Narrative Voices in Modern French Fiction: Studies in Honour of Valerie Minogue on the Occasion of Her Retirement.* Eds. Michael Cardy, George Evans, and Gabriel Jacobs. Cardiff: University of Wales Press, 1997.

————. "Exposing the Imperial Cultural Fabric: Critical Description in Zola's *La Curée.*" *French Studies* 54:4 (2000): 439–52.

Iser, Wolfgang. *Prospecting: From Reader Response to Literary Anthropology.* Baltimore: Johns Hopkins University Press, 1989: 3–30.

Kafka, Franz. *Sämtliche Erzählungen.* Ed. Paul Raabe. Frankfurt: S. Fischer Verlag, 1976.

Klossowski, Pierre. *Les Lois de l'hospitalité.* Paris: Gallimard, 1989.

Kristeva, Julia. *Le Temps sensible. Proust et l'expérience littéraire.* Paris: Gallimard, 1994.

————. *Le Texte du roman: Approche sémiologique d'une structure discursive transformationnelle.* The Hague: Mouton, 1970.

Kuroda, S. Y. "Réflexions sur les fondements de la théorie de la narration." In *Langue, discours, société. Pour Emile Benveniste.* Julia Kristeva et al., eds. Paris: Seuil, 1975: 260–93.

Lacan, Jacques. *Écrits.* Paris: Seuil, 1966.

Ladenson, Elisabeth. *Proust's Lesbianism.* Ithaca: Cornell University Press, 1999.

Lavagetto, Mario. *Stanza 43: un lapsus di Marcel Proust.* Torino: G. Einaudi, 1991.

Le Huenen, Roland, and Paul Perron. "Le système des objets dans *Eugénie Grandet.*" *Littérature* 26 (1977): 94–119.

Lerner, Scott. "Jewish Identity and French Opera, Stage, and Politics, 1831–1860." *Historical Reflections/Reflexions Historiques.* (Forthcoming.)

Lessing, Gotthold Ephraim. *Laocoon: An Essay upon the Limits of Painting and Poetry.* Trans. Ellen Frothingham. New York: The Noonday Press, 1957.

Lorrain, Jean. *La Maison Philibert.* Paris: Christian Pirot, 1992.

Lotringer, Sylvère. "Mesure de la démesure." *Poétique* 3 (1972): 486–94.

Lowe, Catherine. "Salammbô ou la question de l'autre de la parole." *L'Arc* 58 (1974): 83–88.

Lowe, Lisa. "Nationalism and Exoticism: Nineteenth-Century Others in Flaubert's *Salammbô* and *L'Education sentimentale.*" In *Macropolitics of Nineteenth-Century Literature: Nationalism, Exoticism, Imperialism.* Jonathan Arac and Harriet Ritvo, eds. Philadelphia: University of Pennsylvania Press, 1991.

Lucey, Michael. *Gide's Bent. Sexuality, Politics, Writing.* Oxford and New York: Oxford University Press, 1995.

Lukács, Georg. *The Historical Novel.* Trans. Hannah and Stanley Mitchell. Harmonsworth, Middx.: Penguin, 1962 [rpt. 1976].

———. *Studies in European Realism.* New York: Grosset and Dunlap, 1964.

———. *The Theory of the Novel: A Historico-philosophical Essay in the Forms of Great Epic Literature.* Trans. Anna Bostock. Cambridge: MIT, 1971.

Lyotard, Jean-François. *Discours, figure.* Paris: Klincksieck, 1971.

———. *Lectures d'enfance.* Paris: Galilée, 1991.

Macé, Gérard. *Le Manteau de Fortuny.* Paris: Gallimard, 1987.

Marty, Éric. *L'Écriture du jour.* Paris: Seuil, 1985.

McKenna, Andrew J. "Flaubert's Freudian Thing: Violence and Representation in *Salammbô*." *Stanford French Review* 12:2–3 (1988): 305–25.

Mingelgrün, Albert. *Thèmes et structures bibliques dans l'œuvre de Marcel Proust. Etude stylistique de quelques interférences.* Lausanne: Editions l'Age d'Homme, 1978.

Mirbeau, Octave. "Colonisons." In *Contes cruels.* Eds. Jean-François Nivet and Pierre Michel. Paris: Séguier, 1990, 2:268–73.

———. *Le Jardin des supplices.* Ed. and preface by Michel Delon. Paris: Gallimard [Folio], 1988.

Mortimer, Armine Kotin. *Writing Realism: Representations in French Fiction.* Baltimore: Johns Hopkins University Press, 2000.

Moss, Martha Niess. "The Masks of Men and Women in Balzac's *Comédie humaine*." *French Review* 50 (1977): 446–53.

Neefs, Jacques. "Le Parcours du zaimph." In *La Production du sens chez Flaubert.* Ed. Claudine Gothot-Mersch. Paris: Union Générale d'Editions [10/18]: 227–41.

———. "*Salammbô*: Textes critiques." *Littérature* 15 (1974): 52–64.

Nesci, Catherine. "'Le Sucube' ou l'itinéraire de Tours en Orient: Essai sur les lieux du poétique balzacien." *L'Année Balzacienne* 5 (1985): 263–95.

Noiray, Jacques. "L'Angoisse de la chair dans *La Bête humaine*." In *Voix de l'écrivain.* Cabanès, Jean-Louis, ed. Toulouse: PU du Mirail, 1996.

Ovid. *Metamorphoses.* With an English Translation by Frank Justus Miller. Cambridge: Harvard University Press [Loeb], 1950. 2 volumes.

Pasco, Allan. "Literature as Historical Archive: Reading Divorce in Mme de Stael's *Delphine* and other Revolutionary Literature." *EMF: Studies in Early Modern France* 7 (2001): 163–200.

———. *Sick Heroes, Society and Literature in the Romantic Age, 1750–1850.* Exeter: University of Exeter Press, 1987.

Poe, Edgar Allan. *Poetry and Tales.* New York: The Library of America, 1984.

Pollard, Patrick. *André Gide: Homosexual Moralist.* New Haven and London: Yale University Press, 1991.

Praz, Mario. *La Carne, la morte e il diavolo nella letteratura romantica*. 4th Edition. Florence: G. C. Sansoni, 1966.

Prince, Gerald. *Narratology: The Form and Functioning of Narrative*. Berlin and New York: Mouton, 1982.

Proust, Marcel. *A la recherche du temps perdu*. Ed. Jean-Yves Tadié et al. Paris: Gallimard [Pléiade], 1987–89. 4 volumes.

———. "A propos du 'style' de Flaubert." In *Contre Sainte-Beuve*. Paris: Gallimard, 1971: 586–600.

Przybos, Julia. "Délices et supplices: Octave Mirbeau et Jérôme Bosch." In *Octave Mirbeau*. Eds. Pierre Michel and Georges Cesbron. Angers: Presses de l'Université d'Angers, 1992: 207–16.

Ricardou, Jean. *Nouveaux problèmes du roman*. Paris: Seuil, 1978.

Riffaterre, Michel. "Describing Poetic Structures: Two Approaches to Baudelaire's *Les Chats*. In *Structuralism*. Ed. Jacques Ehrmann. New York: Doubleday Anchor, 1970: 188–230.

Rose, Marilyn Gaddis. "Decadent Prose: The Example of *Salammbô*." *Nineteenth-Century French Studies* 3 (1975): 213–23.

Rousset, Jean. "Positions, distances, perspectives dans *Salammbô*." *Poétique* 6 (1971): 145–54.

Sainte-Beuve, Charles. *Nouveaux Lundis*. Volume 4. Paris: Michel Lévy, 1870.

Sartre, Jean-Paul. *La Nausée*. Paris: Gallimard [Folio], 1972.

Scarry, Elaine. *The Body in Pain: The Making and Unmaking of the World*. New York: Oxford University Press, 1985.

Schehr, Lawrence R. *Alcibiades at the Door: Gay Discourses in French Literature*. Stanford: Stanford University Press, 1995.

———. *Flaubert and Sons*. New York: Peter Lang, 1986.

———. *Parts of an Andrology: On Representations of Men's Bodies*. Stanford: Stanford University Press, 1997.

———. *Rendering French Realism*. Stanford: Stanford University Press, 1997.

———. *The Shock of Men*. Stanford: Stanford University Press, 1995.

———. "The Unknown Subject: About Balzac's 'Chef d'œuvre inconnu.'" *Nineteenth-Century French Studies* 12:4 (1984): 58–69.

Schlossman, Beryl. *The Orient of Style: Modernist Allegories of Conversion*. Durham: Duke University Press, 1991.

Schor, Naomi. *Breaking the Chain*. New York: Columbia University Press, 1985.

———. "Details and Realism." *Poetics Today* 5:4 (1984): 701–10.

———. *Reading in Detail: Aesthetics and the Feminine*. New York: Methuen, 1987.

Schuerewegen, Franc. *Balzac contre Balzac: Les Cartes du lecteur*. Toronto: Paratexte; Paris: CDU—SEDES, 1990.

Schwarz, Martin. *Octave Mirbeau. Vie et Œuvre*. The Hague: Mouton & Co., 1966.

Segal, Naomi. *André Gide: Pederasty and Pedagogy*. Oxford and New York: Oxford University Press, 1998.

————. "'Parfois j'ai peur que ce que j'ai supprimé ne se vente'—Gide and Women." *Paragraph* 6 (1986:) 62–74.

Serres, Michel. *Feux et Signaux de brume. Zola*. Paris: Grasset, 1975.

————. *Le Parasite*. Paris: Grasset, 1980.

Simon, G-Eug. *La Cité chinoise*. Paris: Nouvelle Revue, 1885.

Smith-Di Biasio, Anne-Marie. "'Le Texte de la vie des femmes': Female Melancholia in *Eugénie Grandet*." *Nottingham French Studies* 35:2 (1996): 52–59.

Solda, Fabien. "*Le Jardin des supplices*: Récit d'une initiation?" *Cahiers Octave Mirbeau* 2 (1995): 61–86.

Spencer-Brown, G. *Laws of Form*. London: Allen and Unwin, 1969.

Starr, Peter. "*Salammbô*: The Politics of an Ending." *French Forum* 10:1 (1985): 40–56.

Sundquist, Eric. *Home as Found: Authority and Genealogy in Nineteenth-Century American Literature*. Baltimore: Johns Hopkins University Press, 1979.

Terdiman, Richard. *Discourse/Counter-Discourse: The Theory and Practice of Symbolic Resistance in Nineteenth-Century France*. Ithaca: Cornell University Press, 1985.

Villeneuve, Roland. *Le Musée des supplices*. Paris: Editions Azur—Claude Offenstadt, 1968.

Villiers de L'Isle-Adam. *Contes cruels. Nouveaux Contes cruels*. Paris: Classiques Garnier, 1989.

Waller, Margaret. "Disembodiment as a Masquerade: Fashion Journalists and Other 'Realist' Observers in Directory Paris." *Esprit Créateur* 37:1 (Spring 1997): 44–54.

Watt, Ian P. *The Rise of the Novel*. Berkeley: University of California Press, 1965.

Weber, Samuel. *Unwrapping Balzac: A Reading of* La Peau de Chagrin. Toronto: University of Toronto Press, 1979.

Weightman, John. "André Gide and the Homosexual Debate." *The American Scholar* (Autumn 1990): 591–601.

Weinrich, Harald. *Tempus: Besprochene und erzählte Welt*. Stuttgart: Kohlhammer, 1964.

Weiss, Allen S. *Mirrors of Infinity: The French Formal Garden and 17th-Century Metaphysics*. New York: Princeton Architectural Press, 1995.

Wetherill, P. M. "A Reading of *Eugénie Grandet*." *Modern Languages* 52 (1971): 166–76.

White, Hayden. *Metahistory: the Historical Imagination in Nineteenth-Century Europe*. Baltimore: Johns Hopkins University Press, 1973.

Wilson, Emma. *Sexuality and the Reading Encounter*. Oxford, 1996.

Ziegler, Robert E. "Hunting the Peacock: The Pursuit of Non-reflective Experience in Mirbeau's *Le Jardin des supplices*." *Nineteenth-Century French Studies* 12:4–13:1 (1984): 162–74.

Zola, Émile. *La Bête humaine*. In *Les Rougon-Macquart*. Paris: Gallimard [Pléiade (1961)] 4: 995–1331.

# Index

In this index, an "f" after a number indicates a separate reference on the next page, and an "ff" indicates separate references on the next two pages.